HOW GUJARATIS DO BUSINESS

DHANDHA

ધંધા

DHANDHA

ધંધા

HOW GUJARATIS DO BUSINESS

SHOBHA BONDRE

TRANSLATED BY SHALAKA WALIMBE

RANDOM HOUSE INDIA

First published by Random House India in 2013
Tenth impression in 2014

Random House Publishers India Pvt. Ltd.
7th Floor, Infinity Tower C, DLF Cyber City,
Gurgaon – 122002, Haryana

Random House Group Limited
20 Vauxhall Bridge Road
London SW1V 2SA
United Kingdom

978 81 8400 312 3

Typeset in Adobe Jenson Pro by SwaRadha Typesetting

Printed and bound in India by Replika Press Private Limited

A PENGUIN RANDOM HOUSE COMPANY

For Shalaka, Ajit, Mrugali, and Manoj.
May all your dreams come true!
This book is for you.

CONTENTS

FOREWORD

It is nice to receive an appreciable effort by Shobha Bondre in the translated version of the book named *Dhandha*. The success stories are narrated nicely, glorifying Gujarati culture and courage. Their ways to tackle tough situations with tenderness and to enter the world of entrepreneurship are unique but diverse. The traits, tricks, and tolerance for success are the inherent business sense of Gujaratis—with hard work and habit to toil—till the road to success and path for progress is carved out.

The reasons for the roaring success of the Gujaratis is their sharp intellect, tremendous will power, and incredible capacity for hard work. Success has instilled in them the sound values and high sense of responsibility for society. Caring attitude and humane approach reflects in their professional dealing and dedication to service. Once the challenge is taken, there is no looking back—self-confidence is something to be treasured and lasts for a lifetime.

The characters depicted in the book possess the grace, glory, and guts as expected of Gujarati culture. The honesty and hopes, the respect of relationship and fairness in dealings are directing forces for each one's success. The lively language and warm words picked up to portrait the personalities will touch every heart.

I compliment Random House India for a worthy publication as well as the Marathi Granthalaya Association for awarding the Best Book Award to the original version.

I hope *Dhandha* will inspire all to explore and expand the instinct to go ahead in life, with the Gujarati way of branding and bonding.

(NARENDRA MODI)
Chief Minister, Gujarat

INTRODUCTION

As one travels across the length and breadth of Gujarat, one comes to know how kings had built their massive empires from humble beginnings. Today, it's the Gujarati businessmen who have repeated history by building business empires.

Business acumen is something that Gujaratis seem to inherit rather than acquire. Did you know that it was Ranchodlal Chotalal, a Gujarati, who brought the textile industry to India? Or that it was Gujarat's Gondal Maharaja who collaborated with the British for laying down railway tracks for trains? These examples tell us how business flows in the veins of the Gujarati community.

In this book, Shobha throws light on some of the stellar performers in the Gujarati business community. Men who didn't just create wealth for themselves but for the nation as well. Men who didn't just earn money but respect too.

Let's hope this book serves as a source of pride and inspiration for people all over the world.

(signature)

(**AMITABH BACHCHAN**)
Brand Ambassador, Gujarat Tourism

DIAMONDS ARE FOREVER

Bhimjibhai Patel

It was a busy day at the British High Commission in Mumbai in the year 1974. I was among the hundreds of people who had queued up to get a British visa stamped on their passports. The queue was inching forward at a snail's pace. Finally, it was my turn and I handed over my documents to the British officer at the counter.

He glanced at my papers and asked in plain English, 'Why do you want to go to England?'

I was dumbstruck. I hadn't been inside a classroom for more than fifteen days in my entire life, so naturally, I didn't know a word of English.

I requested politely, 'Sahib, Gujaratima bolo.'

He gave me an irritated look and bombarded me with more questions in English—'Do you know anyone in England? Where are you going to stay in England? What is the purpose of your visit?'

I didn't know what to say so I repeated once again, 'Bhai, please speak in Gujarati.'

He continued with his barrage of questions in English and I kept on asking him to speak in Gujarati. This duel went on for a while. Finally, he lost his temper, stamped something on my passport, and flung it to the ground.

I didn't really understand what had happened. I bent down and picked up my passport. I kept thinking to myself, *Has this Gora given me the visa or not? And why did he throw it on the ground?*

I had to find an answer to both questions. I looked around and to my relief, I saw an Indian, most probably a Gujarati lady, at the next counter.

I showed her my passport and asked her in Hindi, 'Ben, can you please tell me what is the matter with my passport? Why did the Gora officer throw it down?'

'Sir, there is nothing wrong with your passport but he has refused you the visa. Here is the rejection stamp.'

I asked her, 'Why has he refused to give me the visa?'

She turned to the British officer next to her and spoke to him in English. He said something to her. She told me in Hindi, 'He says you don't speak a word of English so what will you do in England?'

I said, 'Ben, please ask him, does he speak Hindi? Does he speak any Indian language? If he can work here without knowing the local language, why can't I survive in England without speaking English?'

The lady smiled and narrated the incident to the officer. He looked thoughtful, stared at me for a long moment, and finally broke into a smile.

'Come on, give me your passport.' He stamped my passport once again and said to the lady, 'Tell him he has got the visa. Ask him to come back in the evening to collect his passport.'

On the way back from the British High Commission, I felt as if I was on cloud nine. As the taxi sped along Chowpati, I looked out at the Arabian Sea stretching out till the horizon and said to myself, 'Bhimjibhai, get ready for a new chapter in your life. Very soon, you will cross this ocean and the Atlantic and set foot on a new land. You have to be prepared to face this latest challenge.'

After England, I was going to visit Belgium and Israel. I had big dreams of increasing my diamond business. I rested my head against the seat, shut my eyes, and went back into the past. I was back in my little village in Saurashtra, Hajiradhar. I could see my house, our farm, the marketplace, and there, in front of the grocer's shop, was me, all of ten years old.

One morning, Ba gave me a shopping list and sent me to the grocery store in the village. I gave the list to the shop assistant in Karsanji Kaka's store and waited while he packed the items. Karsanji Kaka was reading *Jaihind*, a Gujarati newspaper. He was the only person in our village who read the newspaper every day. As I stood in front of him, I happened to glance at the paper. Without even realizing it, I began to read the letters. Before I knew it, the letters became words and I was actually reading 'India wins the match at Bombay with two wickets in hand...' Suddenly the paper was pulled aside and I saw Karsanji Kaka's face. He was staring at me, surprised.

'Dikra, do you know how to read?'

'Uh...uh...a little...,' I stammered.

'Do you go to school?' he asked me.

I didn't know what to say to that. 'Uh, I mean I do, but...'

'When do you find the time to go to school, Bhimu? Whenever I see you, you are working in the fields.'

I didn't have an answer to that but luckily at that moment the servant gave me the grocery items and I left without another word.

On my way back, I kept thinking to myself, *Kaka is right.*

Even though I was enrolled in school, I didn't attend classes for months on end. For one thing, the school was almost five kilometres away from my home. It took such a long time to go there and come back. Secondly, since I was the eldest son, it was my duty to help Bapu in his work.

We owned a house and a little land. But the land was not fertile and our farming produce was at the mercy of the vagaries of rainfall. So, in spite of toiling the whole day, we barely managed to grow enough to feed all of us.

That evening, as I was lying down in bed after a hard day's work, I couldn't stop thinking about school. I was feeling sad that I was unable to go to school. The only tiny ray of hope was a Brahmin boy from a nearby village who had been coming to our village on his horse since the last few days to teach boys like me who could not go all the way to the school.

Thanks to his efforts, I could now recognize alphabets, read a little, and do simple calculations. What was even more important was that I developed a genuine passion for learning.

As I tried to go off to sleep, conflicting thoughts clouded my mind and then suddenly I saw a white, bright light. I sat up in bed with a start. I saw a new path open up, one which would help me get an education. My mind was racing with various possibilities and my face lit up with a smile as I found the miraculous answer to my problem. I lay down once again and began dreaming of the next day.

Early next morning, I put on a clean churidar, kurta, and a pagdi. Ba was making rotis for me. When she saw me dressed like that, she was surprised. 'Bhimu, aren't you going to the fields today?' she asked.

'No Ba, I am going to the market,' I replied and ran out of the house before she could question me any further.

When I reached Karsanji Kaka's shop, he was reading the newspaper. He put it aside when he saw me. 'Arrey Bhimu, what do you want today?'

'Your newspaper.'

'Uh, what?'

I felt like laughing when I saw the look of amazement on his face, but I asked him in a serious tone, 'Kaka, what is the price of your newspaper?'

'One anna.'

'Okay. So if I give you half the price that is half an anna every day, will you give me the paper? After you have read it, of course.'

Kaka was amused by my offer but he accepted it.

I immediately put my hand in my pocket and pulled out half an anna. 'Here is the money for today.'

Karsan Kaka realized that I was actually serious about this. He took the money and said, 'Alright, come in the evening to collect the newspaper but you have to return it the next day.'

I nodded my head in delight. I was thrilled. I had actually made my first deal with a seasoned businessman.

When I returned home, I went over my calculations once again. Fifteen annas a month was a big amount for me. Did I have that kind of money?

Even though I was only ten, I was an earning member of the family. Not only did I work in our family fields, I also worked as a labourer in other farmers' fields. I was paid 2 or 4 annas per day for this. I used to hand over most of the money to Bapu but I did keep a little aside for myself.

I had another secret source of income. There was a Hanuman temple in our village. There were often fairs at the temple. Bapu used to give me 8 annas when I went to the fair: 4 for me and 4 to buy a coconut and offer it to Hanumanji. But when I saw the huge pile of coconuts in front of Hanumanji, I would say to myself, 'What will poor Hanumanji do with so many coconuts? He will be happier if I don't give him another one.' So that added to my small treasure.

Finally, after many complicated calculations, I decided that I did have enough money for the newspaper. The newspaper would be my guide, my guru, and it would help me with my learning.

And that is exactly what happened. After a hard day at work, I would pick up the paper from Karsan Kaka and then the evening was spent in trying to decode, read the newspaper slowly, laboriously.

As time went by, my reading speed improved and I began to love going through the contents of the paper. It became my window to the outside world and I began to discover fascinating facts about the vast world beyond my tiny village.

Reading the newspaper after labouring the entire day in the fields was like magic, a form of entertainment and relaxation, and a great source of happiness for me.

One evening, as I was returning home, I met my classmate Govind. He was carrying his school bag, heavy with books, while I had a stack of hay on my head. He made it a point to stop and tell me, 'Arey Bhimu, we have a test in school tomorrow. You will give the test, won't you?'

I replied in the affirmative.

When I told this to Ba and Bapu at home, they were a little worried for me. 'But Bhimu, how will you do the test? It's been ages since you went to school.'

'Let's see. I'll definitely attempt it,' I told them.

Next morning, I put on clean clothes, my pagdi, and went to school. The teacher entered the classroom, looked around, and was surprised to find me there. I quickly went up to him, touched his feet, and offered him a bag with green chillies and jaggery in it. He seemed touched by the simple gift and asked me to sit down.

He went to the blackboard and began writing the questions for the test. He wrote some sums on the board and asked us to read two lessons from the textbook. Not only did I solve the sums in a jiffy but I also read the lessons fluently and confidently. My classmates gaped at me and the teacher congratulated me on my performance.

I was secretly pleased. Little did they know that it was because of reading the newspaper every day that I found these lessons so simple and easy.

The results were to be announced after the break. When I went to the classroom after break was over, Guruji came in and said, 'The boy who has scored the highest marks in the test today is Bhimji Dahya Patel'.

The class was amazed. I whooped with joy but Guruji continued, 'Bhimji, that was the good news. The bad news is that the Headmaster has expelled you from the school. You have barely attended fifteen days of school and that is not permissible. I am very sorry but you cannot come to school anymore.'

I was speechless.

I sat there like a statue while the teacher read out the results of the other boys in class. He left, so did the other boys. Nobody gave me a second glance.

Finally I too got up. With a heavy heart, I left the school, never to enter it again, and made my way back home.

My formal education ended abruptly, but luckily not my passion for reading.

Meanwhile, life went on as usual. Days, weeks, months passed, but our family's plight remained the same. I now had three younger brothers—Shivlal, Kurji, and Dhiru—for company. But as they were still too young, the onus was on me to help my father in his work in the fields. My world was limited to crops, seeds, rainfall, ploughing, sowing, and reaping. My only aim in life was to earn as much as possible and lighten my father's burden. At times, my father had no other option but to borrow money from a moneylender.

On one occasion, he had borrowed money from a moneylender who was actually a childhood friend of his. However, the friend's behaviour changed totally from the day he lent my father money. Those were such difficult times that we often did not manage to repay even the interest on time, forget the capital.

The moneylender asked me to do odd jobs for him to repay the loan. But he treated me more like a slave. When he gave me an order, I had to drop everything else and do his bidding. I felt so angry but I was helpless. I had to do as I was told and not utter a word in protest.

One day matters came to a head. I was watering our fields when he came there and said, 'Here you, go to my fields immediately. We need more hands for the harvesting.'

I replied politely saying, 'Kaka, I will go as soon as I have finished watering our field.'

The Sahukar was furious 'Didn't you hear what I said? IMMEDIATELY.'

I was furious with this selfish and arrogant man. I didn't say a word, but I continued watering the field.

Now he was in a towering rage. He called out to my father 'Dahya…Dahyabhai…come here at once.'

My father came running. The Sahukar told him the story. I tried to explain my point of view to my father. 'Bapu, all I said to Kaka was that I will go to his field when I finish watering ours.'

The Sahukar screamed 'You see how rude and disrespectful he is. He is not even bothered about what you think now.'

Bapu gave me a stinging slap. 'You idiot. I can't afford to repay even his interest and you refuse to do his work? Stop whatever you are doing and do as he says.'

This was insult added to injury. I left with the Sahukar without saying a word.

That day, I worked for the Sahukar from 4 in the afternoon to 2 in the morning. As I was finally leaving, the Sahukar said to me, 'Take these sacks of grain to my house and then you can go home.'

There was no way I could refuse. It took me until 9 the next morning to finish the job. I had worked all this while without a break, without a morsel of food, without a drop of water.

When I reached home, my eyes were smarting, my body numb with fatigue. Ba made me some fresh rotis. But when I put the first morsel in my mouth, my eyes welled up with tears. 'Dear God, I wouldn't wish this fate even on my most bitter enemy.' After a while I calmed down, ate a little, and then with new resolve, prepared to face a new day.

It was after this incident that I decided that in the future, if I was ever in a position to lend money, I would never ever charge anyone interest on it.

Another positive outcome was that I never ever found any chore physically too exhausting to handle after this. My experience at working tirelessly for the sahukar for such a long stretch of time had strengthened me up both physically and mentally.

Many years later, the tide had turned and now there were many who asked me for loans. Once, a friend had borrowed 20,000 rupees from me. A few months later, I was passing by his farm. He called out to me. 'Bhimji come in. I haven't seen you in ages. Let's have a cup of tea.'

I went in, had a cup of tea, and we spent some time chatting. As I got up to leave, he put a bag full of fresh beans in my hands. 'Take this, they are fresh from the farm.'

'Thank you', I said, 'How much do I owe you?'

'Don't be silly', he replied. 'I have not repaid the money I borrowed from you, neither the capital nor interest. How can I take money from you?'

I said, 'My friend, don't ever mention the word interest again. And the loan is a completely different matter. Don't mix it up with this. Tell me how much I have to pay you for the beans.'

But my friend felt too embarrassed to take any money. Finally I said, 'Okay. Return my 20,000 rupees this moment.'

My friend gaped at me.

'You can't at the moment, right? My friend, that is what I have been trying to tell you. You can repay me as and when you can, but don't ever mention the word "interest" to me again. And now tell me how much do I give you for the beans?'

The friend gave in and accepted the money I stuffed in his hand.

However, a lot of water was yet to flow under the bridge before all this happened. But that is another story.

In 1960, my parents got me married to Ramila, a girl from a neighbouring village.

Normally, the days before and immediately after the wedding are magical, filled with romance, hope, and happiness.

Unfortunately for us, Lady Luck still refused to smile on us. That year, there was a terrible drought in Gujarat. The region of Saurashtra where we lived was devastated by the drought, and more specifically, our district 'Amareli' was one of the worst hit by it.

The situation was bleak: no water, no crops, and no food. What was one to do?

Many people from our village left and went to Bhayavdar where one could work as a daily labourer on the farm and was paid 2 rupees per day.

After discussing the matter with Ba and Bapu, it was decided that Ramila and I would go to Bhayavdar in search of work. The bus fare in those days from our village to Bhayavdar was only 5.25 rupees, but we didn't have even enough money for the bus fare for two people. It took a lot of effort but we finally managed to borrow 15 rupees from someone from our village. After paying for the tickets, all we were left with was 4.50 rupees.

Ramila and I decided that the first thing to do when we got off the bus was to find work. Food, a place to live...all that could come later.

Luckily we found both work and a small hut to live in. And so began our married life. The first private conversation we had was about budget and money.

Our earnings put together would be 120 rupees a month. From that, we had to repay the loan of 15 rupees that we had taken, send money to my parents back home, and then manage in what was left.

What a difficult task it was going to be. But one usually finds some hidden source of hope and energy when faced with a challenge.

We settled down quickly in the new routine and life went on. One evening, as we were coming back from work, we saw a sign outside an oil mill saying 'Help wanted'. They wanted someone to work at night. The pay was 2 rupees per night.

When we reached home, I told Ramila, 'I am definitely taking this up. If both of us were to do the job, we would earn 240 rupees a month. But it's up to you. If you feel that you will not be able to manage both the jobs, I won't force you to do it.'

Ramila was vehement. 'I go wherever you go. Do you think I will be able to sleep in peace when I know you are working the whole night? Impossible.'

We started this 'double duty' from the very next day. We worked in the fields tirelessly from 8 am to 6 pm; came back home; had dinner; worked in the oil mill from 9 pm to 4 am; came back home and slept for two hours; got up; cooked; cleaned; packed lunch, and left for the fields. Days and nights merged into one and we didn't realize how time flew. You may take pity on us and think how sad, the poor souls, what backbreaking work. But frankly, those days were filled with endless energy, abounding hope, and a crazy passion for work. And we were young, full of dreams and hopes. Also, there was the satisfaction of knowing that we were supporting our family and were fulfilling our responsibilities as well as we could.

A few months later, the situation in our village improved and we returned. We started growing vegetables like eggplant, gourd, and snake gourd in our field. Once a week, I would hoist a heavy sack full of vegetables on my back and walk to the marketplace in the next village, Damnagar. Once while I was on my way there, I met an old friend from my village. Actually, he was older than me so I used to call him Kaka. I had heard that he was now in Surat. I was seeing him after years and what a transformation. I stared at him and exclaimed, 'Kaka, you don't look like a village bloke at all now. You have turned into a smart Shahari Babu. How did you change so much?'

Kaka laughed. 'Bhimji, the city does that to you. Everything there is different; the food, the language, the lifestyle, and the ideas. One has to change.'

'What do you do in the city?' I asked curiously.

'I am a diamond polisher in Surat.'

'What is that?' I asked.

'Come on; surely you know what diamonds are,' he replied.

'I mean, I know what they are. I have heard of diamonds, one of the hardest and costliest objects in the world, but I have never ever seen one with my own eyes.'

Kaka explained, 'There are many diamond factories in Surat. The diamonds are cut and polished in these factories and that is what makes them precious. I work as a polisher in one such factory.'

'Congratulations, you have really gone up in the world. Can I ask you a question?'

'Of course.'

'How much do you earn?'

'Actually, we don't get a fixed monthly salary in this industry. Polishing diamonds is a very delicate and skillful job. Your income depends on how skilled you are. Now for example, this month I earned 800 rupees and took an advance of 500 rupees from the owner, so right now I have 1300 rupees in my pocket.'

I looked at him in awe and burst out, 'Take me with you to Surat.'

I had expected a negative response but he agreed immediately. 'Of course. Think about it carefully and let me know when you make up your mind.'

That night, I came back late from work. The entire night I couldn't stop thinking about Surat. I couldn't think of a single reason not to go so in the morning, so I rushed to meet Kaka and told him about my decision.

Kaka explained, 'Look here, Bhimji, you will have to get trained in a diamond factory for four months and will have to pay 400 rupees for the training. You will not be paid anything during this period. Once you start working, your earning depends on how skillful and hardworking you are. Are you okay with this?'

I nodded my head, 'This time when you go to Surat, I will definitely come along with you.'

Taking a decision and telling Kaka about it was the easiest thing in the world. The main problem as usual was 'Where do I get the money from?'

As soon I reached home, my calculations began once again. The train fare from Hajiradhar to Surat would be 13.50 rupees and the training charges would be 400 rupees,

I had no idea about the living expenses that I would have to incur in Surat during the training period, but I had heard stories of how living in a big city was very expensive.

Finally I decided that I would need at least 1000 rupees with me when I go to Surat. That would take care of all my expenses during the training period. But 1000 rupees? Who would give me that kind of money and without any security?

I met a friend who was the manager of a co-operative society but he said that their organization could not give me a loan to go to Surat. My face fell but the next moment he said, 'Forget about the co-operative society. I will give you a part of the money myself. I can lend you 300 rupees. So cheer up and think about how you can collect the rest of the money.' I didn't know how to thank him.

I then met a relative who stayed in our village. It was the same man I had borrowed the 15 rupees from when I went to Bhayavadar. He trusted me because I had repaid his money so promptly last time. This time he let me borrow 200 rupees from him.

That evening, when I talked things over with Ramila, she asked, 'Well, you have already managed to collect half of the money you need. What are you going to do for the rest now?'

I replied, 'If I can raise another 500 rupees, I'll be fine. Otherwise, I will have to manage with only 500 rupees. We had only 15 rupees when we went to Bhayavadar, remember? Didn't we manage fine then?'

'Yes, but we started working immediately. Here you will be training in the diamond factory for the first four months. You will need money during that time.'

'I can't work in the diamond factory but who says I can't work elsewhere? I believe that if you have the willpower and determination and the willingness to work, you will never go hungry.'

Ramila looked at me with pride and said, 'You are absolutely right.'

And so I went to Surat with only 500 rupees in my pocket. Thanks to Kaka, I was accepted as a trainee in the factory where he worked. I found lodging, paid 45 rupees, and thus began a new chapter in my life.

All I had left after the train fare, the training fee, and the lodging charges was 41.50 rupees. I decided to take up a part-time job once I had settled down in the training programme. And to my luck, I found work in just a couple of days. There was a Nepali fellow who used to clean the lodge. He was not a good worker and he would always argue with the owner of the lodge. Once I asked the owner, 'How much do you pay him?'

'Why do you want to know?'

'Please tell me.'

'Fifty rupees.'

'I am ready to clean the place if you pay me 50 rupees and I assure you I will give you no cause for complaint.'

The owner was surprised. 'Okay. In fact, I am ready to pay you 60 rupees if you work well.'

They say 'Luck favours the brave'. My money problem was solved and I could now give my undivided attention to learning the craft of cutting a diamond.

The glittering world of diamonds seemed like Alibaba's treasure trove to me. It was like a dream come true to be a part of this brilliant world.

At the same time, it was my first opportunity to educate myself and pave the way for a bright future. And it goes without saying that I was a very diligent student and I gave it my 100 percent.

The main objective of the diamond industry in Surat is to cut and polish rough diamonds and to transform them into brilliant, precious gemstones.

Not only was I interested in picking up the skills of a cutter and polisher, I also felt an insatiable urge to learn all I could about the various aspects of the diamond industry.

Diamonds can be used for two distinct reasons. The most popular and well-known use of a diamond is as a gemstone; these are called 'gem grade diamonds'. These diamonds are valued essentially for their look and beauty.

And then some diamonds are used in industries; these are called 'industrial grade diamonds'. In this type of diamonds, the look of the diamond is immaterial; what is more important is its hardness and thermal conductivity.

The prices for these two types of diamonds are also decided according to very different criteria. For example, the price of a gem grade diamond generally depends on the traditional 4 Cs: cut, colour, clarity, and carat weight.

Diamonds are the most sought after commodity in the world today, but there are only a handful of countries which mine diamonds, cut and polish or trade in them.

Every year, approximately 26,000 kilos of diamonds are mined annually of which almost 50 percent come from mines located in Central and Southern Africa; the rest come from Canada, India, Brazil, and Australia. The De Beers Company in South Africa is one of the largest diamond mining companies in the world and hence it plays a vital role in the world diamond industry. It owns many mines in several countries including the huge Jwaneng mine in Botswana.

There have been diamond mines in India since centuries. Diamonds were traditionally found in Guntur in Karnataka and in the valleys of the Krishna River.

However these mines were exhausted by the end of the 18th century. At present, the diamond mines in India are located in Panna.

Rough diamonds mined all over the globe end up in the wholesale diamond trading centres or exchanges known as 'bourses'. One of the biggest bourse or diamond centre in the world is located in Antwerp in Belgium, so much so that Antwerp is often referred to as the 'World Diamond capital'.

Another important wholesale diamond trading center is in New York City. The centres in London and Tel Aviv are also important.

Rough diamonds are bought and sold in these diamond centres and then sent to the diamond factories for cutting and polishing. It is at this stage that the value of a diamond increases.

According to a survey carried out in 2003, approximately 92 percent of the rough diamonds in the world were sent to the city of Surat in India for cutting and polishing. The rest went to other cities like Johannesburg, Amsterdam, Antwerp, New York, Tel Aviv etc. One of the main reasons for the majority of rough diamonds being sent to Surat is the availability of skilled low cost labour.

A major proportion of the smaller carat diamonds is processed in Surat while the larger or more valuable diamonds are sent to renowned factories in Europe and America. It is here that they are cut and polished and turned into precious gemstones.

The diamond factories in Surat have made a significant impact on the diamond industry. Earlier, cutting and polishing small stones was not financially viable. However, due to the low rates of cutting and polishing in Surat, trading in small diamonds too has become an extremely profitable business proposition. And it is also thanks to the factories in Surat that diamonds have become affordable to vast multitude of people in the middle-income bracket.

The rough diamonds undergo a miraculous transformation in the diamond factory. The most important processes in this transformation are cutting and polishing. Both these procedures are complex and crucial. The cutter first has to make a thorough analysis of the rough diamond and take into consideration its natural shape and weight. If the rough diamond is square or round, the diamond will also be of the same shape. But if the rough diamond is oblong, then the finished diamond could be oval or pear-shaped or egg-shaped. Another crucial decision is which cut should be used: single cut, old mine cut, European cut, basic four sided cut, or the favourite cut these days—the modern brilliant cut.

Markings are made on the diamond to indicate the cuts that have to be made on it. This is a very delicate operation and the smallest error can lead to a loss of thousands of dollars.

Even though a diamond is one of the hardest substances in the world, it is also extremely delicate and brittle. If there is the slightest mistake in marking or cleaving, it can crack or if there is an error in calculating its facets and shape, it may become dull and opaque. Hence, accurate marking is of the utmost importance in the cutting of a diamond.

Along with the shape and weight of the diamond, there are two other factors of equal importance—the clarity and the crystal direction of the diamond.

The next stage is that of actually cutting the diamond. A diamond is used to cut diamonds either with the help of specially-built tools or a lathe machine.

The true worth of a diamond can be achieved only through the skilled technique of an excellent cutter.

To find out more about this process, let us take a look at the following image:

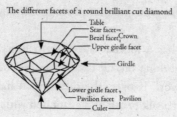

The different facets of a round brilliant cut diamond

Table
Star facet
Bezel facet — Crown
Upper girdle facet
Girdle
Lower girdle facet
Pavilion facet — Pavilion
Culet

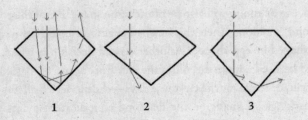

This is an extremely expensive and exquisitely cut diamond. The flat portion on the top is called the table. The shape of the table determines the shape of the finished diamond as seen in the image below.

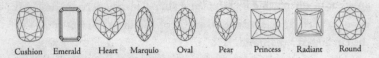

Cushion Emerald Heart Marquio Oval Pear Princess Radiant Round

Below the table is the crown, below the crown is the girdle, below which is the pavilion, and lastly comes the culet.

The crown and the pavilion are cut into many facets. The light enters the diamond from the table; the length, diameter, depth and the angles of the facets influence the brilliance of the reflected light.

That is the reason why the brilliance of the cut of a diamond determines its value.

Small diamonds are weighed and handed over in a lot to the cutter. However, large diamonds are given only one at a time to the cutter.

Every cutter has a locked safe next to him. Apart from the diamond he is working on, all the others are locked in the safe. After the day's work is over, the dust which has fallen down is swept gently with a silk brush and examined with care. The safe is opened and all the diamonds are once again accounted for.

In case of any discrepancy, it is the cutter who is accountable for any loss, so he has to work with total concentration and has to be extremely careful while handling the diamonds.

Even if cutting is a crucial part of the procedure, once the marking is done, it does not take a long time to actually cut a diamond. However, the process of polishing a diamond is a time consuming and tedious procedure. That is why the polishing of the table, the crown, and the pavilion are done by three different persons, each a specialist in his particular area. A polisher has keen eyesight and at the same time an instinctive feel for the diamond. A skilled polisher can tell just by rubbing his fingers over the surface of a diamond if the polishing has been done well.

The methods of polishing a diamond have evolved over the years. At present the 'scaife', a rotating metal wheel, is used to polish diamonds. The wheel is lightly coated with diamond dust and a special tool called 'tang' is used to keep the rear part of the diamond in position while polishing. The table, crown, and pavilion have to be polished to such a degree that the diamond shines its brightest. At times, it takes days to achieve the perfect shine. It is said that African diamonds are the most difficult to polish. But man is known for his passion to take up challenges that nature throws his way. This is absolutely true in the case of the diamond industry.

The months of my training flew past in a blur. There was so much to see, observe, and learn that even 24 hours in a day seemed less. My mind absorbed all the information like a sponge and four months later, I was proficient in the skill of cutting diamonds.

It was my first day at work. I reported to work, full of enthusiasm.

The owner said to me, 'Bhimji, since you have mastered the difficult skill of cutting diamonds on the lathe machine, that is precisely what you will be doing from today.'

I did as I was instructed and went towards the lathe machine. I was supposed to assist the person who was cutting diamonds there. I thought that we would take turns to work on the machine but that was not the way it turned out. That entire day, I didn't get to use the machine myself even once. And it was the same story for the next four days. I was in a real dilemma. *What do I do? Should I speak to the owner? But that might spoil my relations with the other workers. And if I say nothing, how would this situation change?* These and other million thoughts were buzzing in my head.

While I was debating what to do, a golden opportunity presented itself. One morning, as soon as I reached the factory, I noticed an empty place at one lathe machine. I immediately approached the owner and got his permission to work on it.

That day was the real test for me. I said a quick prayer in my mind and began working. I focussed entirely on the job at hand. That evening, the owner carefully examined the diamonds I had cut and exclaimed 'Excellent'. That one word was enough to boost my confidence. From the next day onwards, I decided that I would work as much as I could. For the next month, I worked from 4 am to 9 pm. At the end of the month, when the calculations were done, I had earned 2800 rupees. I couldn't believe my eyes. I had never seen so much money in my entire life and now this was my earning for just one month. My hard work had paid off.

After keeping a little money aside, I sent the rest of the money to my father. A year went by. The situation was gradually improving back home in the village. I repaid the money I had borrowed when I came to Surat, we got the water well on our land repaired, and cleaned and installed a water pump on it.

At the end of one year, Ramila and our two year old daughter joined me in Surat. Our life in Surat began in a small tin shed for which we paid a monthly rent of 25 rupees. It was so tiny that even our family of two and a half people could barely fit in there. A stove, a few utensils and clothes, and a small cot was enough to fill up the entire shed. There was no space left for anything else.

But as they say, necessity is the mother of invention and soon enough, Ramila came up with a bright idea. After the cooking was done in the morning, she used to push the stove under the cot to give us more place to move around. In this way, our kitchen was actually covered by the cot and now served as our sitting area. At night, the same area became our bedroom.

One day Ramila said to me, 'I want to do something too and contribute to our family income.'

I was worried. 'But how will you find the time for it?'

'I'll make time. Anyway it doesn't take me long to finish cooking and cleaning and then I am free the rest of the day.'

The twinkle in her eye told me that she already had a plan in mind.

'You have thought of something, haven't you?'

Ramila explained. 'Many of your colleagues have told me how much they hate the food in their mess. They have had dinner here and they have liked it very much.'

'I am not surprised. You are a great cook.'

'What I mean is why don't we start a mess for them here? Instead of cooking for three people, I will cook for ten.'

I felt so proud of her. That was the kind of the support that I needed from my family.

I talked to my colleagues who loved the idea and our new venture began immediately. Gradually, the mess became so popular that we had 20 regular customers. The charges were 45 rupees per person so Ramila earned 900 rupees per month, a sizeable addition to the family income.

It was difficult to imagine that just a few months ago, Ramila and I were working as farmhands and earning 4 rupees a day. Now our earning had gone up to thousands every month. The days as a labourer were a thing of the past. Ramila now ran a small business and I held in my hands, not a plough but diamonds. Incredible, isn't it? But that is the beauty of life: dark and grim at times, and then all of a sudden, bright and golden.

In a matter of a few months, I came to be known in the diamond industry as an extremely skillful cutter. I was approached by another factory to come and work for them and given a fantastic offer. They tried their best to convince me. They were offering a better pay and finally after a lot of deliberation, I accepted their offer and started my new job.

Gradually our financial situation improved to such an extent that we decided to rent an apartment at a rent of 100 rupees. This apartment had running water, a bathroom, and a kitchen—all the luxuries that we didn't dream of having earlier. Now that we had a big apartment, I called my three brothers to Surat. Shiv had studied up to grade 5, Kurji up to grade 8, and Dhiraj up to grade 9.

They were not inclined to study any further so I thought they could perhaps, like me, do their training in a diamond factory. By then, I knew how the diamond business worked: I was proficient in cutting diamonds, so I suggested that they concentrate more on becoming polishers. In fact, ideally, I thought if one could become a specialist in tabletop polishing, one in crown polishing, and the third in pavilion polishing, it would be excellent for our family's future prospects.

'How is that?' asked Shiv. I smiled, 'If the four of us are experts in these varied areas, one day we could own our own diamond business.'

My brothers were still new to the industry. But I had full faith in them. They too trusted my judgement and did what I had suggested.

In a few months, their training was over and they began work as polishers in a diamond factory. Soon they too became proficient in their trade.

One evening, my friend Kanubhai had come over for dinner. Ramila had made the traditional Gujarati specialty 'Oondhiyo' and puris with it. When Kanubhai realized that all four of us brothers were experts in the four important domains of the diamond industry, he suggested, 'Why don't you start you own factory?'

I replied enthusiastically 'Just what I had in mind. But the problem is where do we get the capital?'

Kanubhai said, 'Don't worry about that. I will arrange the money.'

'If that is the case, we will definitely start our own business. Shiv, Kurji, Dhiraj, are you ready for it?'

The three of them nodded enthusiastically. Kanubhai was true to his word. He introduced me to a businessman who agreed to lend me 20,000 rupees only because he had complete faith in Kanubhai's word and Kanubhai had assured him that I would do everything possible to repay him on time.

I think I have been extremely fortunate in one thing: there have been many who have put their faith in an ordinary man like me and helped me in my times of need. And I too have always kept my word and reaffirmed their faith in me.

Well, we bought a lathe and two polishing machines with the money and started our own factory in a small rented place. I will always remember those first few days; we were the owners and also the workers, we were the sales managers and, at times, even the cleaners.

Initially, we began with job work. The factory owners who knew of my skill as a cutter, started sending their orders to me.

A business, however small it may be, is a source of enormous satisfaction and at the same time it fuels the flames of ambition. The mantra of business is to do more and more work, establish bigger businesses and still have an unending desire to grow.

Luckily, we were never short of work for we never refused any that came our way.

Whatever the challenge, we accepted it as a new opportunity and an adventure. Every such opportunity was also an occasion for us to grow. One by one, we acquired many more lathes and polishing machines. We used to repay one loan and take another to buy new machines and thus expand our business even more. As the number of machines increased, so did the number of workers. And very soon, I rented two huge places; one for us to live in and the other that would become our factory.

One evening, the four of us brothers were analyzing our current position and the progress our company had made.

Shiv said, 'Bhimjibhai, we have done excellent business in the last few months. Work has increased and so has the number of machines. But now, we just don't have the space to put in any more machines.'

I replied, 'That is not a problem. If there is no space, we will have to create it. I believe that where business is concerned, if you stop, you are finished. Most of the huge business empires have been founded on this principle. So, the only way for us is the way ahead. Now that we are on the subject, I want to share my dream with you. We will make our business grow slowly and steadily. However, we should not be satisfied with where we have reached and should always try to aim higher.'

My brothers were puzzled. 'How are we going to do that?'

'See, we will not limit ourselves to doing job work forever. Eventually, I want our company to buy rough diamonds, cut and polish them, and turn them into valuable, sparkling diamonds. I want to sell them not only in the local market but across all the major diamond centres in the world.'

Ramila and my brothers were stunned. Finally Kurji exclaimed, 'Bhimjibhai, do you really believe that this dream will come true?'

'Why shouldn't it? "The word impossible is not in my dictionary", said Napoleon, and I agree with him,' I replied with a smile.

Ramila was still not convinced. 'That Napoleon, whoever he is, can say what he likes. But buying and selling diamonds is not child's play. I think it is too risky. We might fall flat on our faces.'

'I don't think we will. At the moment I am making a detailed study about all aspects of the diamond industry. We will venture into it only when we are completely ready. Don't worry.'

But Ramila gave me a piercing look and asked, 'Tell me, I have been noticing this since the last few days. You go out in the evening and return late at night. Which is this school where one studies late until night? I am really curious to know.'

Ramila had me cornered. I had to tell them my secret now.

'Actually, I go to meet Kantibhai and Keshubhai who come here often from Mumbai. Both are big diamond merchants and our clients. I go to help them but in the bargain, I am also helping myself and our cause because I am trying to learn all that I can about buying and selling diamonds.'

Ramila wouldn't give up. 'I understand that you are learning about the diamond business but what I want to know is how are you helping them out?'

'Alright, I will tell you everything. Once the diamonds are polished, they have to be sorted and graded. This is a very crucial moment and they need people they trust completely, like me. I offered to help them in the grading and sorting of diamonds. My main objective was to learn about a new aspect and increase my knowledge about the diamond industry.'

'So have you fulfilled your objective?' asked Ramila.

'I am on the right track. I am discovering the answers to many questions like what are the things to consider while buying rough diamonds? How should the grading of diamonds be done? And how is the value of a diamond decided?'

'I am slowly learning more and more about the diamond trade. Once I feel confident that I understand its working in all the aspects, we will go for it. Our ultimate goal is to reach the top of the mountain. Worker to factory owner to diamond merchant—that is what we should aim for.'

'"Patel Brothers, Diamond Merchants" that is what we will be known as in the future.'

Everyone was speechless and yet caught up in the same dream and we waited impatiently for the dawn of the next day.

We were facing a space crunch once again. The two flats that we were currently using were not enough for our rapidly growing business. We were planning to buy new machines in order to execute the huge new orders that we were swamped with. I had a lengthy discussion with my brothers. We had a close look at the work and financial situation and finally we came to a conclusion: we would vacate the two flats that we were renting at present and move in to bigger premises.

We found a big bungalow for our family and suitably large premises for the factory and decided to shift both our home and workplace. The owner of the flats that we were renting at the moment belonged to the famous cinematographer Babubhai Mistry. We met him only occasionally. His employee, Mr Mehta, used to collect the rent regularly from us.

The date that we had decided to shift on was fast approaching but for some reason, Mr Mehta did not come around to collect the cheque. We didn't know what to do.

Finally, we decided to go ahead with the shifting. Our belongings were sent to the new place and the two flats were vacated. We felt that we should perform a small religious ceremony to show our love and gratitude to the Goddess Laxmi for looking after us in these flats. We prayed to the Goddess, performed a 'puja', and placed an offering of 11 rupees in front of the idol. We then locked the flats and kept the keys with our nephew who lived close by.

A few days later, Mr Mehta came to collect the rent and was shocked to see both flats locked.

When he asked the neighbours, he was told that Bhimjibhai and his family had moved to a bunglow somewhere and had also relocated the factory.

He called up Babubhai immediately and said, 'Bhimjibhai has shifted both his residence and factory but he has locked up the flats before leaving and has not handed over the keys to me. I am sure he will demand money to hand over the flats to us.'

A few days later, Babubhai came to Surat, found out my new address, and came to see me.

'Aavo, Babubhai,' I greeted him warmly.

Babubhai came straight to the point. 'Bhimjibhai, tell me clearly, how much do you want for the flats?'

'What do you mean?' I said.

'I mean, how much money do you want to vacate the flats? I am ready to give you 1 lakh rupees per flat. Is that okay?'

I replied in a serious tone, 'No. That is not okay.'

Babubhai's face fell. 'How much do you want then? Name your price.'

'I don't want any money Babubhai.'

But he still didn't understand. 'What do you mean?'

'I mean, I was only renting your flats. Now that I have vacated the flats, why should I take any money from you?'

Babubhai replied saying, 'All the tenants do. They demand money to vacate the property.'

'They might do that but I can't. I have no right to such kind of money. In fact I feel grateful to you for renting out the flats to me when I needed them the most. That is why we performed a puja there and didn't feel like leaving the flats unlocked. We locked them and gave the keys to our nephew. Please take them from him. If Mehtaji had come around as usual, all this confusion wouldn't have happened.'

Babubhai almost had tears in his eyes. He shook my hand and said, 'Bhimjibhai, I have several properties and flats in Surat, Baroda, Madras, and Bombay and there are tenants in almost all those properties. But the tenants always expect to be paid a hefty amount for vacating the premises. I have never seen a tenant like you and I don't think I ever will again.'

Babubhai and I became very good friends after this episode and our friendship deepened with the passing of time. When I used to go to Mumbai, he would invite me on the sets to see his shooting. He would introduce me to all the bigwigs of the Hindi film industry. 'This is my friend Bhimjibhai Patel. He is a big time diamond merchant. And what is more special is that he is a rare diamond himself,' he would say.

Money is extremely important. I, of all the people, considering my background, know of its importance. However, I can say in all honesty that to me it has never been more important than people.

Anyway, to come back to the story, our diamond cutting factory in Surat was doing very well indeed; we now had 60 lathe machines, 120 polishing machines, and around 300 employees. It was time, once again, to expand. My trips to Mumbai now increased with this goal in mind. In addition to doing job work, we now bought the raw material, the rough diamonds, ourselves and sold the finished diamonds in Zhaveri market. I was now personally involved in the actual buying of rough diamonds and selling of polished ones. These were very complicated and risky transactions but my years of experience as a cutter and then factory owner and my knowledge of the stones stood me in good stead. To think that only some years ago, Ramila and I had made our first journey with only a sum of 15 rupees in our pocket which had been borrowed. If anyone had told us at that time that in 10 years' time, we would own our own diamond factory and deal in diamonds, I would have laughed out loud. But that is the beauty of life. It changes tracks when we least expect it to and before we even realize it, we are on the fast track.

In 1970, I decided it was time to buy a home in Mumbai and also branch out the business and set up a unit in New Delhi. The children could live in Mumbai with Ramila because the education there was very good. I would try and spend a major part of my time in Mumbai. My three brothers could run the show in Surat. It was possible to dream so big and achieve those dreams mainly because of the solidarity in our family and the unquestioning support of my brothers.

By 1974, everything was running according to plan, so I now looked overseas for new challenges. I wished to see for myself the diamond renowned markets in London, Antwerp, Tel Aviv, and New York. I wanted to learn how the transactions took place, how rough diamonds were bought in the wholesale market, and how polished diamonds were sold.

'Sahib, do you want to get down here, or go ahead?' I was jolted from the past into the present by the voice of the taxi driver.

'I want to go way ahead.' The words were out of my mouth before I realized I had said them.

'Eh? But you had said…' Confusion was written all over the taxi driver's face.

I came out of my reverie with a jolt and said, 'No, I will get down here.'

I got down from the taxi and started walking towards our home with a spring in my step. How happy everyone would be when I told them that I had got the visa.

Epilogue

It was Bhimjibhai's first trip abroad. He landed at Heathrow airport. His nephew Jitu had come to receive him. Jitu had migrated to England from Africa and had now settled down in London. Jitu drove him home where his wife welcomed them with the traditional hot cup of Gujarati 'masala chai'.

For a moment, Bhimjibhai felt as if he was back home in Gujarat.

Jitu wanted to know more about Bhimjibhai's plans for his Europe trip. When Bhimjibhai explained that he wished to observe and learn the various aspects of the diamond trade and even buy some rough diamonds, Jitu looked worried. He glanced at his wife and said, 'Uncle, your plans are good, but frankly how will you manage all this when you don't speak any European language?'

Bhimjibhai was confident. 'I know diamonds and that is the most important language in this business.'

Jitu and his wife didn't seem convinced and were still worried that Bhimjibhai would have trouble communicating with people or that someone might cheat him. Jitu's wife said, 'Uncle, you will have a problem and you will find it difficult to communicate when you visit different countries, stay in strange hotels.'

Bhimjibhai smiled. 'Actually, those people will have a problem. See, I am their client, so it will be in their interest to make sure they can communicate with me.'

Jitu burst out laughing. 'Uncle, you have a point there.'

'Don't worry about me, Jitu. I too will make an effort to communicate with them. In fact, I have prepared thoroughly for this visit. I have got important information about myself and our business written down in English. I have a list of names, addresses, and telephone numbers of the people I need to contact. Most important of all, I have a written list in English of all the questions to which I seek answers about the diamond trade here. And last but not the least, I have made arrangements for a broker to accompany me in each of these markets and these brokers are Gujarati and they also speak the local language. So, I am 100 percent sure I will not have any problem getting my work done.'

Jitu looked impressed and was finally convinced.

He and wife wished Bhimjibhai all the best for his venture and assured him that they would help in any way they could.

The first trip was a great success. In the years to come, Bhimjibhai made so many trips to the diamond markets all over the world, that travelling abroad became a routine matter for him. He became an expert in cutting the best deals—whether it was buying or selling of diamonds—and he soon made a name for himself in the world of diamonds. People talked with great admiration and respect about Bhimjibhai Patel, the diamond merchant.

Bhimjibhai's dreams had materialized and the credit for this goes to his inherent talent, his genius, his passion for learning, and for his capacity for hard work, his integrity, and his unshakeable confidence in himself and his abilities. His incredible journey from the very bottom to the highest peak of success is awe inspiring.

At the same time, one wonders if he ever tripped and hurt himself in this climb to the top?

Wasn't he ever defeated by circumstances, by bad luck or accidents? Naturally, there were several such instances in Bhimjibhai's path to success. The story of any business or indeed, any person, would be incomplete without such incidents.

Bhimjibhai narrates one such instance. He had set up an office in New York as a part of his expansion plans. He was in search of an experienced and trustworthy person who could take charge of the office. Just then a young Gujarati man came to see him. He was looking for work and he had been referred by an acquaintance of Bhimjibhai. He was originally from Ahmedabad but had been living in the US for some years now. Bhimjibhai spoke to him at length.

He had quite a few years of experience so Bhimjibhai decided to entrust the responsibility of the New York office to him.

Initially, everything went off smoothly. Bhimjibhai used to visit the office frequently and see that everything was on track. However, as the days went by, there was a subtle change in the man's behaviour. He seemed a little distracted, careless, and unwilling to put in any extra effort.

Bhimjibhai also realized that he was reluctant to submit accounts and generally avoided giving clear answers to any question. He had even stopped picking up Bhimjibhai from the airport as he used to earlier.

One day, he just disappeared from the scene. It was only then that Bhimjibhai learnt that he had been cheating the company. He had fudged the office accounts and had siphoned off a tidy sum for himself.

Bhimjibhai frankly admits that he himself was entirely responsible for this incident. He should have checked the man's background more thoroughly and verified all his references in Ahmedabad before entrusting him with such a big responsibility. Had he done that, this unfortunate incident could have been avoided. Bhimjibhai certainly learnt a lesson thanks to this unpleasant experience.

Another instance that comes to his mind is after he began visiting the diamond market in Antwerp and established a solid reputation for himself there. Bhimjibhai, like several other Indian diamond merchants, used to buy diamonds at wholesale prices there, get the grading done, retain the good quality stones, and finally return the inferior quality stones to the wholesale dealers.

The employees who sorted and graded the diamonds, whether they were Belgian or Indian, strictly followed the norms laid down by the Belgian Government. All workplaces were closed for the weekend in Belgium and hence the diamonds had to be returned to the owner by Friday evening. In the hurry to leave for the weekend, sometimes inferior quality stones got mixed with the good quality ones and vice-versa. In both situations, the loss was borne by the owner. And the loss was substantial, often running into lakhs of rupees.

Bhimjibhai had found out a unique way to tackle this situation. The sorting and grading premises of the diamond centres were empty on Saturday and Sunday. Bhimjibhai used to go there and grade and check the diamonds very carefully himself over the weekend. He thus ensured that he received only the best possible stones. Everyone in Antwerp praised his initiative and respected him for his efforts in rechecking the diamonds himself.

A very big diamond merchant from Mumbai was in Antwerp. He heard of Bhimjibhai and was impressed by his astuteness. He too had had to face severe losses a couple of times due to the employees who did the grading. So he appreciated all the more Bhimjibhai's careful approach to the business. He felt that if the two of them got together, the sky would be the limit for them.

Eventually the two met and after a lot of discussion and deliberation, decided to become partners in the diamond business. When two such talented and enterprising persons got together, it was only natural that their dreams would be larger than life and they would succeed in turning these dreams into reality. The result of this partnership was the immense, impressive, state of the art 'Diamond Nagar' in Surat which was spread over a massive area of 120 acres.

Diamond Nagar lacked nothing. It was equipped with every facility you could think of. Naturally the diamond factory itself was ultra-modern, with the latest equipment and machinery. Diamond Nagar also had spacious and comfortable housing facilities for its employees, a huge dairy, a factory that made dairy products, a textile unit, a service centre for vehicles, big farms which produced vegetables, fruits and flowers, and even a factory which made the specialized machines needed in the diamond industry.

Diamond Nagar was an ideal, prosperous, rich, picturesque, and self-sufficient township. Visitors from all over the world, including scores of VIPs, made it a point to visit it. It was the realization of Bhimjibhai's ultimate dream. It was the highest point on his success graph. Bhimjibhai had spared no effort to turn his dream in to reality. However, sometimes even reality can be an illusion. In a few years, the partnership ran in to bad weather and was dissolved. With it, Diamond Nagar became history.

But Bhimjibhai takes everything in his stride. 'That is life. Every business has its ups and downs. But one's feet should always be planted firmly on the ground. Money, assets, and material things may come and go; the one richness that will always remain with me is my knowledge and experience of diamonds. If I look at it in that light, I will never ever lose the treasure I have accumulated.'

Today Bhimjibhai, in his seventies, is as dynamic and active as ever. It is a source of great satisfaction and pride to Bhimjibhai that his three brothers are still with him. 'My brothers have complete faith in me and always trust my instinct. They know that if I decide on something, there is always a valid reason for it. That is why they implement my orders without question. Of course, I eventually explain the reason for my decision and they understand it.'

Their family has offices and residences in Mumbai, New Delhi, and Chicago and the next generation of Patels—highly educated and qualified—have joined the ranks to take the business to new levels of success. Bhimjibhai's son Lalji, did his MBA in the US and now looks after the Chicago branch along with his wife. Shivlal's son Ravin looks after the business in New Delhi.

Along with diamonds, the family also has a textile unit in Surat which Shivlal handles. Dhirubhai and Kurjibhai head the Mumbai office. The youngest generation is at present enrolled in universities in the US and Taiwan and they have yet to chart out their future.

Bhimjibhai himself is back in his village 'Hajiradhar' and back too in his role of a farmer. He does farming on the 14 acres of family ancestral land. He also runs 'Lalji Dairy and Farm Private Ltd' which produces dairy and farm products.

Bhimjibhai keeps a close watch on the various aspects involved in farming and at the same time also goes frequently to Surat, Mumbai, Chicago, New Delhi, London, Antwerp, and other places all over the globe to keep track of his diamond business.

Along with official documents and papers, he carries a heavy load of books when he travels. These books too have travelled the world with him. Zhaverchand Meghani in Gujarati and Dale Carnegie (he has read the Gujarati translations of his works) are his favourite authors. He reads all kinds of books published in Gujarati and they are still a source of information and inspiration for him.

The latest and certainly not the least of Bhimjibhai's achievements is the Mongi Bai Dhaya Patel school in Hajiradhar, which he has set up in the memory of his mother. Almost 700 students study in the school at present. The school is especially significant when one considers the fact that Bhimjibhai could not receive a formal education because there was no school in their village. Today, no child in Hajiradhar need suffer a similar fate. All thanks to Bhimjibhai's vision and initiative.

THE CIRCLE OF LIFE

Mohanbhai Patel

It was the year 1958. I was facing an extremely busy morning since I had received my first major order for collapsible aluminium tubes from the Himalayan Drug Company. I was a small-time producer then, manufacturing tubes used for packaging toothpastes and other drugs or medicines. The factory was working on a war footing to successfully execute the order. While I was supervizing every small detail personally to ensure that everything went off without a glitch, the telephone rang.

'Hello. This is Mohan Patel speaking.'

A voice at the other end said, 'Good morning, Sir. I'm calling on behalf of Mr Cochran Barnett, the Managing Director of Metal Box Company. Mr Barnett would like to meet you. When would you be available?'

I was taken aback. I wondered what the Managing Director of Metal Box could possible want from me.

Metal Box was a highly reputed British company, the leading producer and supplier of collapsible aluminium tubes in India. In contrast, I was a new entrant in this field compared to big guns like them.

Since Mr Barnett was my senior in age, experience, and position, I offered to go to the Metal Box office myself. I fixed up an appointment with Mr Barnett's secretary and went there at the appointed hour.

Mr Barnett came out personally to greet me and escorted me into his office. It was just him, his secretary, and me in the cabin. Giving me a broad smile, he gestured for me to sit.

'Young man, I have heard a lot about you. I know that you passed with a first-class degree from the prestigious Faraday Engineering College in the UK. You were then invited to join the Tata group of companies in India on a very high post. That's spectacular.'

I was bewildered. *Why is Mr Barnett praising me to the skies?*

Fixing me with a stare, he continued, 'Thanks to your intelligence and abilities, you have proven that you are an extremely talented and dedicated person. That is why I am all the more surprised that you decided to give up a fantastic job with the Tatas to start your own enterprise.'

His tone had now turned razor sharp. His words were laced with heavy sarcasm. 'Look here, I am going to be very frank with you. Our company doesn't tolerate competition. We are the leading producers of collapsible aluminium tubes in India and we will do everything to ensure that it stays that way. We will make sure that any company that dares to stand up to us is destroyed.'

What arrogance. I thought.

I was both shocked and angry. However, keeping a check on my emotions, I replied in an even tone, 'Mr Barnett, there are seven companies making aluminium tubes in England. But they do not waste their time fighting among themselves. If a customer likes the products of a given company, the company gets the order on the basis of the customer's preference. And if such healthy competition is acceptable to all there, why should it not be acceptable in India? Ours is a big country. You need not feel threatened by another small company like mine setting up shop. You look after your customers' needs and I will cater to mine.'

Mr Barnett was livid with anger by then and said angrily, 'That is what everyone says in the beginning but very soon, they try to steal our clients from us. I will not tolerate such nonsense. I will not allow a nobody like you to interfere in our business.'

But I was firm. 'That is your problem, Mr Barnett. My decision to start my own business has been taken after a lot of careful consideration. I have put in a lot of efforts to make it possible and I am not going to shut it down because of your threats. Goodbye, Mr Barnett.'

And with that, I got up to leave. All of a sudden there was a change in Mr Barnett's tone. 'Mr Patel, please listen to what I have to say. It will definitely benefit to you. Firstly, we will give you double the amount of money that you have spent to set up your company. So, you see, you will not lose a penny and in fact gain double of what you invested.'

I stood there is silence while he continued in a conciliatory tone, 'That is not all. Your company will be absorbed into Metal Box. You will be given a very senior post here and double the salary that you were getting in Tata—3000 rupees. Since you have studied in England, you will also get all the benefits and perks offered to a senior British manager. What do you think?'

I was actually amused by the bribe that was being offered to me in the guise of this proposal, but I replied with a straight face, 'Thank you very much for the generous offer, but...I'm afraid I cannot accept your proposal. You see, I am a Gujarati. I come from the trading community. Securing a job holds no importance for us. It is every Gurajati's dream to start his own business. We believe that being successful in business proves the mettle of a person. So whether you threaten me or try to tempt me, my answer will be the same: I will not close down my business.'

Mr Barnett was speechless with anger. Finally he said, 'Okay, Mr Patel. If you want to commit professional suicide, so be it. Have you heard of the Orient Can Company? It had dared to stand up to us as a competitor. Where is it now? Nowhere. It has closed down, leaving its owner bankrupt. If you fail to see reason in what I said, you will meet with a similar fate. Even today, most pharmaceutical toothpaste industries have a European management board. We can bring pressure on them directly from Europe to ensure that they do not buy your products.'

'Secondly, one of your most important raw materials—aluminium slugs—is produced by the Indian Aluminium Company, Indal. The Director of Metal Box is also the Chairman of Indal. Does that tell you something? You will not get the raw material you need from Indal.'

'Thirdly, and finally, there is only one company which makes the plastic caps for the collapsible tubes—the Indian Plastic company. We are its biggest client. We will make sure that they do not sell the caps to your company.'

I could not restrain myself from laughing.

'Mr Barnett, please do not demean yourself with these ridiculous threats. I have thought of each and every single eventuality that you have mentioned. And this is what I have planned: Firstly, there are many European companies producing pharmaceuticals and toothpastes in India. However, there are also several Indian companies like Sarabhai's, Alembic, Zandu, and Bengal Chemicals which are growing at a rapid pace and establishing themselves in the market. More importantly, there are many officials in these companies who take pride in being Indian. They will not bow down to foreign pressure and will do their utmost to encourage Indian entrepreneurs. In fact, there are also many foreign companies who have no problems about giving work to Indians. My products will speak for themselves. If they are of a superior quality, they will find customers—Indian or European.'

'Now for your second threat: Indal. This is not a recent problem. You have already put that threat into practice a long time ago. You have bought raw material from Indal far in excess of your demand, only to prevent me from procuring it. In fact, you have even taken on rent the Kamani company warehouse since you don't have enough space to store all your raw material. And now that your agreement with Kamani is due for expiry, you are getting impatient to settle the matter. Well Mr Barnett, you are welcome to keep the raw material, because you see, I have signed a deal with Indal according to which they have agreed to supply the raw material to *my* company.'

'For your third and final threat: the matter of the plastic caps. What a trivial issue. Just so you know, from now on I will be producing all the plastic caps that I need for my business in-house. I do not need to depend on anybody else for such small matters. In fact, I do not even need to pay anybody else to produce these caps for me. Plus, doing so will also double my profit.'

Mr Barnett face was drained of all colour, making me even pity him. But there was one final score to settle.

'Mr Barnett, one expects at least a modicum of decency from an educated and "cultured" person like you. But today, I have been disillusioned. If I had stooped to such low tactics and done the same to you in your country, how would you have felt?'

Mr Barnett was now sweating profusely. His secretary looked at him and tried to intervene. 'Mr Patel, I think you have misunderstood us. That is not what Mr Barnett meant.'

I replied, 'Madam, with all due respect, please stick to what you know best—making coffee for your boss—and don't try to come to his rescue. You too have been a witness to his threats. But I would like to make it clear once again: I am not someone who gives in to threats. Good day.'

And I stepped out of Mr Barnett's cabin.

1980

Twenty two years have passed since that heated discussion in Mr Barnett's cabin. The small company that I had started back then is now an integral part of the Patel Extrusion Group of Industries comprising of 11 large-scale companies. We produce all kinds of collapsible tubes in our factories. Our head office is in Goregaon, Mumbai, close to the Western Express Highway.

I'm again reminded of the day when I was in my cabin, going over some documents. My secretary entered and handed me a letter. It was from the European Packaging Manufacturers' Association. It said:

Congratulations, Mr Patel. We are pleased to announce that your company has earned the distinction of being the highest producer of collapsible tubes in the world. It is our pleasure to invite you to be the Chief Guest at our worldwide meeting to be held in England next month. We would also like to extend a warm invitation to your wife. The details of the meeting, including the date, venue, and time, will soon follow.

I felt extremely proud and honoured. After all, it is the public recognition of one's work that counts, isn't it?

I immediately called my wife Chanda and gave her the good news.

The venue for the function was a picturesque island near London. The arrangements for our stay and sightseeing were truly impressive.

When we reached the venue of the meeting, one seat in the first row had especially been reserved for Chanda. As I entered, the Head of the Association walked over and escorted me to my place on the dais.

The meeting soon commenced. The Chairman welcomed all the members, outlined the agenda, and introduced me to the audience.

'Please welcome our honourable Chief Guest, Mr Mohan Patel from India. His company is the leading producer of collapsible aluminium tubes in the world, used for toothpastes and pharmaceutical products.'

This statement was greeted with thunderous applause.

Mr Chairman turned towards me and continued, 'Mr Patel, It is a tradition in your country to welcome guests with a garland of flowers. We do it in a slightly different way. I wish to salute your achievements and hence, I offer you my chair for the day.' The Chairman stood aside and with a gesture invited me to begin the proceedings for the day.

I was overwhelmed. What an unforgettable moment. This temporary chairmanship was more precious to me than any gilded memento or certificate. It was an occasion which proved that there is poetic justice in this world after all.

Dhandha

Ever since I can remember, I always wanted to become an Indian Civil Service (ICS) officer and achieve the highest glory possible in my chosen profession. At the time I had no intention of becoming an engineer and I certainly had no idea what a collapsible tube was.

Such are the quirks of fate.

And, in fact, why should my fate be any different? Even Lord Ram did not have any idea of what the future held in store for him. On the eve of his coronation, he was a Prince waiting to take over the administration of a huge, prosperous kingdom. Little did he know that the very next day, he would have to leave behind his home and his kingdom and go to the forest for a long period of fourteen years and lead a life of hardship and danger.

Returning to the subject of my childhood dreams, the reason why I was so fascinated by the Civil Services was my awe-inspiring neighbour—H. M. Patel.

Muljibhai Patel lived in the bungalow next to ours at Jogeshwari. He was always singing praises of his son Hirubhai (H. M. Patel) and justly so.

Hirubhai's career graph was exemplary. He was always first in his class in school and college. He then went to England and passed the ICS exam with flying colours. He had held many important posts in the ICS on his return to India and was at the time a Textile Commissioner in Delhi.

Hirubhai was my idol, my greatest hero in those days.

I still remember how excited everyone would be when Hirubhai visited his family. His father, Muljibhai, couldn't do enough to welcome him. Hirubhai likes this... Hirubhai loves that... And so on and so forth.

The entire household would be busy for days preparing for his arrival, as if he was not the son but the precious son-in-law of the family. Our family too participated in these festivities with equal enthusiasm. Muljibhai would tell my father, 'Ishwarbhai, don't forget to get patra (a savoury snack that Hirubhai liked very much) from Bhuleshwar.' And my father would make it a point to go in the evening all the way to Bhuleshwar at the other end of town and get two kilos of patra from one particular shop.

When Hirubhai would finally arrive home, our little lane would be bustling with life. I was awestruck by the long line of cars parked below his house (from Hirubhai's official car to all kinds of impressive foreign cars belonging to the VIPs who came to meet him) and by the elegant, richly dressed people who got down from these cars. I was fascinated by the aura of power he exuded.

So when I finished the Matriculation exam, I announced my plans for the future: I would complete my B.Com, then go to London and give the ICS exam.

But in reality, I didn't even have to wait until I finished B.Com. Immediately after the Inter-Commerce exams, my father decided to send me to London to complete the rest of my studies there.

My father paid 900 rupees and got me a ticket aboard the military ship S.S. Franconia. After a forty-day long voyage, the ship finally docked at Southampton port in 1946.

Mr Rambhai Patel, a family friend of ours, was there to receive me. Rambhai was the General Manager of Bhavnagar State Railways and was presently in England to buy some engines for the Railways. In those times, it took almost two hours to reach London from Southampton and we started chatting during the journey. Rambhai asked me in Gujarati, 'London avianu karan?' (Why have you come to London?)

I immediately launched into a detailed explanation of my future plans: Bachelors in Commerce from London University; Law at Lincoln Inn; and last but not the least, the ICS exam.

Rambhai looked at me strangely and said, 'Well, the rest is fine, but it will take you at least three to four years to complete all this and by that time the ICS exams will be stopped.'

I was speechless. 'What do you mean?'

'I mean that at present the last batch of candidates is preparing for the ICS exams to be conducted in London and this is the last year that these exams will be held here. From now on, the exam will be called the IAS (Indian Administrative Service) and candidates will be able to appear for these exams in India itself.'

All my dreams were shattered in the space of a moment.

Rambhai asked me 'What will you do now? Return home?'

What terrible luck. I had only just arrived in England and there we were, already talking about going back home. I shook my head vehemently.

Rambhai started to laugh, 'I am not suggesting that you go back right now, son. Take your time, think it over and then decide what you want to do.' After this, he started talking about other things. I pretended to listen to him when in fact I had no idea what he was saying. My head was reeling.

But by the time we reached Victoria Station, I had made up my mind. I announced my decision to Rambhai. 'I have given up the idea of becoming an ICS officer. I have now decided to do my B.Com, become a Barrister, and then pursue a career in Law.'

Rambhai nodded his head without saying a word.

The following day was a Sunday. I got up late, had breakfast and then left with Rambhai to do some sightseeing in London.

We started the day by visiting a lovely park near the place where I was staying. We strolled around and then sat on a bench. Shortly, Rambhai asked me, 'So, what have you decided? Are you going to be a lawyer?'

I replied firmly, 'Yes.'

Rambhai didn't seem to approve of my decision to pursue law. He was silent for some time. Finally he said, 'So, you are going to become a lawyer. You will become an expert at twisting the truth.'

I was taken aback, 'There are so many lawyers in the world today. They command respect and they are very successful in their profession.'

Rambhai replied, 'Yes, of course. But what is the key to their success? Their ability to spin a web with words. They have to ignore the call of their conscience. I could give you so many examples. Who benefits the most from a property wrangle between two brothers? The lawyer. Who saves a criminal and helps him get away with his crime? The lawyer.'

My head was reeling once again with confusing thoughts and emotions. 'But, what do you suggest I do then?'

'Why don't you become an engineer?'

'An engineer?'

'Yes. What our country needs above all today is engineers. You are perhaps aware that very soon the British will leave India. Independent India will need many new industries. If you love your country and want to make a positive contribution to its development, then you should become an engineer and play a dynamic role in its progress. I hope you understand what I am trying to say.'

I did understand the point that he was trying to make but I didn't know what to say.

We got up and went off on our tour of London. But my mind was in turmoil. The same questions kept repeating themselves in my mind—*What do I do now? Which profession should I choose?*

However, by Monday morning I had finally come to a decision. During breakfast, I told Rambhai, 'I have decided that I will become an engineer.'

When I had arrived in England on Saturday, I had plans of becoming an ICS officer. Within two hours of my arrival, I had decided to become a lawyer, and now I was saying with conviction that I wanted to become an engineer. What strange turns life takes.

However, Rambhai did not seem to find anything unusual about my decision. He was very glad, in fact, and said, 'Okay. Now that you have made up your mind, I will see what is to be done.'

The very next day, he took me to the prestigious engineering college, Faraday House.

We met the Registrar there who was a retired Brigadier of the British Army. He listened to us, had a look at my certificates, and declared, 'Sorry. But you do not have the right background to be an engineer. You have been a commerce student until now. What made you change your mind all of a sudden?'

I replied, 'I am interested in engineering and I am willing to put in all the necessary effort to become an engineer.'

'All right then. You will have to study the technical subjects required for engineering and give the Matriculation exam here once again. The Matriculation exam will be held in four months' time. If you score 75 percent marks in this exam, you will get admission to the Engineering course here.'

Now I was really scared. The wheel seemed to be turning backwards. Although I had already passed the Inter exam, I would now have to sit again for the Matriculation exam. That too with new subjects and only in four months' time.

Only then could I hope to enter an engineering college. I didn't know what to say. But Rambhai replied on my behalf. 'Yes, of course. He will do it.'

Considering the confidence that Rambhai was showing in me, I now had no other option but to give it my best shot and become an engineer.

Five years later, I became an electrical engineer. I immediately started work as a trainee.

By then, my family had begun pressing me to get married. The truth was that I had already chosen my future life partner a long time ago. I was only 17 and Chanda 14 when we fell in love with each other. We were neighbours then and our families knew each other well, so they were happy when I announced she was the girl I wanted to marry. During the five years I spent in London, we had not even spoken to each other over the telephone, let alone meeting her. But we were still firm in our decision to get married. We regularly wrote letters to each other during this period as a means of staying in touch. These letters, an expression of our love, had only served to deepen the bond between us.

So after finishing my engineering studies, I came to India on a whirlwind trip of eight days, got married to Chanda, and returned with her to London to begin a new, happier phase in my life.

My work was interesting and I had a loving wife. Life seemed complete. But as soon as one begins to feel content about having achieved a milestone in life, there comes a feeling of 'What next?' Man is always looking ahead and dreaming new dreams. Now that I was well-settled in London, happy with work and home, I had started nurturing dreams of returning to India.

Around this time, Sir Norman Redford, head of the London office of the Tata Limited Company, received a letter from

Mr A. D. Shroff stating that they were looking for a young, dynamic British engineer for their Bombay office.

Sir Norman Redford in turn contacted the Principal of Faraday House, Sir John Adams, and asked him to recommend a suitable candidate for the post.

Sir John was perplexed at the request and enquired, 'I understand you need a young, dynamic engineer. But why do you insist he should be British? If nationality is not such an issue, I would like to recommend one of our best students, Mohan Patel for the job.'

Sir Norman held Sir John in high esteem and agreed to meet me on his insistence. I had taken my certificates and other documents with me. But Sir Norman gave them a passing glance before looking at me intently and announcing, 'Yes, young man. You are selected.'

I was surprised. 'Pardon me, Sir, but don't you want to interview me?'

Sir Norman smiled and shook his head, 'No. I had never intended to interview you. After the glowing recommendation given by the Principal of your engineering college, it seemed hardly necessary.'

I was overwhelmed. 'Thank you...thank you so much, Sir.'

'You are welcome,' he replied. 'I will write to the Bombay office immediately and inform them of your selection. In the meantime, you can start working in our office here, get to know the workings of a Tata enterprise, and then join the office in Bombay later. Your salary will be 1800 rupees in addition to which you will receive all the facilities and perks that a British engineer would enjoy. Is that okay with you?'

I nodded in approval. I was over the moon about my selection for it marked an important achievement in my career.

I had attempted to climb a mountain (however small) and had successfully reached the summit. I promised myself that this would certainly not be the last or the highest glory that I achieve in life.

Bombay suddenly began to look so much within my reach.

A few days later, Sir Norman asked me to come and see him again. On my way to his office, I thought to myself, *Sir Norman must have received a reply to his letter from the Bombay office confirming my appointment. In fact, I might even get the appointment letter today itself and I can start work immediately.*

I entered Sir Norman's office and as I had thought, he handed me a letter saying, 'Here is the letter from the Director of the Bombay office, Mr A.D. Shroff. He wants to bring you on board. However…'

I was puzzled. *What could the problem be now?* I asked myself. I was getting increasingly impatient and wanted to know what Mr Shroff had said.

'Well, Mr Shroff is of the opinion that you are certainly an appropriate and deserving candidate. However, since you are an Indian, you should not be given the same salary and facilities given to a white British engineer. Instead of 1800 rupees, they could offer you a salary of 800 rupees. This is quite a comfortable salary for a young man of your age in India.'

Sir Norman was looking at me closely as I read the letter. He now asked, 'Well, what do you think? Do you think it is alright?'

I really didn't know what to think. It had been more than four years since India attained Independence, but nothing seemed to have changed much for white skinned people were still being considered superior to those who were brown skinned.

The Parsis (the community to which Mr Shroff belonged) in particular were known for their admiration for all things British and they firmly believed in the saying, 'If you are white, you are right.' They were impressed by the superiority of the British culture and tried to emulate the British and their language, customs, and mannerisms.

In answer to Sir Norman's question I said, 'I do not know if their offer is right. However, I will now have to decide what the right thing for me to do is.'

Sir Norman persisted, 'And what have you decided to do?'

Without giving the matter any further thought, I declared, 'I accept the offer and the job.'

'Nonsense.' said Sir Norman in a rising tone, his voice echoing in the room, 'The Principal of one of the most reputed engineering colleges in England thinks you are his best student and you're still ready to accept 800 rupees instead of the 1800 you should rightfully be getting. Why? Indians always accuse the British of putting them down and discriminating against them. Now who is the one discriminating against Indians? An Indian himself. And in spite of being fully aware of the situation, someone as intelligent and deserving as you is still ready to give in to his demands? No way. I will not be a party to it. I do not agree with the racist attitude of your superiors in India. If you are ready to take things lying down, it is your responsibility to communicate your decision to them. I will have nothing further to do with it.'

He held out the letter towards me. I was ashamed of myself and realized what a grave mistake I had made. At the same time, my respect for him grew manifolds. 'You are very right, Sir. It is not right to forego my self-respect and accept a demeaning offer like this just because I am eager to return to India,' I said and left his office.

Several heated discussions between Sir Norman and Mr Shroff followed. I do not know the minute details of their conversation.

However, I was ultimately told that I would be offered a salary of 1500 rupees to work as an engineer in the Bombay Tata office. Without stretching the matter further, I accepted their offer and prepared to leave for Bombay.

I joined the Tata office in Bombay at a salary which was 300 rupees less than the salary of a British man. But I had no regrets.

Firstly, 1500 rupees a month back in 1953 was considered a princely sum. In spite of leading a very comfortable life, we spent only 300 rupees on our monthly household expenses. That meant a massive saving of 1200 rupees every month.

Of course, our idea of a 'comfortable' life was quite simple in those days. It meant a first-class train pass from Jogeshwari to Churchgate. We would work for half a day on Saturday. Chanda would reach my office by 1 o'clock. We would then enjoy a delicious 'thali' at the nearby Chetana restaurant for only 5 rupees. Then we would watch an English film at the Regal or Empire cinema, followed by a walk at Chowpati beach. We would be back home in Jogeshwari by 10.30 pm after a perfect day together.

Another important reason why I was so happy in those days was the work satisfaction that my job at Tata gave me. I had been given the position of Head of the Electrical Engineering Department. This was a very big responsibility for a young man of 25 years and I was certainly aware of it. That is why my aim was to make optimum use of every single moment of the time spent at work. Our office would open at 10 am. However, I would reach office everyday by 9.30 am to do my homework, plan my day meticulously, and also read international journals and magazines in the field of engineering to keep myself up-to-date with the latest developments. By the time everyone arrived in office, I was ready to tackle the challenges of a new day.

As soon the staff members arrived, it was time to get to work. Laziness and shirking from work were a taboo in my department. Very soon, I earned the reputation of being a demanding taskmaster.

It was now six months since I had returned to Bombay. One day, the Director, Mr A.D. Shroff, sent me a message asking me to meet him immediately. When I went to his office, he said, 'Patel, when you were working at our London office, you were handling a rolling mill project, weren't you?'

'Yes Sir. I had prepared a project report for the rolling mills, including details of the machinery, projected expenses, budget for the project etc,' I said.

Mr Shroff nodded his head, 'Okay. Well, we are now going to start a pilot plant of these rolling mills. We are going to order the machinery from London. Since you already have an idea about this project, I think you should handle it. You will be in charge of the entire project and will have full responsibility.

I was very enthusiastic about the job and accepted it immediately.

I began corresponding with our London office regarding this project. My work was now being looked after by Hayles, a British man. I asked him to send me the latest figures for the project. While I was reading through the documents sent by the London office, I noticed that there was a revised quotation for the purchase of machinery for an amount totalling 75 lakh rupees. I was astounded because only six months ago I had prepared a quotation for the same machinery for 38 lakh rupees. *How could the price have almost doubled in such a short span?*

I wrote to Hayles asking him for a clarification. He replied stating that the figures he had sent were correct. But I knew something was not right. So I sent repeated letters asking for all the details regarding the purchase of machinery. Even after several such letters, Hayles stuck to his guns and was not ready to concede my point.

A few days later, I got another message from Mr Shroff asking me to see him in his office.

When I entered his cabin, he said in an irritated tone, 'Patel, what do you think you are doing? Why are you not agreeing to the quotation sent by the London office? Our project is being delayed all because of your stubborn attitude.'

I explained the reasons for my insistence but he refused to see the point I was trying to make.

'There must be some misunderstanding on your part. If Hayles has sent a quotation of 75 lakh rupees, it must have been based on appropriate calculations. He *must* be right.'

Now, I was really angry. 'White is right' was still a firm, unshakeable belief in our country. I looked into Mr Shroff's eyes and said in a firm voice, 'I had made the appropriate calculations as well. In the past six months, none of the prices I had considered in my quotation have doubled. As the person in charge of this project, I say once again that I cannot approve of the purchase of the machinery at these prices.'

I awaited the explosion of anger. Mr Shroff was one of the most senior and respected directors of the Tata Group of Companies. He was known to be knowledgeable in financial matters. Why would he listen to the words of a young, inexperienced pup like me?

But to my surprise, he was silent for a moment and then, in a conciliatory tone, said, 'If you are so firm in your belief, I suggest you go to London, meet Hayles personally, and get to the bottom of this matter. The important thing is to resolve this issue at the earliest. Our project should not be delayed under any circumstances.'

I was slightly mollified by his words but the stubborn streak in me refused to give in, 'Why should I go to London? Hayles is my junior. He should come here to discuss the matter.'

Mr Shroff gave me some advice, 'Patel, remember one golden rule. Work comes before any personal issues. Ego hassles shouldn't come in the way of work. If we take a step forward and in this way ensure that our work doesn't suffer, there is nothing wrong in it. Listen to me. Go to London and get to the bottom of this matter.'

I took into consideration Mr Shroff's age and experience and nodded my head in agreement but I was still not too happy about having to travel all the way to London to prove my point.

The first thing I did after arriving in London was to go and meet Sir Norman who had retired from work by then. When I explained the situation to him, he told me that, 'Do not give up if you are convinced that you are right. Get to the heart of the matter, investigate each aspect in detail, and prove your point.'

I met Hayles and started to discuss the matter. Initially he refused to change his opinion. It took me four meetings, a detailed analysis of the figures given by him, and clear proof of the errors in these figures before he accepted that he had indeed made a mistake. Now whether the mistakes were genuine or intended to be so was for the company to decide.

I had achieved my objective. The quotation finally settled at 44 lakh rupees. I had succeeded in saving the company a sum of 42 lakh rupees, no less.

Without any further ado, I placed the order for the machinery.

An important consequence of this episode was the increased confidence that Mr Shroff now had in me.

He was convinced that I only had the company's benefit in

mind and that my actions were always driven by that motive and not by my ego or selfishness. This incident marked the beginning of a long standing relationship based on mutual trust, confidence, and respect between Mr Shroff and me.

I had now settled down and was enjoying my work at Tata. In the course of my work, I was often required to visit other companies. I would get to meet successful entrepreneurs who had created some of these companies and was mightily impressed. Gradually, a desire to be like them and own a successful business of my own took root in my mind.

But I kept thinking to myself—*Which business should I venture into? Which business would still be successful a few years down the line?*

Around this time, the company received a big order from the Railways. We had to supply them with vitreous enamelled reflectors, which we were going to source from the Bengal Enamel Company.

I soon realized that enamelled reflectors were required in large quantities not only by the Railways but also to light up roads, factories etc. So I decided to begin a company that produced these very enamelled reflectors.

Without wasting any time, I gave an advertisement in the newspapers asking people who had knowledge about this specific field to contact me.

In reply to the advertisement, a Mr Rasik Lal Dave came to see me. He said to me, 'Patel Saheb, why are you setting up a new factory in Bombay? Such a factory already exists in Dadar, though it is not operational at the moment. Why don't you take over this factory instead of starting from scratch?'

Rasik Lal's words made sense. I made detailed enquiries about the factory and found out that it was closed since the last two years due to financial problems. The owner lived in Calcutta and the factory was currently mortgaged with Dena Bank.

When I showed an interest in taking over the company, the Trade Union Leader, Mr Bandivdekar, met me, spoke at length about the situation of the company, and then requested me to re-employ the old staff and workers, as these people had been out of work for the past two years.

I told him, 'When I start the company again, I will take the same workers and pay them the same salaries they were getting earlier.'

Bandivdekar said, 'But Patel Saheb, these people have been unemployed for the past two years and through no fault of theirs. Can you offer them some compensation for that?'

I decided to clear this issue at the outset. 'Bandivdekar, the past is the past. That is not my responsibility. I can only guarantee the workers a fair deal in the future. Think over it.'

Bandivdekar was a sensible man and saw the point I was trying to make. Even though he was a union leader, he realized that inciting the workers and convincing them to demand and fight for compensation would not serve their cause. He realized that it was in the workers' best interest to start work right now. This positive attitude of his paved the way for a solid and stable relationship between the workers and the management of the company in the future.

The workers were delighted that the Indian Enamel Company would begin functioning once again. The management of Dena Bank was equally delighted.

The company owed a sum of 1,10,000 rupees to the bank. If I took on the responsibility of repaying this amount, it would be a relief for the bank as well.

During my meeting with the Dena Bank officials, they probed and asked me a number of questions about my background and my current position—'Do you have any previous experience about the industry? What is your current salary? At present what are your expenses? How do you plan to repay the loan amount?' and so on.

They were duly impressed by my experience, my designation in the Tata group of companies, and my income.

I promised them saying, 'Initially I will repay 1200 rupees per month to your bank. And once the company begins operations and starts making a profit, I could repay a larger amount every month and clear the loan at the earliest.'

There was an audible sigh of relief from the bank officials and I was given the permission to take over the running of the company. The Indian Enamel Company was now officially mine.

From then began the real battle of making this business run successfully once again. But I had decided that I would do everything possible to achieve this dream.

I had to literally give it all I had because I invested almost my entire savings in the company. I negotiated with the owner and gave him the sum agreed on. I then supervised the repairs of the machines and ordered the raw materials needed. It involved a lot of hard work but at the same time, there was also the thrill of finally handling a business on my own.

For a long time I managed to do both—managing the Indian Enamel Company and my job at the Tatas. Then, there was also my responsibility to my family, my wife, children and parents. At times, I felt guilty that I took them for granted. So I decided to resign from my job with the Tatas. However I realized that I would have to discuss the matter with my family and take them into confidence first. So, one evening, I went back home early. After dinner, I interrupted our casual family conversation and dropped the bombshell.

'Bapu, I am handing over my resignation to the Tatas.'

Just as I had expected, a shocked silence followed. No one knew how to react or what to say.

Finally my father found his voice and declared, 'Mohan, everything is going so well for you. Why do you want to upset it all? You have a job which people would kill for at a prestigious company like Tata, a senior position of responsibility, and a fantastic salary. What more can one ask for?'

I had anticipated this reaction from Bapu. His whole life, he had run a small business and it was a matter of pride for him that his son had been educated in England and had such an envied job with an iconic company like the Tatas. He was so impressed by my air-conditioned office and the chauffeur driven Chevrolet car given to me by the company. He used to proudly announce to everyone, 'My son is a Bada Saheb now.'

Bapu was really upset. He continued to voice his dissent, 'What is the point of starting one's own business when one already has such an excellent job? Actually, I was going to ask you this very question when you bought the Indian Enamel Company, but since you said that you will be managing both the job and the business at the same time, I didn't say anything. Now why this sudden decision to quit the job?'

I did understand Bapu's point of view. But at the same time, I too had my dream and I was eager to see it turn into reality. I said in as gentle a tone as possible, 'Bapu, I want to start my own business. For the past few days, I have been managing both my job and the business but I cannot continue like this forever. At some point in the future, I will have to take the crucial decision:

job or business. Well, I have already made my decision. I want to be a businessman.'

And the argument continued.

I refused to change my mind and Bapu refused to let go of his opinion. Finally, he shook his head and in a defeated tone said, 'I will be brutally honest with you, dikra. As a businessman, you will not always get the respect that you now get because of your prestigious job in Tata. This may sound crude but, in fact, there are times in business when you will have to lick the puchadu (backside) of a person whose face you cannot stand seeing. So, think well before deciding anything.'

But I was firm in my decision. The next day, I went to see Mr Shroff, placed my resignation on his desk and explained the situation to him. He listened to what I had to say and then, instead of picking up my resignation, said, 'I understand the strain that you are going through. But why do you want to give up such a good job because of it? I have an excellent idea. Why don't you work half day here in our office?'

I was taken aback.

Mr Shroff continued, 'Don't think too much about this. I am suggesting this for your own good. Come to our office for half a day and then spend the rest of the time in your company. Once the business begins to run well and you start making a profit, well, think about resigning then.'

I thanked Mr Shroff and left his office after having torn up the resignation.

When I came back home and related the incident to my father, he didn't say a word and only gave a small smile.

Then it was back to the same gruelling routine of office- factory-home-office.

But I could now give a lot more time to the business.

At the end of the month, I received my monthly pay cheque from Tata. I was stunned to see the same amount as before. I immediately went to see Mr Golwala, the chief accountant, 'Mr Golwala, I think there is a mistake in this cheque. I now work only half day here so I shouldn't be paid my entire salary.'

Golwala smiled and replied, 'No, No, Mr Patel, There is no mistake at all. Mr Shroff has specifically instructed me not to deduct anything from your salary and to make out the cheque for the entire amount.'

I didn't have words to express my feelings. Mutely, I took the cheque and left the office.

It was a few months later. I was in my cabin at Tatas, reading an engineering journal. One particular advertisement caught my eye. It was by a German company called R. Lechner. They were looking for an Indian company or an individual in India to market their aluminium collapsible tubes for them.

These hollow, light, aluminium collapsible tubes were made of very thin foil of aluminium and were used for packing toothpastes and other medicines. Since they had to be sent by ship, their packaging had to be carefully done in order to ensure that they were not damaged during transit. However, if the German company was sending these tubes all the way to India even with this added cost, I was sure that it was because it was a profitable deal for the German company and that there was a large demand for this product in India.

This advertisement set me thinking. *If there is a large demand for these tubes in India, why shouldn't we make them here? We would save a lot on the transport and make double the profit.*

I got up like a man possessed and started pacing the length of the room thinking how to go about it.

In the following days, I obtained more information about these collapsible tubes. I found out that there was only one big company in India which was producing them: Metal Box.

But the demand for collapsible tubes in India far exceeded the quantity being produced and hence companies like R. Lechner exported these tubes from Germany and sold them in large numbers here.

My interest was aroused. I decided that I would set up a factory to produce these collapsible tubes in India. Of course, the easiest thing to do is to decide on something. The real challenge is tackling the seemingly insurmountable odds that come up while setting up any new venture. But I have also realized one thing: the bigger the challenge, the greater your will power to overcome it and in such a situation one seems to possess an infinite amount of energy and determination.

A job at Tata, the Indian Enamel company, and now the creation of a new enterprise: it was like walking a tight-rope. I suddenly started feeling that 24 hours in a day were not enough.

The Indian Enamel Company was running well. Production had begun and we had good orders for the reflectors. There was only one problem: procuring the raw material. In order to get the steel plates needed for producing reflectors, we had to repeatedly knock at two doors.

One was the office of the Directorate General of Technical Development (DGTD) in Delhi to procure the license and the second was the office of the Iron and Steel Control Board in Calcutta.

We had to face the typical red tapism and bureaucracy prevalent everywhere in India.

At the D.G.T.D, the officials would unconcernedly 'sit' on your file for days without doing a thing about it. Only after repeated visits and prolonged wrangling over the size of their 'cut in the deal', would they deign to approve the application for the license. Even after everything would be agreed upon, there were still some officials who would hold up the license on some flimsy excuse.

One such officer was Mr Tomar. Once a file was on his table, it was difficult, nay impossible, to hope that it would be cleared early, if ever at all. And trust our luck—our file had to land up on his desk. We were so dejected. However, to our relief and joy, an official memo was issued by the Ministry of Industries saying that no file should take more than 40 days to be cleared.

I was thrilled. Now it would not take more than 40 days to receive the license. But sadly, it was a case of counting the chickens before they had hatched. After 35 days, I got a letter saying that a few details had not been included in my application and that I would have to submit a new application.

And with that went up in smoke my dream of getting the license on time. I had no other option but to start all over again with a fresh application.

And this was just the beginning of the nightmare. Receiving the license after that intense battle was not a cause for joy. Because, now began the even more terrible ordeal of getting a quota approved from the Iron and Steel Control Board in Calcutta.

In those days, there was no direct flight from Bombay to Calcutta. An Indian Airlines aircraft would leave from the four major cities of India—Bombay, Delhi, Calcutta, and Madras and these four aircrafts would arrive in Nagpur at around the same time. In Nagpur, both mail and passengers would be transferred to the appropriate aircraft which would then take them to their destination. Hence one reached Calcutta at 6 am only after a tiring all night journey.

I used to freshen up quickly and land up at the office of the Iron and Steel Control Board only to be greeted by a closed door on most days.

The office was officially supposed to open at 10 am but the Bengali Babus, lazily chewing paan and holding up their dhoti with one hand, would casually stroll into the office only around 11 am. This would be followed by the usual vociferous fight over seats and it always ended with the Superintendent having to barge in to resolve the issue. By the time this daily farce was dutifully enacted, it was already noon. We then charged and valiantly battled to get our job done. It usually took four to five such arduous trips to Calcutta to obtain a quota for 100 tonnes of steel.

Every time I had to go to Delhi or Calcutta, I had to take leave from the Tata office. When it became embarrassing to take leave so frequently, I redrafted another resignation and walked into Mr Shroff's office. When he saw the letter in my hand, Mr Shroff asked me, 'What is this?'

'My resignation, Sir.'

'What is the problem *now*, Patel?'

'Sir, I often have to go to Delhi and Calcutta for my business and I cannot come to office. This is not right, Sir.'

'Says who?'

I didn't know what to say.

Mr Shroff continued, 'I would in fact suggest that since you have to go to Delhi and Calcutta often, you could also finish our pending work in these cities. For instance, we have submitted a tender of 30 lakh rupees to the D.G.T.D office in Delhi. Anyway,

I have to send someone to Delhi to follow it up. Why don't you do it? Do you get my point?'

Once again, I was left speechless. Mr Shroff seemed very pleased with his innovative idea. With a twinkle in his eye, he said, 'This saves us some money and a lot of time and in fact, it saves you double the money. Since you will be going to official Tata work, the office will also pay your airfare. So your work is done and you also save on the airfare. Isn't that great?'

I tried to protest, 'But, Sir…'

But he wouldn't let me get a word in.

'Don't say anything now. Tear up that resignation and throw it in the dustbin.'

Once again, I left Mr Shroff's cabin, my resignation letter crumpled up in my hand, amazed and overcome with gratitude at the warmth of this man.

Things at the Indian Enamel Company had settled down much earlier than expected and I was delighted, as was my father, to see that after just one year of production, we had made a profit of 75,000 rupees which was twice of my annual income at Tata. My father was relieved. He was now sure that I would become a successful businessman.

Now that I was confident of the success of the Indian Enamel Company, I threw myself completely into the research of the collapsible tubes industry and made preparations for my entry into this field.

I began by contacting the German company R.Lechner. I wrote to them saying that I was an Indian entrepreneur who was interested in producing collapsible tubes in India and asked them if they could guide me in my venture.

Being such a big company, I didn't think they would even respond, but was surprised to receive a very cordial reply from them. In spite of the fact that I would eventually be their rival in the field, they assured me that they would do their best to help me and guide me. And they were true to their word. Over the next few months, they gave me a lot of valuable information about the machinery that I would need for producing collapsible tubes. I was impressed by their professional approach.

I then contacted another German company called Herlan and fixed up a deal to buy the machinery from them.

I then began efforts on a war footing: on the one hand I applied for an import license for the machinery to the D.G.T.D in Delhi and at the same time I also started to scout around for someone to finance my project.

Thankfully (and for a change) I was in the right place at the right time. The Government had recently launched a scheme to promote small-scale industries in India. The Small Industries Corporation, used to buy the machinery and give it on a hire-purchase basis to businessmen. I approached them and finalized everything.

Now there remained another important issue to fix: space.

After a long search, I leased a place in Malad, a Bombay suburb.

Just as the preparations for the launch of the venture were almost in place, I received another letter from Herlan asking me to come to Germany for a month. The purpose of this visit was to tie up any loose ends of this deal as well as to undergo the training necessary to understand the functioning of the machinery.

Once again, I was back in Mr Shroff's office, resignation in hand. This time, he asked me in an irritated voice, 'Well, what is it now?'

'Sir, I have to go to Germany for a month and I simply cannot ask you for a month's leave.'

Mr Shroff replied, 'You are right. And I simply cannot give you a month's leave.'

'That is why, Sir, I request you to please accept my resignation.'

'No way, Mr Patel. I will not accept your resignation because I am sending you to England.'

He saw the puzzled look on my face and taking pity on me, explained, 'Patel, if you want to go to Germany for a month, then do so. In fact it will be good because on your way back, you can stop over in England and wrap up a pending matter for us with the Manchester Lancashire Dynamo Company. Now get ready to leave. I will send across the relevant documents to you as soon as possible. Oh, and by the way, please throw this resignation of yours in the dustbin on your way out. That is the perfect place for it.'

On my return from Germany, I threw myself deep into work. My day used to begin early in the morning at 6 o'clock by going to the Indian Enamel Company in Dadar which had now been renamed Lance Metal and Enamel Works. I used to spend two to three hours there and then go to Churchgate to my office at Tata where I would work for four hours a day. After this I would once again return to Lance and from there go to the new factory at Malad in the evening.

We had decided to name the new company Patel Extrusion. The factory had just been built and the machinery had recently arrived from Germany. We were now faced with the daunting task of getting the machinery started. Since electricity was available at this factory only at night, I used to begin my work there in the evening and stop almost every day at dawn.

Due to such a hectic schedule, I had almost forgotten what it felt like to go home. The task of getting the machinery working was so riveting and absorbing that the workers and I never realized how the night flew by. I used to have my morning tea and breakfast in the factory itself and then would began another hectic day. Running to catch the local train from Malad to Dadar to Churchgate to Dadar to Malad—the routine continued day after day. During those days, the only sleep I got was in my train journeys from one point to another.

Once, when it was more than a month since I had gone home, my father packed his bag and said to my mother, 'My son doesn't seem to have the time to come home. So I might as well go and stay with him at the new factory. In fact, I will do whatever I can to help him there.'

And he was true to his word. He stayed with me at the Malad factory for six months. It was also a big relief for me because now there was someone trustworthy to supervise the work while I was away.

Since both her husband and father-in-law had decided to stay at the factory, Chanda began getting us our dinner to the factory. On one such occasion, she got the children along with her. It had been many days (or was it months?) since I had met the kids. As soon as they entered the factory, they began to look for me but couldn't see me anywhere. Finally she asked my father who was sitting outside where I was. He pointed to some workers working on a machine. Their clothes were covered in grease and their faces were black and grimy. Chanda had a tough time identifying me from the lot. She burst out laughing. I noticed her and waved my hand. She waved back and showed me the tiffin she had got for dinner.

I must admit that those were magical days where one lost track of time, hunger, and thirst. It was a lot of hard work but I could see my dream coming true in the near future and this spurred me on to inch closer and even closer to that dream.

However, there came a day when I felt I was going round in circles. My life was nothing but work, work, and more work. I was not getting a minute's rest. I had not gone home in six months and had not been able to spend any time with my family. Thankfully my wife, children, and parents understood but finally there was a limit to how much one could stretch their patience.

Once again, I wrote out my resignation and stood before Mr Shroff, my hands joined together in appeal. He immediately guessed why I had come to see him.

He began interrogating me. 'Has the machinery arrived?'

'Yes, Sir.'

'Has the production started?'

'Not yet, Sir. That is what we are trying to achieve right now.'

'I see. If the production is yet to begin, that means no income, no profit from the factory as yet, right?'

'Yes Sir. There is still a long way to go before we make any profit.'

'Well, then why are you in such a hurry to resign?'

'Sir, I can no longer bear the burden of this triple responsibility. So this time I request you please accept my resignation and free me of at least one responsibility.'

This time Mr Shroff did not argue and accepted my resignation. I was overcome with relief and gratitude. When I thanked him for all that he had done for me, he patted me on the back and said, 'Patel, I hope your dream comes true and you achieve every success you wish for in life. You certainly deserve it.'

As I walked out of the Tata office building, I couldn't help turning around for a last lingering look.

What a great company and what a great boss.

I promised myself that these would forever be my ideals when I ran my own business in the future.

The machinery had arrived from Germany and I was now caught up with the complex and delicate job of its installation and commissioning. At the same time, I was also planning for a big inauguration ceremony.

Even though the Indian Enamel Company was my first business venture, in a way it was not entirely my own creation. But Patel Extrusion was my own baby. Right from the idea of setting up a factory to produce collapsible tubes, to struggling to get the entire show on the road, all the effort was mine. Naturally, I wanted to have a grand inauguration ceremony for it.

We had already received our first major order from the Himalayan Drug Company. The raw material needed was ready. Once the machinery was commissioned, production could begin in full swing. We set a date for the trial.

A set of dies had been sent along with the other machines from Germany. However, when we decided to conduct a trial we realized that the specifications of these dies were in inches while we had done all the other calculations in millimeters. We had to redo all the calculations which meant a loss of several days.

Finally the day of the first trial of the machines arrived. We were going to be producing the first batch of collapsible tubes in our factory.

The workers, experts, and I had all taken our positions. There was palpable excitement in the air.

As a pressure of 200 tonnes per inch was applied on the aluminium disc, there was a huge cracking noise. For a moment all of us stood still in shock. Then we ran towards the machine. The machine tool had broken.

We didn't know what to do. Instead of seeing our dream come true, it had literally shattered right in front of our eyes.

I made a frantic telephone call to Germany and asked them to make a new tool for us and to send one of their technicians to India to help us install it. They were very helpful and promised to send someone at the earliest. However, when they told me how much the cost of all this would be, I was heartbroken.

In the present scenario, it was impossible to even think of paying such a huge amount. So, finally, I had to abandon that plan. I decided that we would make the tool ourselves. Production plans were put on hold and we addressed ourselves to the more urgent task of making the tool.

The special kind of steel that was needed for making the tool was available only in Austria. When we contacted the company, they said that they could supply us the steel but the delivery would take three months. It meant that we would get the steel only by December.

The problem was that we had planned the inauguration for September. Mr Manubhai Shah, the Minister of Industries for the Central Government, had already accepted our invitation to inaugurate the factory. Several other important industrialists, friends, and relatives were also going to be there. But how could there be an inauguration without the machinery being commissioned?

I was in a real dilemma. I discussed the matter with my family.

Bapu said, 'Mohan, I think we should go ahead with the inauguration as planned.'

I was not so sure, 'But Bapu, the machinery is not yet ready for production.'

He insisted, 'That does not matter. It is the inauguration of our factory. We are not claiming to have started production. The factory building, the machines are there for all to see. That is enough.'

I was still not convinced so in his typical way, he gave me an apt example from our culture: 'You know how in India, the wedding ceremony goes on as planned even if an old lady in the family passes away. Everyone puts on a brave act until the wedding is over. The funeral, the grief is dealt with later. And the same applies to business as well.'

I had no other option but to agree (albeit reluctantly) to this practical point of view. I too realized that it would shake my clients' confidence in me if I postponed the inauguration.

So, ultimately, the inauguration ceremony went on as planned. It was a grand affair. The Minister, several V.I.P s, our friends and family were all present on the occasion. I showed everyone around and finally requested the Minister to press a button to start the machinery. The sound of the machine starting was drowned in the roar of applause that followed. Nobody realized that the machine was not actually producing the tubes.

The steel for the tool arrived from Austria in December and after a lot of back-breaking, we managed to make the tool.

Once again, it was the day of the trial—January 17, 1958. It was my wedding anniversary. But there was another reason that this day became unforgettable for me: This time, we were successful in producing the first collapsible tube in our factory.

Our first order was for 2,500 tubes for the Himalaya Drug Company. The incident that I narrated at the beginning of the story took place when this order was almost ready for delivery. After that explosive meeting with Mr Barnett, I worked tirelessly for I had a point to prove.

Our first order was executed on time. But do you know how the delivery was made? In a bullock cart.

After that first order, the next few months were extremely dull as we did not have too many orders. Business was not really picking up. Then all of a sudden, we got a challenging order from Alembic, a leading pharmaceutical company, for ophthalmic nozzle tubes. (In layman's terms, these are tubes used for packing eye ointment.) In those days, these tubes were made from tin which was far more expensive than aluminium. Hence the cost of these ophthalmic nozzle tubes was also prohibitively high: Four hundred rupees for 100 such tubes.

I felt that if we made these tubes out of aluminium, it would greatly reduce its cost and eventually prove to be very beneficial to the common man who would buy the eye ointment. I wrote to the Herlan company in Germany and explained my idea. However, they were very categorical in their reply: It would not be possible to make ophthalmic nozzle tubes from aluminium as it is a hard metal.

These tubes needed to be made out of metal sheets of only a thickness of 1/10th millimeter. It would be impossible to get aluminium sheets so thin. And finally, nowhere in the world were these tubes made from aluminium. So it would be in my best interest to forget such an idea.

I reread the letter a dozen times but still couldn't help thinking that there must be a solution. I decided to follow my intuition and began a very detailed research of the tubes—their design, size and specifications, the dies and tools required for their production—by reading books and making experiments in the factory.

The Circle of Life

In the meantime, we had received a large order of 5 lakh ophthalmic tubes from Alembic. I gave them a choice—they could order the tubes made from tin which would cost them 400 rupees per 1000 tubes. Or they could go in for aluminium tubes instead which would cost them 80 rupees per 1000 tubes—one-fifth the price. I assured them than both tin and aluminium were equally safe for packing these ointments.

Naturally the lure of the financial benefit succeeded in convincing the company and they finalized an order for 5 lakh aluminium tubes. It was impossible for me to turn back from here now.

After all the calculations were done, the tiniest details worked out and checked several times, we were ready to produce the first batch of aluminium tubes. The tension in the factory was tangible.

Finally, the moment we all had been waiting for was here. I placed the dye in the machine and pressed the lever. Everyone was holding their breath...but alas, there was a cracking sound and the dye broke.

The disappointment was visible on everyone's face. I too was dejected. But then I thought to myself that I would not let this one incident deter me. I would try again and surely succeed one day.

We redid our calculations and remade the dye. But once again, it was the same story. The dye cracked and broke into pieces. We repeated this process not once, or twice but 30 times. And every time we were faced with the same scene: the dye broken into several pieces.

It was on the thirty-first attempt that the machine finally started working and one tube came out after another. We managed to make 7 tubes before the dye broke. This time we were not dejected about it breaking because we could now see light at the end of the tunnel. A month of feverish work, another trial, and this time we succeeded in making 250 tubes before the dice gave way.

More efforts, more calculations, and then finally the day dawned. The machine produced 1,600 tubes and the dice had still not broken. We could not believe our eyes. For a long moment, there was a stunned silence. And then all of us erupted with joy. Managers, workers, technicians, accountants, peons…we were all screaming with joy, tears streaming down our faces: 'We have done it. For the first time in the world.'

We were all clapping our hands like small children. To tell you the truth, we did not completely realize the importance of our achievement then and how the tube was going to make history and change my life forever.

Once the Alembic order had been successfully executed, we were swamped with large orders for ophthalmic nozzle tubes, not just from the big pharmaceutical companies in India like Sarabhai, but also from abroad.

Nowhere in the world were these tubes made from aluminium and we were making the cheapest tubes in the market. Hence the terrific demand for them.

As I mentioned earlier, these tubes changed the course of my life.

And in a way, an error in calculation on my part only helped to add to the success story. I had made some basic calculations and quoted a figure of 80 rupees per 1000 tubes to Alembic. In reality, after I had completed the order, I realized that the cost to me was approximately only Rs 40 per 1000 tubes. I had made almost double the profit I had imagined. But before I could do something to rectify the mistake, I had already given quotations to several other companies based on the earlier calculations. So this time, for a change, even my mistake made me a lot of money.

Anyway, to cut a long story short, I was soon acknowledged as the worldwide king in the field of ophthalmic nozzle tubes and I can proudly claim the title even today.

When I look back at the past, I realize that the odds against me had been almost insurmountable. The key to my success was my perseverance and the unshakeable belief I had in myself. Every time, I encountered an obstacle, I did not lose heart and kept going until I reached the peak that I had identified as my target.

Naturally I am proud of my achievements. At the same time, I have to confess that in the long run towards the winning post, many precious moments in my personal life passed me by. I always regret that I could not devote enough time to my family and especially to my children during their growing up years. I couldn't enjoy their childhood with them and for them too, Papa was like a meteor who flashed through their life from time to time.

I remember one incident in particular. It was during one summer vacation when the children were quite small. As usual, some of our friends had planned to go to Lonavala for holiday with their family. All my friends had taken a month's leave and would take their kids on long walks and exciting treks. But our family was the only one where 'Papa' was not a part of the plans. I had told Chanda and the kids to go ahead with our friends and enjoy themselves. And I had promised them that I would join them every weekend. Of course that 'promised' weekend never arrived. The kids used to wait eagerly for me to arrive every weekend and every time, they would be left disappointed.

One day, Chanda was chatting with our friend and well-known writer, Gulabdas Broker. He asked her in a tone of banter, 'Chanda Ben. What is this? Why does Mohan always give you hollow promises which he never keeps?'

Chanda of course took my side as always and said, 'No. Actually Nayan's Papa was going to come here but there was an order to be delivered and he had to be there.'

Gulabdas said, 'Its ok. I was just joking.'

But little Nayan quipped, 'Mummy. Come on, let's change this Papa.'

For a moment both Chanda and Gulabdas were stunned by the little boy's outspoken words.

Even when Gulabdas returned home, the words were ringing in his ears. It is interesting to note that he later on wrote a very poignant story with the title: 'Let's change Papa.'

At times like these, I felt so guilty. But on the whole I have to admit that everyone in my family—my parents, wife and kids— have been exceptionally supportive of my efforts and have always understood me.

The biggest credit goes undoubtedly to Chanda. She was firm in her belief that whatever I do will be in the best interest of the family. And she had shown this confidence in me from the very beginning.

When we decided to get married, initially her family was not very happy about it because they were quite well off in our comparison. But Chanda had told her father firmly, 'I will marry only this boy because I am certain of one thing: even if he has only one morsel to eat, he will first offer it to me.' And this confidence was never breached in all the time that we have been together.

Another person who always supported me during all the uncertain times when I first launched my business was my father.

He had always been a small businessman but he was extremely astute about judging people. Whenever I had to deal with any kind of difficult situation, I turned to him and he always gave me the correct advice in his rustic and inimitable way.

Some of his favourite Gujarati proverbs taught me a lot:

Dikra, namyo to gamyo.

One should always be humble and respectful. People like a person who speaks respectfully. Arrogance only breeds enemies.

Kharkartinu chayanda na levo.

A leafless tree like the 'beri' cannot offer shade to others. Do not depend on someone who is weak himself. Another principle he firmly believed in was that one should always lead a simple life.

Of course, in those days I did not agree whole heartedly with this principle of his.

Three or four years after I started the business, money was flowing in and I was quite successful. Naturally I was proud of my achievement. I decided to splurge and built a house for my parents in our village. Here, I must explain that no matter where we are or what we achieve, we Gujaratis always remain firmly connected with our roots. We ensure that at least one-fourth of what we earn goes back into the village where we came from. We build a home there, invest in agriculture there, give donations to the local schools, temples etc. We make sure that we make a positive and constructive contribution to the development of our village. So when a group of Gujarati businessmen meet, the favourite topics of conversation are business, share prices, and what they have done for their respective village.

Anyway, to come back to the principle of simple living advocated by my father.

81

In those initial heady days of success, I too gave in to temptation and bought a brand new imported white Impala car, which was considered a status symbol in those days. Only film stars or Maharajahs were seen driving around in them.

As expected, my father did not approve of this extravagance at all. He was of the opinion that why should one buy a new car when the old one was working fine?

I did not argue with him but I had no intention of giving up my precious Impala either.

To tell you the truth, I used to be thrilled with all the attention I got from the onlookers when I drove by in my posh car. Coincidentally, the famous film star of the time, Dilip Kumar, too, had a white Impala. So when I used to go by in my car, the children on the street would yell: 'Hey. That is Dilip Kumar.' I used to preen and secretly think that I must in some way resemble him. Well, one day, my car stopped at the Vile Parle railway crossing and as usual, a crowd collected around the car, shouting: 'Dilip Kumar, Dilip Kumar.'

But just then, one smart (or over smart) kid peered inside the car and shouted, 'Arrey. No. It's not Dilip Kumar. It is just some "Phaltu admi," a "nobody".'

I came down to earth with a bump.

When I narrated the incident to my father, he couldn't help saying 'I told you so. Showing off money is a sham. The only reality is work and work alone.'

This time, I agreed with him and sold off the Impala. From that moment, flashing wealth has never been my reason for buying a car. If someone asks me today, which car do you have? I say, 'I don't know. I know my driver and I go in whichever car he is driving. The make or the model of the car is not important to me.'

Since then I firmly believe that the sole purpose of a car is to take me from one point to another.

It is impossible for a businessman to compartmentalize his life. A businessman cannot say 'I will work only from 9 am to 5 pm' and put the thought of work out of his mind when he returns home. It is not as easy as a salaried person for him to say 'I have had enough. I am now going to retire.' He cannot afford to slow down, to stop. A businessman who slows down, who stops, is out of the running.

Of course there are times when one feels like listening to one's inner voice and doing something different. I am one such lucky businessman who had the luxury of being able to stop when he wanted to. And for this I have my two sons to thank. Nayan and Kartik, my two sons, began working with me even while my business was growing. So when I felt that I had done all I could and had achieved what I wanted in the field of collapsible tubes, I handed over the baton to my sons. It was now up to them to continue and expand the business according to their vision. Fortunately my sons gave me this opportunity to pursue my other interests.

After handing over the reins of the business to my sons, I devoted myself to other issues close to my heart—working towards making a constructive contribution to society, particularly in the field of education and science. However, one day, I realized that once again I was swamped with work. I did not have a moment to spare. I did some soul searching and found out that what I wanted above all was to take a breather, in the literal sense of the word. I wanted to get away from the crowd and the hectic Mumbai life and take a deep breath of pure, unpolluted air.

Dhandha

I used to dream of a small house, away from the noise and hustle-bustle of Mumbai, yet at the same time within easy reach of the city. The more I dreamt about it, the easier it became to envisage: A small, cozy house, against the backdrop of hills, surrounded by green fields, hundreds and thousands of trees, a little stream or river flowing through it…

Very soon I became obsessed with this dream and set about in search of my ideal home. For once, my family was totally in agreement with me. So everyone became a part of this mission.

My son Kartik was very enthusiastic about location hunting. So every Sunday, he and I would set out early in the morning and visit several possible locations in the Mumbai suburbs of Vasai, Virar, and Dahanu. We used to have some information about available lands before setting out and we used to find out about many more while we were actually there at the location. In the afternoon, we would sit beneath a tree, eat the 'theplas' we had brought along with us from home, and enjoy the cool shade, the peace and quiet.

Once, we went to see a piece of land in Dahanu and liked the place. The only problem was that it was a little too small for what I had in mind. The caretaker informed us that there was a huge plot of 250 acres at a distance of hardly 5 kilometers from there which we should visit. So, we went off to investigate further.

We reached the village of Amboli-Karanjgaon where the land was located. We met the old caretaker there, Bhaskar, who was more than happy to provide us with the desired information. It was a very big piece of land that seemed to stretch as far as the eye could see. There were small hills on it, little brooks and streams flowing through it. At one end, there was a tall mountain, with, believe it or not, a historic fort on the top.

The Circle of Life

The old man launched into his story: 'Saheb, this fort originally belonged to one of the Sardars of King Shivaji (the famous Maratha king) and this land was also his.

Unfortunately, his descendants were not as capable and they divided the land into smaller pieces and sold them as and when they needed money for their extravagant habits. The present owner of the entire land is a Marwari, Mr Punmiya.

We did not feel like leaving the place until we had climbed to the top of one of the hills and we did not have cause to regret our decision. It was a breathtaking view. Since it was the monsoon season, the entire area was shining with the glow of an emerald. I was enchanted by the amazing shades of green. Kartik echoed my thought when he said softly, 'Papa, this is like a second Switzerland.'

The next time, Chanda and my daughters-in-law also came with us to see the land and just like us, they too, immediately fell in love with it. Everyone agreed that we had to buy this land.

When I contacted Mr Punmiya to ask about the land, he seemed unnaturally eager to sell it off to me. I was puzzled by this. We quickly agreed on the price and the terms and conditions of the transaction. I was surprised by the speed with which he worked on the formalities and ensured that the deal be finalized at the earliest. Once we had to meet the District Officer regarding the deal. The District Officer pulled me aside and whispered, 'Sir. That land is not auspicious. Why are you buying it and inviting trouble for yourself?'

I did not pay any attention to his words and the deal went through as planned. One fine day, Kartik and I met Punmia and very soon, all the formalities were complete and the Patel family was now the proud owner of the land.

I said to Mr Punmiya, 'I would like to go to our land and officially receive the papers of the land from your hands there.'

Mr Punmiya looked as if he had been struck by lightning. He shook his head vehemently, 'No, no. That will not be necessary.'

I did not understand what he meant and tried to explain to him: 'Punmiya Sheth, buying a piece of land cannot be just a dry business deal. It forms a link between the two of us and it makes it more meaningful if we are actually standing on our land as it is transferred from one owner to the next.'

Mr Punmiya looked at me as if I had taken leave of my senses. He was now trembling with fright. He said, 'No, no, I don't want to go there. The Adivasis there are terrible and I am scared of them.'

I used all my persuasive powers to finally convince him to come with me to the land near Dahanu. As we left behind the Western Express Highway and approached the area, we saw that the road had been blocked by stones and boulders and both sides of the road were lined with ferocious looking Adivasis who were glaring at us.

We pretended not to notice the tension, got down from the cars, and began clearing the road so that our cars could pass through. Punmiya seized this moment and said, 'Mohanbhai, I think I will go back now.'

But I stopped him and said in a clear, firm tone: 'No, we are going ahead. We will sit in the old house in the clearing, have some snacks, and then you will hand over the papers to me. Only then will we leave.'

Punmiya followed me with the air of a sacrificial lamb being led to the slaughter.

While we were having lunch, we could see the Adivasis gathering around us.

After a while there was quite a huge crowd. Their leader, a man with bloodshot eyes, stepped forward and with an aggressive air cried: 'Hey, you. Come out.'

I asked Mr Punmiya who he was. He replied that his name was Ladkya and that he was the Adivasis' leader. He was also the local representative of the Communist party. Everyone was terrified of him because he was believed to have committed two murders in the past.

Ladkya yelled once again, 'Sheth, can you hear me? Come out.'

I went towards him, looked him in the eye and calmly said, 'You come in here if you want to talk to me.'

He came inside the clearing stamping his feet, followed by several Adivasi men with spears and sickles in their hands, and started firing questions at Mr Punmiya, 'What is going on? Why did you sell the land?' He then turned towards me, 'And you. The new Sheth. Why did you buy it?'

Shantilal Punmiya cowered before him. Ladkya kept on repeating the same questions again and again: 'Why did you sell the land? Why did you buy it?'

Finally I lost my cool and shouted back at him: 'Who is the one who has sold this land? And who is the one who has bought it? It's none of your business. And by the way, who are you? Everything has been done legally and I am now the owner of this land. And not just the owner in name only. I am going to build a house and live here, with my family.'

Ladkya was glaring at me. The men behind him took a step forward and started threatening us: 'Who do you think you are? We will bash your head in, break your legs...'

I could feel the situation turning ugly.

I took Kartik aside and told him to quietly leave from the back door and go straight home.

When he protested, I pushed him towards the exit and went back towards the Adivasis. For a long moment, there was silence.

Both sides were taking stock of the situation. Then, suddenly, Ladkya said to me: 'Sheth, if you have any common sense, don't come back here tomorrow.'

He then turned towards his men and gestured for them to go back. One by one they followed him.

Shantilal Punmiya was mopping his brow, 'I told you they were dangerous.'

I didn't reply. I was thinking about this new turn of events and wondering how to tackle it. Suddenly I noticed Kartik. He had not left.

He said, 'Papa, how could I leave you alone and go home in a situation like this?'

I was touched but I replied, 'I was concerned for your safety. What if something had happened to the two…'

But he cut me short, 'But nothing happened, right? So let's not talk about it. Let's go home now.'

The very next day, I decided to go back. But this time, I was not taking any risk. I took along several security men from the factory and asked them to carry their guns along too for security reasons. Chanda was firm. She too wanted to come along and be with me. So we decided that we would stay the night in the new house and come back the next morning.

As the gun-bearing security men took their positions around the house, there was a strange stillness in the air. This display of power-play had worked.

I could sense the Adivasis peering at us through the trees but nobody dared to approach any closer.

Chanda and I spent the entire day walking around, inspecting the area, making plans, having a leisurely lunch. The 'Grihapravesh' was to take place in the evening. As we entered the house for the first time by the flickering light of the lantern, we saw the sorry state it was in. The plaster on the walls was peeling off, the doors creaked, and rats had dug up the floor in some corners.

It is true that the house was more than a 100 years old but it was in this pathetic state only because no one had taken care of it at all over the years. But whatever the condition it was in, it was now our home. We spread the mattresses on the floor and lay down.

I got up as usual at dawn and came out of the house only to see hundreds of Adivasis staring at the house in silence. They seemed as shocked to see me. Finally I couldn't help myself and I asked them, 'What is the matter? Why are you all waiting here?'

One of them stammered, 'Sheth. You are alive?'

'What do you mean? Can't you see me? I am standing right here, in front of you, hale and hearty.'

'No, Sheth, actually…we thought…'

'What did you think?'

And then the whole story came out.

It was in this very house that Punmiya Sheth's father, Kaluram, had been murdered. Kaluram had many vices; drinking, women, etc. He used to come to this house, drink, and ask the Adivasis to send him any woman that caught his fancy. Once he forced himself on his servant's wife. The servant was mad with anger. That night, he poisoned Kaluram. The next morning, Kaluram's dead body was found by the other servants, and it had turned as black as his name because of the poison. From that moment onwards, the Adivasis thought that Kaluram's ghost lived in this house and killed anyone who entered the house.

'That is why when you stayed the entire night, we were surprised and we thought…'

Anyway, the end result of this incident was that it convinced the Adivasis that the new owners were different from the previous one—honest, full of guts, spunky and courageous.

An old dilapidated house and 250 acres of empty land overrun with wild grass: this was the beginning of my 'SUPA Farm'.

The previous owner was not at all interested in the land and only used to come there rarely when the grass had to be cut and sold. This was a boon to the Adivasis who lived in the surrounding area. They had encroached on small pieces of land wherever they wanted and even did a little farming for their sustenance. They certainly didn't want an interfering owner who lived there permanently.

I changed this situation. I began to go there regularly. I wanted to build a haven for my family there.

Gradually, the Adivasis got used to my presence. They used to also listen to my plans for developing the land and discussed these among themselves.

I had plans of planting trees, cultivating the land, etc. But before all this could be done, it was imperative to cut the grass and clear the land. The Mamaledar (the government official in the village) informed me that men were paid 10 rupees per day and women 8 rupees for their labour.

I promised the Adivasis that I would pay them all, men and women both 10 rupees per day. The Adivasis discussed the matter amongst them and agreed for they were in dire need of the money. But this time it was not the Communist party worker Ladkya, but the self-proclaimed 'King' of the village, Dharma, who was creating obstacles and throwing his weight around.

He would tell his fellowmen, 'Don't you dare go to Patel Sheth's land for work. I will break your legs and chop off your head if you do.'

Finally the Adivasis were forced to listen to him and I had no other option but to get the labourers from Talasari village which was about 14 kilometres away. The first day 70 labourers began the task of cutting the grass. But the Adivasis threatened them and created such a scene that the next day none of the labourers returned.

The third day hardly 30 labourers came from Talasari but again, they were threatened and so they too, disappeared. It was the same story for the next few days. The men who came from far away villages had to run back for their life in the face of the ferocious threats of the Adivasis. Once things really came to a head. That day, Dharma was standing on top of a hill facing the workers. He started pelting stones at them. When the workers came running to me and told me what was happening, I decided I had had enough.

I took along 5 or 6 men and went to Dharma's field, which incidentally was also part of the land belonging officially to me. There was freshly harvested rice in Dharma's field. I instructed my men to take these bags and put them in my house. At the very moment that Dharma was throwing stones at my workers, I was taking his rice back to my house. When he was informed of this, Dharma came running down the hill and came directly to my house with a couple of his men.

I thought the situation might turn violent and I was ready to face it, but to my great surprise, Dharma ran towards me and threw himself at my feet, begging, 'Please, Sheth, don't do this. I am sorry. I made a mistake but don't take my rice from me.'

I was wondering what could be responsible for this turnaround in his attitude. Perhaps he realized that he had no real power or it could be the fact that he saw that I would not give in to threats.

I said to him, 'See Dharma, you can take back your rice. I don't want it. But you have to keep one thing in mind. Don't interfere in my work.'

That was the end of the 'Dharma' episode. After this, the Adivasis gave me no more trouble and in fact started working for me.

The end of this hostility proved beneficial to both of us: the Adivasis got regular employment and I could now proceed with my ambitious plans to develop the land.

First of all, the land had to be cleared; a lot of trees had to be planted. I wanted to do farming, plant orchards, grow vegetables. Not just that, I wanted to build embankments across the river and create lakes and canals which would ensure an adequate water supply to the crops throughout the year.

A 100 odd Adivasi men and women from the Amboli-Karanjgaon village started working on the land and I was filled with renewed enthusiasm. Work on all my projects began methodically and gradually I achieved many of the targets I had set. I could see my dream slowly turning into reality. The Adivasis were more than willing to cooperate. Because perhaps for the first time in their lives, they had a regular job and income and they realized the importance of stability in their lives.

In fact, a few days later, Dharma himself approached me and requested me to give him work. As he had been considered the head in the village, I asked him to work as a 'Mukadam' or a Supervisor. Now that this foe had turned into a friend, there was no opposition against me and my plans at all from the Adivasis, all of them being convinced that it was to their benefit to work with me and not against me.

But, just as things were falling into place, something happened. One day, as soon as I arrived from Mumbai, Bhaskar came running towards me and said, 'Sheth, please go back. Tomorrow there is going to be a 'morcha' here and it might get dangerous.'

I wondered what could be the problem now. It seemed that the local Corporator, who in other words was the elected representative of the area of the State Legislative Assembly, was planning to hold a protest march against me. But I stood my ground and declared, 'Let them come here. I am not going to budge from here.'

This time though, I took the precaution of informing the police in advance about the protest. The next afternoon, a few people from the neighbouring villages, sticks and sickles in hand, gathered in front of my house and started shouting slogans:

'Sheth, go back.'

'We don't want an outsider here in our area.'

'Who is the owner of this place? Come out.'

The police were ready and I was ready too, to face the protestors. I went outside and stood in front of the mob.

A giant of a man, who appeared to be the leader, asked me in a rasping voice, 'Sheth is this land yours?'

But I countered with another question, 'Who are you to ask me this question?'

'My name is Laniya and I am the Corporator from this region. What is your name and where are you from?'

'My name is Mohan Patel. I have factories in Goregaon and Malad, in Mumbai.'

Laniya seemed stunned. He looked at me closely and asked, 'Sheth, do you know Mrs Mrinal Gore (a senior politician)?

'Yes, I know her very well.'

Laniya came near me and joined his hands humbly, 'Please excuse me, Sheth. I didn't recognize you before.'

Now I was stunned. What could be the reason for this change of heart? The protestors and the police too gaped at this transformation.

Laniya explained, 'Sheth, Perhaps you are not aware of it, but after the Emergency, when I contested the elections from this region, it was thanks to your contribution that I won.'

Now I was genuinely puzzled. *My contribution? How come I knew nothing about this?*

As Laniya's story unfolded, the riddle was solved.

When the Emergency was lifted and elections were announced, Mrs Mrinal Tai Gore, a senior and respected politician, met me and asked me if I could help her. She needed some financial help for the election campaign. When I asked her how much money was required, she asked me to donate a sum of 2 lakh rupees for the cause of the elections. I assured her that I would arrange for the money. I talked to several businessmen and convinced them to contribute to the campaign. We managed to collect 2.5 lakh rupees which we handed over to Mrinal Tai. A couple of days later, I met Mrinal Tai, who said, 'I will not need more than 2 lakh rupees, so please take back this extra 50,000.'

But I did not take the money and told her, 'Several of us together have contributed and collected this money. We don't need it back. Please keep it and use it for some other useful purpose.' I trusted Mrinal Tai completely and was sure that she would put the money to good use.

I had totally forgotten about the extra 50,000. Now I realized that Mrinal Tai must have given the money to Laniya to help him with his election campaign. And today he was the elected representative from the region.

Laniya apologized once again, fell at my feet, and begged for forgiveness and went back with his men.

What an irony. The same men who minutes ago had been shouting, 'Patel Sheth Hai, Hai.' were now shouting: 'Patel Sheth ki Jai.'

It was after this incident that the Adivasis truly accepted me and considered me their friend. In fact, this incident made me famous among the Adivasis not only in the region but everywhere else in Maharashtra as well.

Here I would like to narrate one occasion which is very special to me. The Chief Minister of Maharashtra was chairing a meeting at the Mantralaya. Names of people who would be members of the 'Adivasi Development Board' were being proposed and finalized. All the members belonged to the Adivasi community. When my name was proposed, the Chief Minister was surprised, 'Are you sure? Mr Mohan Patel? He is not a member of your community and in fact, he is a "Zamindar" (landowner). Will he be accepted by the Adivasis?'

But the Adivasi leaders were very firm, 'Even if he is a Zamindar, he is not like the others. He does not behave like a Zamindar. Today, thanks to him, hundreds of Adivasis in the Dahanu region have stable jobs and a good income. Some of the Adivasis, who could not dream of owning even a bicycle earlier, today ride a scooter or motorbike and it is all because of Mohan Bhai. He has built schools, dispensaries, and done many other things for our development. We don't consider him an outsider. He is one of us.'

And it is a matter of pride and satisfaction to me that, to date, I am the only non-Adivasi who has become the Chairman of the Adivasi Development Board.

Epilogue

The story of a man's life begins with his birth and ceases to be important the day he retires and stops working. It is very rare to see the most crucial part of a man's story beginning after he retires from active 'work'. Mohanbhai Patel is one such extraordinary man, whose life seems to have come around full circle and whose story continues ahead with full steam even after the age of 60.

After having completed one full circle, a new phase has now begun. Mohanbhai has played several roles to perfection: successful entrepreneur, social worker, ardent supporter of education, firm believer in science and so on. And then at the age of 60, when most people seek retirement, he took on a new role: that of a farmer. And he has been enthusiastically playing this part for the last 24 years now. During this period, he has established and strengthened his bond with Mother Earth.

When people ask him, 'Why this sudden interest in agriculture?', he replies, 'Not sudden, no. It is in my genes. I come from a family of farmers and spent the best part of my childhood years in a small village amongst lush green fields. I ventured out and explored new avenues. But finally I had to come back to my roots, to this soil. I could not ignore the call of the earth and it is now that I feel truly at peace.'

He has named his farm 'SUPA Farm' after his two daughters-in-law, Sunita and Parul. It was spread initially over 250 acres of land. Over the years many tiny pieces of land were added to it and today the total area of SUPA Farm is approximately 400 acres. SUPA Farm can only be described as 'heaven on earth'.

If Lord Indra, the King of Gods, were to descend on earth, even he would envy the beauty of SUPA Farms and would ask himself what he could do to create something as beautiful in Paradise.

In 1984, it was a barren piece of land overrun with grass and wild bushes. Today, you name a plant, a flower, a tree, a crop, a vegetable, a fruit, and you will surely find it on SUPA Farm. This is because Mohanbahi has created SUPA Farm with the same passion and vision with which he built his business empire. Mohanbhai is a perfectionist and he believes in dreaming big. He is never satisfied with even a 96 or 97 percent. For him, it has to be 100 percent.

These are the reasons why even today he is still considered the Numero Uno manufacturer of collapsible tubes. Today, he has 11 companies spread out over India in Mumbai, Silvasa, Vadodara, Wapi, and Goa. He believes in producing all the machinery needed for his factories indigenously. He has also helped to set up several collapsible tubes factories on a turnkey basis in Russia, Sri Lanka, Bangladesh, and many countries in Africa. Today, collapsible tubes made by the Patel Extrusion Group are exported to around 40 countries all over the world.

This is an achievement every Indian can feel proud of.

Mohanbhai's motto is: Excel in everything that you do and this is the key to his phenomenal success not just in business but also where SUPA Farm is concerned.

Today SUPA Farm boasts of 10,000 mango trees, 10,000 coconut trees, 15,000 custard apple trees, 25,000 teakwood trees, 2 lakh bamboo trees, 3 lakh pine-apple trees, 4 lakh eucalyptus trees to name just a few. In addition to this, hundreds of other types of vegetables, leafy vegetables, fruits and flowers are grown here.

Around 150 workers—including men and women from the neighbouring villages—take care of this green bounty. In addition to them, there are also some supervisors from the region who oversee the work, a skilled manager like Nipun Patel who looks after the entire farming operations, and of course Mohanbhai Patel hiself, the Managing Director-Chairman, who turns dreams into reality with his vision and driving force. All these people work together as a team to contribute to the success of SUPA farm. It also helps that the Chairman does not restrict himself to his seat but works hands on and is also one of the most knowledgeable persons on the various aspects of farming.

Another aspect which has helped SUPA Farm to grow to such a height is Mohanbhai's firm belief in research, education, and continuous training. He is always been in search of new methods and techniques and never hesitates to implement them on his farm.

When he learnt that Ashoka trees help to block the wind, he did some careful calculations and along with the teak and eucalyptus trees, planted a lot of Ashoka trees at the appropriate distance. This offers protection to the other crops and fruit-bearing trees. He has 200 bonsai mango trees, which bear fruit, growing on the terrace. He has also experimented with seedless mangoes and there are now 50 such trees growing on SUPA Farm.

Not only is Mohanbhai today a world-renowned expert in the field of collapsible tubes, he is also well informed about the trees, their properties, and other characteristics.

Someone who is not aware of his achievements in the collapsible tubes domain, would be right in thinking that he is a Professor of Botany or the Head of an Agriculture college. One is impressed by the amount of innovation and research going on at SUPA Farm. They have developed a new strain of excellent quality rice, Gujarat 17; a new fruit which is a hybrid product of the orange and tangerine; seedless oranges; a flaming orange variety of papaya; and lemons as big as oranges.

What is truly amazing about Mohanbhai is his quality of sharing his knowledge and expertize with everyone. So the benefits of his research and innovation are not limited to SUPA Farm alone, but are also extended to the poor Adivasis of the neighbouring areas. These Adivasis used to grow a coarse variety of rice. But thanks to Mohanbhai, today these same Adivasis take the seeds and knowledge from SUPA Farm and grow Gujarat 17, excellent quality rice, and that too double the quantity they used to produce earlier.

Managing SUPA Farms has given Mohanbhai an insight into the problems and travails of the Indian farmer.

He gives an example: 'A year after we started growing fruits and vegetables at SUPA farm, we had an excellent yield of high quality tomatoes. I thought that even the Adivasis from the neighbouring areas could grow tomatoes and we could sell them in the Mumbai markets. So I approached some traders in the Mahatma Phule Market in Byculla and told them that we could supply one truckload of high quality tomatoes, grown from hybrid seeds on a regular basis. They agreed to buy the tomatoes but I was stunned when they quoted the price: a mere 80 paise per kilo. This at a time when the retailers were selling the tomatoes at 6 rupees per kilo. I objected and insisted that the farmer should get at least 3 rupees per kilo because he is the one who has put in the maximum effort, so he should get at least half of what the customer pays.'

'But the traders couldn't care less and replied arrogantly that this was the price; take it or leave it. Otherwise they were not interested in buying from us. I was outraged at the injustice of it all and certainly could not accept it.'

'So I thought of another option. I started a small outlet to sell our produce near the Western Express Highway which borders SUPA Farm. Here, we sell all the vegetable and fruits produced daily on

SUPA Farm. Word quickly spread that the vegetables and fruits grown on SUPA Farm are of an excellent quality. So now there are hundreds of people who make it a point to stop at SUPA Farm and buy our products. At the same time, we also save money on transport. I would like to say though, that I have never looked at SUPA Farm from a commercial point of view. The main aim behind selling the farm products is to make enough money to cover the overhead costs of running SUPA farm such as workers' wages, fertilizers, electricity etc. SUPA Farm is run on a "no profit no loss" basis.'

'But I must admit that the profit earned from SUPA Farm is clear in my mind: peace of mind and infinite satisfaction. Satisfaction which is invaluable because it cannot be measured in terms of money.'

Mohanbhai Patel, who is an octogenarian today, would put the youth to shame with his unceasing enthusiasm and passion to dedicate himself to new projects. New ideas and innovative techniques to be introduced in SUPA Farm, innumerable lectures and articles on various issues like science, education etc, exchange of thoughts and ideas with the thousands of people who come into contact with him…the list of Mohanbhai's interests is never-ending. When it comes to Mohanbhai, the circle of life seems to be eternal.

Mohanbhai, tame mharo pranam.

MOTELIER BECOMES MAYOR

Dalpatbhai Patel

A few years ago, if someone would have told me that I was to become a motelier one day, I would have laughed out loud at the absurdity of the idea. But not only did I become a motelier, I was also elected as the Mayor of a city in the US.

After getting a Civil Engineering degree from Baroda University, I went to the US for higher education. I was soon hired after college and had a very well-paying job in a big engineering firm which specialized in building railway bridges. So where did a motel fit into the scheme of things?

I still remember that evening at Maganbhai's place in Philadelphia. It was May, 1970. I had just returned from my office at Turnpike Engineering Company.

As soon as I entered, my son Chetan ran towards me. The whole day long, he had only Neeta for company. So, in the evening as soon as he saw either Maganbhai or me, he insisted that we take him out.

I put him in the stroller and took him for a walk. By the time we came back, Maganbhai had returned from office. Both of us sat down to have dinner while Neeta retreated to the kitchen to make fresh and hot rotis for us.

Maganbhai exclaimed, 'Oh great. Today you have made bitter gourd. Where did you get that?'

'From the Chinese store.' Neeta said.

Maganbhai laughed: 'Look at the irony, Dalpat. Here in the US, we do not get any of our Indian vegetables except for potatoes and green peas. To get a typical Indian vegetable of our choice we have to go to the Chinese store. We should open Indian stores here. Not only will it make life easier for us but it is sure to be a profitable venture looking at the huge Indian community here.'

I was amused, but for a different reason. Maganbhai was an electrical and mechanical engineer. He had pursued his studies in the US and had an excellent and well-paying job in a reputed engineering firm but his passion was and always would be 'business'. He saw an opportunity for business in every situation.

Neeta was asking me 'Do you want some more kadhi?' But my thoughts were elsewhere. When I did not reply, Maganbhai asked 'What are you thinking about, Dalpat?'

'Nothing.' Then after a few minutes' silence I said, 'I saw a couple of places today while coming back home. They were really small 2 bedroom apartments, but nothing below 25,000 dollars.'

Maganbhai sighed 'Whatever else happens, the real estate prices always seem to be sky high.'

There were a few moments of awkward silence. Both of us continued to eat. But then Maganbhai took one look at my dejected face and said in a consoling voice, 'Dalpat, what's the hurry. Things are fine the way they are.'

I replied 'No, Bhai. It is high time I became independent. I could come to the US and study only because of your support. But now, I have to shoulder the responsibility of my family on my own. I am sure you will agree.'

'I do agree. But how do we solve the problem of finding a place for you to live?'

And then I saw a glint in his eyes. 'What if we bought a place where you could live and at the same time earn something from it too?'

'A home and business at the same place? How is that possible?'

'It is possible. I have been thinking about this for the past few days. Dalpat, we buy an old motel, even one that may not be doing too well, and run it. In this way, you not only get a place to live but we earn from it too.'

'But Maganbhai, who will run it? Do we give up our jobs for that?'

Maganbhai had an answer to everything. 'No, not at all. Until the motel shows a profit, we do not give up our jobs. We will work in the motel after office hours.'

'And who will look after it while we are in the office?'

'Neeta. She is at home the entire day. Chetan too is not a baby any more. During the day, while we are in the office, she will manage the front desk and take care of other things as well.'

I looked at Neeta. Her face mirrored her shock and apprehension.

'M…me?' she stammered.

'Yes, why not?' Maganbhai was vehement. 'Women do all kinds of jobs here in the US and Champak will help you out.' Champak was our nephew who was studying at University there.

Maganbhai told us about a Gujarati-run motel in San Fancisco which he had stayed in. He explained to us in detail about how the entire family chipped in and worked in the motel and how it could be a very profitable business proposition. He then looked at me and asked 'So, what do you think?'

It was all so sudden that I didn't know what to say. Realizing I was still in shock, Maganbhai asked pointedly 'I am the only one talking. Aren't you going to say something?'

For a moment, I didn't react. And then, without a word, I got up and left the room.

Maganbhai Patel
I called out after Dalpat who had just stormed out of the room 'Dalpat, Su thayu?'

But he did not reply. This was typical of him. If he got upset or angry about something, he wouldn't say a word. He would just walk out.

I shrugged my shoulders and continued eating. There was no point in going after him right now. Neeta served me the rest of the meal but I could see that her mind was on something else. I finished dinner and went to sleep.

Neeta Patel
How did this conversation, which had begun so innocently from the topic of bitter gourd, suddenly turn really bitter? Maganbhai only had our well-being in mind, didn't he? Then why did my husband get so upset and leave his dinner unfinished.

Maganbhai made a pretence of finishing his meal but I knew that he ate the rest of his meal half-heartedly.

I was in a fix. *What should I do now?* I couldn't eat either. My eyes filled with tears. Finally I got up from my seat, cleared the table, and went to lie down in the bedroom. I could not hold back my tears anymore. I pushed my face into the pillow and started sobbing.

Maganbhai Patel

That night, I did not realize when I finally drifted off into an uneasy slumber. My mind was in a turmoil.

In 1960, after completing my Electrical Mechanical Engineering from Baroda University, I arrived in the US for further studies. I had great dreams about a perfect life in America. But when I started my life as a student here, reality struck me.

Getting to America didn't necessarily translate into success in life. Coming here was an opportunity given only to a select few. It was then up to each one to work hard and ensure that one's dreams were achieved.

Everyone feels lonely in the first few months abroad. But in the 1960s, there were only about a 1000 Indian people in the whole of the US. Most Indians preferred to go to England then. In a way, one can say that Indians had still not 'discovered' America.

So evidently in such a situation, getting to know Indian people in the US was like hunting for a needle in a haystack.

One such search during the summer holidays landed me in San Francisco. I had heard that there were some Gujarati families running profitable motels there and I wanted to work in one of their motels.

These motels had small individual rooms but shared bathrooms. The entire Gujarati family worked to the bone to run the motels. And then there were always some relatives from back home, or students like me, who would stay for a while and help them out. I observed the lifestyle of these Gujarati moteliers. It was a hard life but there was a lot of profit in this business. That is when the idea of me and my family becoming the owners of a grand hotel one day first struck me.

Neeta Patel

The next day morning, Maganbhai got up earlier than usual and left for office. My husband got up and got ready as usual, but I could see that he was not in a good mood.

I handed him his tiffin filled with spinach theplas and chutney and plucking up courage said, 'Talk to Maganbhai in the evening and tell him frankly what is on your mind.'

He said, 'I am definitely going to talk to him about his proposal. I will not be at peace until I do.'

His words only added to my tension.

Ours is a family which is quite open-minded, easygoing, informal, and fun loving. That is why it was so easy for a traditional girl like me who came from a small village in Gujarat and had studied only up to the 11th grade to fit in so easily here.

I still remember the time I arrived in the US. It was three years after my wedding, in 1968, and I was extremely nervous and scared to death. My mind was filled with doubts: *What will this new country be like? I don't even know the language. How will I manage a household here?*

Maganbhai had a 2-bedroom apartment in Philadelphia. My husband was staying there with him and this is where we were to begin our new life. As I entered the apartment behind him, I heard Maganbhai say, 'Aao, Neeta, Welcome home. Welcome to America.'

I pulled up my sari to cover my head and bent down to touch his feet. Maganbhai gave us his blessings and then with a smile said, 'Neeta, you don't need to cover your head here. Our customs and traditions in India are different and here they are different. Anyway, you will gradually learn everything.'

I did learn everything eventually but from that moment, I was completely at ease. My respect for Maganbhai, who was my elder brother-in-law, increased even more and I no longer felt scared of him.

In fact, it was Maganbhai who initiated me into cooking Indian food here in the US. It was very difficult, then, to get our Indian vegetables, spices, grains etc. Maganbhai taught me how to make best use of the ingredients available here cooking traditional Indian food.

My work increased even more after Chetan was born. There were no other women to fuss over me and the baby like we do in India, nor did we have maids to help in the household chores.

I have to admit that both the men in the family helped me a lot. Especially Maganbhai, who took such good care of Chetan. Right from giving him the milk bottle, to changing his nappies, he did every single thing lovingly.

During weekends, he would say to us, 'Dalpat, Neeta, go out wherever you feel like, for a party or something. I will look after Chetan.'

His marriage had broken up. His wife had never come to America and they were now divorced. But he did not feel envious of us and in fact, was always concerned about our well-being. That is why I did not like it when my husband hurt him like that by walking out on him during dinner.

Dalpatbhai Patel

The day was passing by uneventfully as usual, but at the back of mind was the constant thought of the motel.

During the Second World War, the road network spread its tentacles through the length and breadth of the country and Americans started to travel more frequently by road. While travelling long distances, travellers needed to take a break in their journey and motels became a convenient and inexpensive option. Motels were a smaller and more compact version of a hotel. Usually, they consisted of 15 or 20 rooms built in a row on the ground floor. Motels provided lodging but there was usually no room service or restaurant. Some motels, to cater to the needs of the clients and to make additional money, would run a small café or restaurant in the premises.

Motels here are known as the 'Mom and Pop' business. In short, a couple is capable of running a motel on their own. The owner's family usually lives in the motel itself. Barring a few motels in San Francisco, the motel industry was still the domain of white-skinned Americans who ran almost all the motels in the country. So, I was naturally apprehensive about venturing into this uncharted territory.

I had a thousand doubts in my mind—How does one run this business? How profitable is it? How much will we need to invest? And so on. Until I had an answer to all my questions, I couldn't even think about entering this business.

Once again during dinner, Maganbhai and I were seated at the table, eating our food in silence. Neeta signalled me with her eyes to talk to Maganbhai.

'Uh...uh...Maganbhai, I am sorry that I left without saying a word to you yesterday.'

'It's okay. That was yesterday. Are you ready to talk to me now?'

I nodded.

'Good. Then go ahead.'

His words released the tension in the air.

'Bhai, I didn't mean to hurt you or show you any disrespect. But your idea of buying a motel was so unexpected that I didn't know how to react.'

Maganbhai smiled 'I know you very well, Dalpat. You needed time to think. But you couldn't say so openly, isn't it?'

Once again, I nodded.

'Well, now that you have had the time, what do you think?'

I told him about all the questions that were troubling me since yesterday and then I added 'Bhai, we are one of the first Gujaratis to enter this business. So who will guide us? Another important question in my mind is that if we buy an old, run down motel, how can we guarantee that we can turn it around and make it successful?'

Maganbhai was deep in thought.

After a long pause, he said, 'Dalpat, At the moment I don't have an answer to any of your questions. All I have is this "gut feeling" that it is the right decision for us. If you believe in our typical Gujarati capability of taking up challenges, our hard work, our honesty and determination, say yes. Otherwise, I promise, this is the last time, we will talk about this topic.'

This time Maganbhai left the room first, leaving me even more confused and troubled than yesterday.

The next morning, I told Maganbhai 'I am ready to go along with your idea. Let's start looking for a motel.'

I contacted a good realtor in two days but when I told him that we were looking for an old motel which was not doing well, he looked at me like I had lost my marbles. Nobody must have ever asked him for anything like this. But being an American, he believed firmly in the principles that 'The Customer is always right'. So he immediately said, 'Yes, of course Sir.'

He called after two days. 'There is a motel for sale in Bordentown in New Jersey. It seems to be just what you are looking for. So when should we go and see it?'

The next weekend, Maganbhai, Neeta and I went to see the motel in Bordentown.

On Route 206 which joins the main I 95, we saw a huge sign which said 'Imperial Inn'. This was place we were looking for. We got down from the car.

Roger Bradley, the then owner of the motel, came forward to greet us. After the initial introductions were over, we first saw the area around the motel. I felt that the location of the motel was a great asset from a business point of view. The I 95, which stretches an incredible 1300 miles from Canada in the North right down to Miami in the South, was only a few minutes away from the motel. So, there wouldn't be any dearth of customers here.

The motel had a very big yard and the most pleasing aspect was the view which included the vast green corn fields in the background. This town, which is a part of Mansfield Township, consisted mainly of farmers. So there were beautiful green fields as far as the eye could see, dotted with small houses, a church, and a long-winding road.

'Reminds me of our village in Gujarat, doesn't it?' Neeta said.

I looked at her and smiled 'Just what I was thinking.'

We went inside the motel. It was old but in quite a good condition.

I couldn't help myself so I asked Roger 'Why are you selling this place? It is so nice and in such a good location.'

Roger replied 'I am tired now. It's been so long since I opened this place. My wife and I have literally slogged in this business for the last 25 years. Now we feel like taking it easy.'

What an irony. Roger planned to live a peaceful, quiet life with the help of the money he would get from selling Imperial Inn, whereas we were planning to work night and day for the next few years to make this business successful.

We finalized the amount, the date of the deal, and left after saying bye to Roger.

Maganbhai Patel

As I lay down to sleep, I kept thinking to myself, *Tomorrow, July 1, 1970, the deal would be finalized. Dalpat and I would then officially be the owners of 'Imperial Inn'.* A new chapter in our life was about to begin.

Until then, we had lived within the framework of a salaried job. We were successful but it was in the narrow and limited scope of a regular job. I was sure that if we worked hard and took the right decisions, the sky would be the limit. I was filled with enthusiasm for the future.

The last few days had been so hectic that we had had no time to think. The first important matter was raising the money. Even though it was an old and rundown motel, it was still worth a whopping $1,85,000. We had to arrange for an initial down payment of $55,000. The rest would be paid by mortgage at the rate of $2000 per month.

When Dalpat and I calculated our savings, they came up to $35,000. We borrowed the rest of the amount needed for the down payment in small values of $1,000 or $2,000 from our relatives and friends.

The amounts involved were huge for us and seemed a risk at the time. Dalpat was more cautious and careful about money matters than I was. Once he told me, 'Bhai, we have put in our entire life's savings and also taken loans from our friends and the bank. What will we do if we cannot repay this money?'

My mind too was racked by similar doubts. But if I had voiced them at the time, all our dreams would be over even before they started.

So I put on a confident act and assured him 'Dalpat, if it doesn't work out, we will think that we have bought ourselves a huge 29-room house.'

Once we had arranged for the money, we informed the realtor and asked him to prepare the necessary documents.

The realtor was happy that we were ready to finalize the deal. But he couldn't help himself and said to us, 'Mr Patel, I am going against the principles of my business but I sincerely feel that you should think about it once again, very carefully.'

I was stunned. 'Why do say that?'

He replied 'I am scared of racial discrimination.'

'How is that?'

'What if the customers go back when they see an Indian owner? Racial discrimination is against the law but it is not always easy to change people's thinking. If people stay away from the motel because of this, you will be ruined.'

It was ironical that someone who stood to make a good deal of money from this transaction was giving us this advice. But he seemed genuinely concerned for us.

I reassured him 'Mr Kenwood, I appreciate your concern and thank you for it. But both my brother and I have thought carefully about this and we want to go ahead with the deal. On the decided date and time.'

Dalpatbhai Patel

A new chapter in our life was about to begin.

I thought of that other phone call from Maganbhai five years ago which had changed my life at the time.

In those days, a phone call from America was a big event. It would happen rarely, just about once a year. We would receive a letter from Maganbhai fifteen days earlier, informing us of the date and the time at which he would call. We had to go to the nearest Post Office, which was not in our village but in the nearest taluka or district town. Nobody in our village had a telephone in those days.

On the appointed day, Ba, Bapu, the children, and other relatives would travel to the taluka. During the journey, we would sing songs, laugh, crack jokes, and have a great time. The entire atmosphere used to be festive, almost like a picnic.

Ten to fifteen of us would wait outside the Post Master's office. Whenever the phone rang, we would peep in. The Post Master would pick up the phone and then shake his head to tell us it was not ours.

We would all troop out and the wait would continue. Finally, the Post Master would call us 'Aao. Tamara phone.'

We would run in. But instead of handing over the phone to us, the Post Master would keep on talking to Maganbhai himself.

'Maganbhai, kem cho? Aaiya barsat bau che. Tya keu che? Baki maja ma?' We could barely conceal our impatience but the Post Master was so thrilled to be speaking to someone abroad that he would shoot a volley of questions without realizing that there were others in line.

It was Maganbhai who would finally lose his patience and ask the Post Master 'Master Ji, I can't wait to hear my mother's voice. Can you put her on the line please?'

It was only then that we could talk to Maganbhai.

In 1966, during one such telephone call, Maganbhai gave me a piece of good news.

'Dalpat, you have got admission in the Villenova University in Philadelphia. You will hear from them soon. As soon as you get their letter, apply for a visa and come here.'

When I kept down the receiver, I realized that a new chapter was about to begin in my life.

A series of letters followed. I made a trip to Mumbai for the American visa and then finally on September 9, 1966, I left for the US.

That day, there was a news item along with my photograph in the district newspaper: 'Dalpat Patel, young engineer from Malekpore village, goes abroad for further education.

The previous evening, I had visited several elders in the village and touched their feet to take their blessings. But it seems like that was not enough. The next day, apart from my family members, there were around a hundred people from our village standing with garlands and bouquets in their hand, at the Surat Railway Station, who had come to see me off. My face was almost hidden under all those garlands. The compartment was filled with flowers. The other people travelling in the same compartment looked at me with respect.

Actually, I was pretty nervous. It was true that Maganbhai was in America. But I was leaving behind my parents, brothers and sisters, and my wife Neeta whom I had got married to barely a year ago. Now, I didn't know when I would meet her again.

In those days, there was no direct flight to America. I had a night's stopover in London before my flight to America.

Luckily, my cousin who stayed in London came to take me to her house for the night. I reached Heathrow airport the next morning to catch my flight to America. As I entered the airport, my name was being called out over the PA system 'Calling Mr Patel...'

My cousin pushed me and said, 'Hurry, or you will miss the flight.'

I ran like crazy and finally caught the flight with hardly a second to spare.

It was the first time I was travelling such a long distance and for such a long time in an aircraft. By the time we got down in New York, my head was spinning. I was feeling dizzy and so tired that I was scared I would just collapse at the airport itself. I called up Maganbhai.

He said, 'Good, you have reached? Now catch a flight to Baltimore. I will pick you up at the Baltimore airport.'

I couldn't bear the thought of another travel by plane. I stammered 'No, no, not a plane again.'

Maganbhai started laughing 'Okay. Then come by bus. But that will take you four more hours.'

When I got down from the bus and saw Maganbhai standing at the depot waiting for me, I heaved a sigh of relief.

Maganbhai took me home. He had invited some of his friends over especially to introduce me. His friends greeted me with 'Welcome to America.'

One of them pushed a glass in my hand, filled with some orange coloured liquid. Everyone raised their glass and said 'Cheers.'

The glass in my hand shook violently. I put down my glass and said softly 'Sorry, I don't drink alcohol.'

Everyone burst out laughing. One of them said, 'Don't worry, Dalpat. This drink is not alcoholic. It's only orange juice.'

'Orange juice?' I repeated like an idiot.

'Yes, orange juice made from oranges. You know those round, orange fruits? Drink up. You will feel refreshed' and they all laughed.

Forget about feeling refreshed, I felt even more conscious and dazed now. It struck me that the distance between Malekpore to Baltimore was not to be calculated only in miles, it was a journey from one culture to a totally different one. I realized that I would make mistakes like these while settling down into this new way of life. I picked up my glass and started sipping the orange juice.

After some time, when I had freshened up and changed my clothes, I peeped in to the kitchen. Maganbhai, with an apron around his waist, was frying puris.

I could see the rest of the meal laid out on the table: shrikhand, a potato curry, and salad.

When he saw the look of surprise on my face, Maganbhai said, 'We have to do all these things ourselves here. Right from cooking to washing to driving. You will learn everything gradually.'

When Maganbhai dropped me off at Villenova University the next day, for the first time in my life I felt absolutely alone. Except for Maganbhai, everyone who was close to me was thousands of miles away. The only means of communicating with them was by letters. But letters took at least fifteen days to reach in those days. The wait was pure agony.

Until now, all I had ever eaten was typical Gujarati vegetarian food. Here in the University, no one seemed to even understand the concept of vegetarian food. So there was no other option but to cook myself. My attempts at cooking were pathetic and very often there was either too much or too little salt or spices. When I would sit down to eat such bland food alone, all by myself in an alien land, I would be pushed to tears.

To add to my woes, I felt totally lost in the classroom as well. I couldn't understand a word of what the Professors were saying. Sometimes I would feel so frustrated that I would wonder what the hell I was doing there. But as the cliché goes, every dark cloud has a silver lining.

My most important source of comfort was Maganbhai. He looked after me and loved me like a father and always gave me courage to face my new life. He would explain to me the American way of life and was always there for me whenever I needed him.

After a few days, I felt a little relieved because even though initially all that the Professors said seemed Greek to me, I gradually realized that no matter what language it is, the basic principles and concepts of science will always be the same all over the world. So here too, the basis of all knowledge was what I had learnt before in India.

Another source of comfort was the huge number of Indian students on the campus. More than half the students in Villenova University were Indians. For example in my class, out of 14 students, 9 were Indians, and of these 7 were Patels. In fact sometimes Maganbhai would rag me: 'I don't understand why you feel lonely. When I came here, I had to hunt for an Indian face. Now things are so different.'

Most of the Professors in the University were quite well-informed about India. In fact some of them even knew a few words in Hindi or Gujarati. They would greet us with small sentences in Gujarati 'Kem cho?' and try to put us at ease by saying 'Saru che.'

'Aav jo.' These small gestures helped to make me feel at home.

One Professor in particular had a very interesting way of announcing the grades. He would say: 'Navin Patel, you have got an A for Ahmedabad.'

'Dalpat Patel, you have got a B for Bombay.'

'Andrew Williams, you have got a C for Calcutta.'

'And Devang, you have got a D for Delhi.'

Everyone around me said that college life is the most carefree period of one's life because there are no responsibilities. It is to be enjoyed to the fullest.

But not for me. I saw the fun and revelry going on all around me. But I felt that this kind of carefree life was a not a luxury that I could afford. I had to finish my education as soon as possible, become independent, and support my family. So every time I spent money on frivolous purchases, I would ask myself 'Is it really necessary?' Two miles away from the University, I used to share an apartment with three other boys. There was a bus which went to the University from there. The fare was only a quarter of a dollar or two rupees.

For a few days, I took the bus. But then one day I thought to myself, *My elder brother back in our village gives two rupees for an entire day's work to the daily labourers. If these people can toil the whole day for two rupees, can't I walk two miles to college? I will be saving that much more of my family's money.*

From that day, I never took the bus to go to college. I always walked to the University campus.

During my last year at University. I decided to do a summer job during the vacations, and applied to one company in particular. My three flatmates also sent their application to the same firm. All of us were not only called for an interview but were also selected for the job.

In those days in the US, anyone finishing college education could immediately get a job. One didn't even need an American qualification and it was possible to get work even with an Indian degree.

When the summer vacation came to an end, I didn't give up my job. Who would give up a job which paid $3.75 per hour. It was a princely sum then and I didn't want to let go of that. I decided to study on my own and give the last exam. We had that option at Villenova University.

I was managing my job and studies quite well and then suddenly an unexpected problem came up.

The private consultancy firm I was working for had got a contract to design a railway bridge and I was entrusted with the job of designing it.

I conducted a detailed geographical study of the proposed site and then prepared the design. However, the State Government rejected this plan citing some technical reasons which were not acceptable to our company. The matter went to court. I was the one who knew all the details of this project so I was summoned to give evidence in the court on behalf of the company. Even though I was not an accused in this case, I was very nervous and my heart was pounding as I climbed up the stairs of the court on the due date. I was upset because if the decision went in favour of the State Department, it would amount to a personal defeat for me.

Our company's lawyer was doing his best to reassure me. 'Don't worry, Mr Patel. You only have to talk about the technical part of the design. Leave the rest to me.'

I entered the court and sat down. Another case lined up before ours was in progress. As I observed the proceedings, I was relieved to find out that it was not a bit like the courtroom scenes I had seen in the Hindi films where the lawyers grilled the witnesses and often reduced them to tears. The atmosphere here was friendly and cordial. I felt a little more relaxed now.

Our case came up and it was my turn to be in the witness box. The State lawyer, Mr Redford, asked me a lot of detailed questions about the technical aspects of the design for the bridge, but I thankfully had an answer to each and every question. Finally he asked me: 'Mr Patel, if this bridge is built according to your design, can you prove without a doubt that it will not be dangerous and not harm anyone in any way?'

For a moment I was speechless, but then I gathered my wits and rallied with another question: 'Can *you* prove without a doubt that this bridge will pose a threat to human life?'

There was a stunned silence in the court and then everyone burst out laughing. Now it was the State Department lawyer's turn to be speechless. He didn't know how to counter my question so he pretended to look through some documents in order to buy himself some time.

Finally the judge asked him 'Mr Redford, do you have any other questions for the witness?'

'No sir.'

'Then please say so and do not waste the court's time.'

The case wound up shortly and as you can guess, the decision went in our company's favour.

It seems trivial now but at the time, it seemed like an enormous hurdle that I had overcome. It was the first crisis of my life. But even this small victory increased my confidence.

I had stuck to my convictions and won in this foreign land and I now decided that I would prove myself whatever it took.

Eventually I finished my Masters from Villenova University and got a stable job. I got Neeta here from India and settled down into a comfortable routine.

Now that everything was going smoothly, we brothers had taken up a new challenge: we would be moteliers. Only time would tell if this venture would make us or break us.

We signed the legal documents on July 1, 1970, in the presence of our realtor and our lawyer and completed the necessary financial transactions. Maganbhai and I were now the official owners of Imperial Inn.

Roger Bradley, the earlier owner, had promised to stay on for 15 days and show us the ropes. After the legal formalities were over, Roger and his wife Liz moved into one room in the motel, while Neeta, Chetan, and I moved into the spacious 3 bedroom apartment meant for the owners.

The next morning, I dressed up in my formal office clothes and went to the front desk, ready to start the day.

One look at me and Roger burst out laughing. 'Hey Dalpat. You don't need to wear a tie. You are not in your office, you are in a motel. Your customers are going to be primarily truck drivers or middle-class travellers. It will be better if you wear informal clothes while dealing with them.'He then gave us very useful tips about managing a motel, including how to manage the front desk, how to keep the accounts, what one needs to enter in the register, how to clean the rooms and how to make the bed and arrange the blanket and cushions in the correct fashion.

Roger's advice was a great help but there were several other unvoiced questions which played constantly on my mind— *Why was this motel not a success in spite of the fact that it was so close to a highway? What should be done to ensure that it is a success?*

I realized that it was up to me to find out the answers to the questions.

Neeta Patel

I had just tucked in Chetan in his bedroom and was about to start cutting the fruit when I heard Him calling 'Neeta, are you done? We cannot start the meeting without you.'

Maganbhai was here for the weekend and we had decided to have a meeting in the evening after finishing all the chores for the day to discuss some issues regarding the motel.

I suddenly felt very important. Until now, words like 'meetings' and 'business' were not a part of my vocabulary. I was an ordinary housewife. But now I too had a role to play in this business. From Monday, I would be managing the motel all by myself throughout the day. The very thought made me tremble.

I had the tendency of getting tense and nervous even if something went wrong at home or while I was cooking. Now I had the responsibility of running an entire business on my own. What scared me most was the fact that I did not speak the language of the customers. But I had to communicate with them, face them every day, understand their needs and demands, and look after the money matters as well.

And I had to do all this while looking after Chetan, with no help from anybody at all. I really didn't know how I was going manage things.

I put down the fruit bowl and went for the meeting. I could almost hear my heart pounding. As I entered, I looked at Him. He gave me a reassuring glance and said, 'Don't worry Neeta. You will manage fine. There are two boys who will help out with the cleaning of the rooms right now as it is their summer holiday and Maganbhai will step in to do the jobs of a handyman.'

Maganbhai nodded, 'I will come here every weekend and check all the rooms: lights, fans, boilers, ACs, heaters etc, and see to it that everything runs without a glitch, okay? All you have to do, Neeta, is look after the front desk during the week. So, what do you think? Will you be able to manage?'

I said 'Yes' but I mustn't have sounded very confident because Maganbhai smiled and said, 'Neeta, there is no need to feel nervous just because you don't speak the language. Make an effort to communicate and I am sure you will gradually learn enough English to get along in the job. Until then, it will be a great help even if you write the accounts and maintain the register accurately.'

Maganbhai's words boosted my confidence and I began to feel a little better.

Now He said to Maganbhai 'Bhai, I have thought a lot about how we can make this business a profitable one. The first thing I have realized is that we have already made $36,000 a year on it.'

I was so surprised that I couldn't help asking 'How is that?'

Both the brothers began to laugh. Maganbhai said, 'Roger had employed a man to look after the front desk. His salary was $36,000 per year. Now we will be managing the front desk ourselves and you Neeta are going to play a major role in that because you will be in charge of the motel most of the time. Dalpat and I have to do our jobs and we will be able to give only our free time to the business. So actually this first contribution to our business is yours, Neeta.'

He added, 'Bhai, another thing in our favour is that we will be manning the front desk throughout the day and night. Even if a customer comes to our motel at 2 o'clock in the morning, he will get a room to stay.'

Maganbhai agreed, 'Of course. This is something we will have to do. Roger and Liz used to put up a 'No Vacancy' sign outside the motel at night. We cannot afford to do that. Luckily we don't lack manpower. You, Neeta, Champak, and I will do our best to see that the customers are attended to night and day. This will be a boon to the truck drivers or other people who travel at night and wish to relax for a little while and it will be great for our business as well.'

The two brothers discussed other business matters, put forward new plans and ideas. As I listened to them, I could see a new world opening up in front of me. I was thrilled because I too was now a part of it.

When there was a pause in the conversation, I said timidly 'May I suggest something? We should pay attention not only to the cleanliness of the rooms but more particularly to the cleanliness of the bathrooms. I have noticed one thing since we arrived here. The customer first checks if the bathroom is clean when he comes to see the room.'

Both the brothers liked my suggestion a lot. Maganbhai said 'Dalpat. This is the advantage of having a woman as a part of the team. They have a different way of looking at things.'

We didn't realize how time flew and it was past midnight when we finally retired to our rooms. It was late but I just couldn't fall asleep. All I could think about was the business, our motel, my work. Finally I gave up trying to sleep and gave free rein to my ideas. It seemed hours later when my mind calmed down and I fell into a deep slumber.

Dalpatbhai Patel

It was now 15 days since we had bought the motel. Roger and Liz had left. Maganbhai who had come over to help during the weekend had also left. I had taken two weeks off from office, so that day, I too had to go to office. But I couldn't concentrate at all on my office work. All I could think about was the motel. Fifteen rooms were occupied at the moment. I thought that some of the customers might want to check out or there might be new customers coming in. *How was Neeta going to manage all this and manage to look after our little son Chetan at the same time?*

I could picture the scene when I went back: Neeta in tears, because she had had to manage everything all by herself the whole day. She would probably scream 'Enough. Look after your business yourself. I cannot do it.'

When I entered the motel, an entirely different scene greeted me: Neeta was standing at the front desk, a pleasant smile on her face. Chetan was playing happily nearby. Neeta smiled mischievously, and asked 'Hello Mr Patel, would you like a room?'

While we were sipping tea, we talked about how her day had gone by and I understood why Neeta was so happy. Some of the guests had checked out in the morning but there had been many new guests who had come in and at present 25 rooms were occupied.

I was very happy. 'It's an excellent beginning. I hope it continues like this.'

Neeta said, 'Actually, the motel could have even been full but some people who came in seemed surprised to see me. They asked me some questions. I understood what they were saying and tried to answer them but they left anyway. I am sure they didn't like the idea of an Indian lady, wearing a sari, being in charge of the motel. Don't you remember the realtor had said the same thing? People will go away when they see the colour of our skin.'

I tried to console her 'Don't worry. Every new idea faces opposition when it is introduced for the first time. It's basic human nature. With time, the idea takes root and is accepted by everyone. It will be the same in the case of our business. Gradually, Americans will accept the fact that an Indian is running the motel.'

At the time, I had no idea how prophetic my words were going to be. Today, if an American doesn't stay in a motel and goes ahead because he sees an Indian face at the reception, he may regret his decision because the next motel he goes to will most probably belong to another Indian. If it is not run by Dalpatbhai, it is likely that it will be run by Chaganbhai or Nareshbhai or Sureshbhai or Rajeshbhai and if the surname is not Patel, it will be Shah.

Anyway, to come back to 1970, living in a motel and managing it changed our entire lifestyle and it took us a while to adjust to it.

Neeta was in charge of the front desk for almost 12 hours, from 8 in the morning to 8 at night. When I came back from office in the evening, she would prepare dinner and put Chetan to sleep. I used to have dinner, freshen up, change into another pair of trousers and shirt and go to the front desk. And I would remain there throughout the night, dressed in the same formal trousers and shirt. I didn't change into my night clothes because I had to be ready to answer promptly in case a guest arrived in the middle of the night. When I look back at all those years of settling down, I realize how neither Neeta nor I must have had a proper night's sleep.

Normally, we employed school or college students, or at times, regular employees to help us to make the beds and clean the rooms but there were times when we had to do all these jobs ourselves as well.

It was very hard work but since we were making a good profit, we also had the enthusiasm to work tirelessly.

Our motel was a success from the beginning and one of the reasons was the timing: it was summer holidays. Weekends and holidays are precious to Americans. In the office too, I would notice that the American staff would enter the office on Friday morning with plans already in mind for the weekend. The main topic of conversation on Fridays was the coming weekend. They would start wrapping up their work much before it was time to go.

Monday morning was taken up by descriptions of the weekend spent.

It was the same with summer holidays. It is a custom here to travel for a couple of weeks with the family during the summer holidays. Plans are made days in advance. Come summer time, the entire family gets into the car and is off for a holiday. So summer was boom time for the motels. Even though we were Indians, our motel didn't lack business.

There were a few Americans who looked at the colour of our skin and went away but luckily for us they were a small minority.

I had been very apprehensive about getting into this business initially, but I soon realized its advantages. The first one being: Cash in hand. Even if the motel was not full, or even half occupied, it was possible for us to repay the loan on time and even make a decent profit for ourselves. The other advantage was the opportunity to meet so many different people. We met people from all walks of life, had such interesting experiences, and I think it was invaluably helpful in understanding human nature.

Neeta Patel

I was very happy when I started working in the motel. It was no doubt very hectic and involved a lot of hard work. But that didn't matter to me so much. Maybe because I was used to physical hardships as I come from a small village where we used to work in the fields with our father, come home, and help our mother in the kitchen, walk for miles to go to school etc. So I wasn't scared of hard work and I could easily manage the motel, housework, and looking after Chetan at the same time.

What scared me initially though, was the idea of talking to the Americans in English.

But then I tried to build up my confidence and told myself: 'You don't have to give a lecture in a college. All you have to do is answer a few basic questions.' Now when I remember the hilarious mistakes I made while attempting to speak in English, I can't help laughing at myself.

It must have been only two months since we bought the motel. A truck driver came in and started speaking to me. I couldn't understand a word of what he was saying. Finally I understood from his gestures that he was asking 'How much? How much for the room?'

I replied, 'Nine dollars.'

He probably thought that was too much. So he started complaining in a loud voice. I listened to him for some time but finally I lost patience. So I said to him in my brand of Gujarati mixed English 'Takeva hoi to take, nahi to go.'

As soon as I spoke, I felt so ashamed at my funny English, but I think I must have made myself very clear to him because he didn't say a word more and gave me nine dollars.

The only respite we got from the back breaking routine was when Maganbhai and Champak, our nephew, came over on weekends to help us out.

It was only after 18 months that Maganbhai decided it was time for him to give up his job and look after the business full-time. However, he advised Him, 'Dalpat, don't give up your job just yet. It is better if at least one of us has a stable job for some more time.'

Maganbhai had remarried a few months ago. He resigned from his job and Manju Bhabhi and he came to stay with us at the motel. There were now more of us at home but then there were also more hands to share the work and in fact my responsibility became less after they came.

I got along very well with Manju Bhabhi. Both of us helped one another at home and in the motel. Once Manju Bhabhi said to me 'Neeta, some people see the two of us in saris and go away. That is not right. We should do something about it.'

'But what can we do?'

'There is one solution. We can wear western clothes like the American ladies.'

I was shocked and scared. This was a really big step for me. But then we reasoned it out.

We were living in a foreign country. If we needed to change a few of our habits in order to blend in with their culture, there was no harm in it. We were still following Indian customs in the things that mattered the most. We still spoke our mother tongue at home, ate our kind of food, and most important, our values were still Indian. So it didn't really matter what clothes we wore.

When the both of us wore western clothes for the first time, I have no idea about what Maganbhai's reaction was, but He was definitely shocked. I think He didn't like the idea very much but I didn't pay much attention and went ahead with it anyway.

Slowly we realized that Manju Bhabhi's suggestion was very good. In those days, when an American entered a motel and saw a traditional Indian lady at the front desk, he was taken aback. Some were not too comfortable with the idea and went away immediately.

But our change in attire had made a difference. They came in, talked to us, and took a decision only after having a look at the room. We too felt more confident now.

Manju Bhabhi and I were both young women and we were managing the motel confidently. We never had a bad experience, except on one occasion.

One night, I was at the front desk. Champak was there with me as well. A rough looking black man came in and enquired about the rooms. While I was answering his questions, he suddenly took out a revolver and pointed it at me. I was stunned.

'Give me your cash.' he shouted. I panicked and handed him the cash box.

Champak was looking in my direction, scared, and for a moment, he didn't know what to do. But when he saw the man walking away with the cash box, he yelled and ran after him. I was trembling. *What if the man fired at Champak?* I started screaming. There was total chaos. The man ran. Champak ran after him. The others got up because of our screaming, and came to see what was happening. But it was too late. By this time, the man had already jumped into his car and left.

This incident made us realize the danger that we faced in this business. After discussing the matter, it was decided that a bullet-proof glass partition would be installed to protect the person who was at the front desk.

Dalpatbhai Patel

Some customers would haggle about the room rent whereas there were some who requested politely for a discount. I slowly learnt to judge whether the person was genuine and really couldn't afford the rent. In such cases, I would give them a discount.

There were two reasons for this—one, it was better to let out the room at a lower rent rather than get no rent if it stayed vacant and two, this way I could help a person in need at no great loss to the business.

Each one of us added his or her own way of thinking to the business but all the ideas were worked out to our benefit and we slowly turned the business into a success.

Soon the news of our 'Imperial Inn' being a great success spread within the Gujarati community all across the country. Several Patels and Shahs visited our motel. These included not only our friends and relatives, but also Gujaratis we didn't know, who dropped in to see how we were running the business and pick up some tips.

We made everyone feel welcome. They would stay and eat with us and have a look at the motel. But in addition to this, we made it a point to talk to them in detail about how and why we had got into this business, its pros and cons, etc. We never hesitated to share with them the secrets of running a motel successfully.

First one Gujarati and then another and another, slowly several Gujaratis began to buy old, run down motels and run them.

Meanwhile Maganbhai had also started working as a realtor, so he got the Gujaratis some very good deals. If someone did not have enough capital, we even helped them out financially. We hadn't forgotten the help our friends had given us when we first started out. Now it was our turn to help others in the same way.

People often wonder: Why are Gujaratis so successful in business?

The key to their success is, to put it simply, determination, hard work, their readiness to learn, and their practical approach. But above all, what is most important is their willingness to help one another to make the business a success.

When we decided to start our business, Maganbhai had said to me 'Dalpat, the two of us are highly educated and will definitely get good jobs. But we have two other brothers who are not well qualified. If we want to help them and their families, we will have to get into some business and make it grow.'

He was absolutely right. As soon as our 'Imperial Inn' started running well, we called first our brothers, then our nephews to the US. They in turn helped others to come here and settle down. Slowly they all bought their own motels. All they needed was the initial helping hand. Once they got a foothold here, they all added their own special touch, took the initiative, and became successful in their own right. We can proudly claim today, that we didn't limit our success only to ourselves. Our entire family put together today owns 65 motels.

A famous Indian saint has said, 'If we join hands and work together, the road to success is easy.'

And we Gujaratis have put this saying into practice and proved him right.

As the years passed, we saw innumerable facets of human behaviour and learnt invaluable lessons in humanity.

A very important thing that I learnt was that communicating and reaching out to people was as necessary as being practical and having sound business sense.

A truck driver who came into the motel, weary and tired, immediately felt better when he was welcomed with a warm smile and a few friendly words like ' Hi. How are you doing?'

The elderly guests also felt nice when we talked to them and enquired after their well-being.

Once guests realized that the rooms in the motel were clean, reasonable, and well-maintained and the staff caring, friendly, and open-minded, they became our loyal customers and always came back to our motel. More important was the excellent feedback they gave their friends and family and this word-of-mouth publicity increased our customer base.

Of course, in addition to all this, we visited several factories, companies, business houses etc in the region and gave them presentations about Imperial Inn. We offered tempting discounts and other facilities.

All this contributed to the steady growth of the motel and we never had a lack of guests.

I must have met thousands of people during these years. It is not possible to remember everyone but there are some who I cannot forget.

I remember this particularly young couple who had checked in with their little son. The man was an engineer. Both the young man and wife were from aristocratic 'nawab' families of Lucknow, in India. They stayed in our motel for several months as they couldn't afford to buy their own place at the time.

The husband would go off for work early in the morning. The wife had a tough time running after the little one. When it was time for the husband to return from work, she would get nervous. She would say to Neeta 'I don't know what to do. Nawab Saheb will come back at 6 o'clock and ask me what I have made for dinner. But I don't know what to say to him. I haven't been able to cook anything at all.'

Neeta asked her 'Why didn't you cook?'

The poor girl was almost in tears 'I get so tired just looking after my son. And frankly, I don't know how to cook. I come from an aristocratic family where there were more servants than family members in the house. Forget about making a cup of tea, I have never ever picked up my own cup of tea and put it in the sink. My father thought an engineer living in America was a fantastic match for me. Little did he know that here we have to work like servants and do everything ourselves. Cook, clean, do the dishes, and buy the grocery.' She couldn't hold back her tears. She started sobbing 'My life is ruined.'

I must have heard these words at least fifty times from her and they left a lasting impression on me. It is true that many come to America thinking it is paradise and they are left feeling disillusioned.

What they do not realize is that America is a land of opportunities. But it is in our hands to make the most of these opportunities, work hard, and create our own paradise here. Those who understand this are able to live here happily.

As the I 95 highway was close to Imperial Inn, we got a lot of people from the north and south of US coming in to our motel. Most of the people from the New England states in the north were prosperous, rich, white Americans. They usually did not bargain about the room rents. On the other hand, the people from the southern parts like Tampa, Florida, New Orleans etc were not so well off. They used to haggle a lot about the room rent.

They would ask 'Why is it so much? Please lower the tariff.' It was not always possible to give in to their demands. At such times, they became angry or sarcastic. 'I'm not asking you the rent for the whole motel, you know. I want to know the rent for only 1 room.'

Finally I too started speaking their language: 'If you can't afford the rent for 1 room, why do you want to talk about the whole motel?' Sometimes one has to give it back in the same coin if one doesn't wish to be taken for a ride.

At times, some guests would get really angry. 'This is highway robbery.'

Sometimes, the scene could get ugly 'You want to stay in this country don't you?' I normally did not respond to such provocations.

But once I was stretched to the limit.

A black man from the South came in and enquired about a room. I said, 'Sorry. All the rooms are occupied.'

He lost his temper and started shouting 'You are refusing to give me a room because I am black. This is discrimination and it is against the law. I will complain about this to the cops.'

I put my arm next to his and tried to calm him down 'Look at the colour of my skin. It is as dark as yours. Why will I discriminate against you because of your colour? If you don't believe me, look in the register. There really is no room vacant.' But he was in no mood to listen. He started yelling and cursing at the top of his voice. Finally I lost my patience and I yelled in a voice loud enough to match his 'Get the hell out of here. If you say one word more, it is I who will call the cops.' He took one look at my red face and left. Later, Neeta said to me 'Why did you shout like that at him? What if he had lost his head and done something terrible?'

She was correct. One hears often of such instances in the US where the argument is ended by bullets. There have been times when motel owners have been attacked or shot dead. I was lucky to have got off safe.

All the guests have to note down their name, address, contact details, profession etc in the motel register. However, there is no way these can be verified. So, one often reads in the newspaper or sees on TV about a murder or some other crime taking place in a motel. Motels are also convenient for secret rendezvous in illicit relationships.

No motel owner can totally control what goes on in the rooms in a motel. All he can do is pray that nothing bad happens. I too was no exception. But in spite of all my prayers, there was such an incident.

Once, a white American family of German origin took a room in the motel. The man was an Army officer. The family was returning to Washington after spending a nice vacation in the North. In the morning, the husband went out with the children. When he came back, his wife was not in the room. The bathroom was locked and he could hear the shower running inside. He called out 'Ruth, we're back.' He waited for some time and then when she still didn't come out, started banging on the door. But there was no reply.

Finally he came to the front desk to ask for help. Neeta ran and opened the door with the master key. The woman was in the tub, dead.

What a mess it was then. Doctors, cops, rigorous questioning followed.

Finally the body was sent for a post-mortem. The police questioned the motel staff and grilled us as well. The Army officer left with his children. Was the lady's death an accident or was it suicide? We never found out. And we didn't follow it up either. The sad truth was that a woman had lost her life in our motel.

We thought it best to accept the fact and leave it at that. The incident slowly faded out from my memory but what I cannot forget is the look of shock on the children's faces and I can still remember their pitiful cries of 'Mom'. Memories like these always leave me disturbed.

One person who came in as a guest and slowly became a member of the family was Peter Dada. We bought Imperial Inn on July 1, 1970. The earlier owners had left, after training us for 15 days. But Peter stayed on. Peter had been staying at the motel since the last 6 months. He was a retired army officer who had returned from the war in Vietnam. The rate for 1 room at that time was $9 per day. But since Peter was almost a permanent guest, he paid a special rate of $35 a week for his room.

When Neeta, Chetan, and I shifted into the motel, Chetan was the first to become friends with Peter. Gradually we all came to know him well and he became our Peter Dada. Peter was an American Jew. Over the years, thanks to his friendship with us, he learnt Gujarati.

He came to love Gujarati food and to understand our customs and traditions. When he saw me, he would say in his American accent 'Jai Shri Ram, Dalpat' Sometimes I would rag him 'How long are you going to live alone Peter? Get married.'

He would answer 'Why? Do you wanna get rid of me? But I'll stay here until I die.' And his words came true.

My three other brothers and I stayed for 24 years in the motel with our respective families. Then in 1994, all of us built houses nearby and slowly moved into them, but Peter stayed on in the motel. He was now 85 years old and hardly ever went out.

We used to get him everything he needed. Sometimes he would go himself to the military hospital when he did not feel well. We would visit him daily in the hospital. As his health started to deteriorate, the doctors asked him 'Do you want us to send word to your family?'

He replied, 'Dalpat Patel and his family is my only family. Call them.'

Neeta and I had gone then to visit Chetan in Washington. As soon as we got the call, we went immediately to the hospital. Peter took my hand in his and then breathed his last.

We were grief stricken and sobbed as if we had lost a close member of the family.

I was the one who claimed his dead body. He had expressed the wish to be cremated so that is what we had decided to do. He was given the traditional military salute. It was I who pushed the button at the electric crematorium and bid farewell to my dear friend.

I was just about getting used to idea that Peter Dada was no longer with us, when one day I got a call from his lawyer. Peter had made a will in which he had written 'All the money in my bank account should go to Dalpat Patel. Dalpat will have the freedom to do what he chooses with that money and I am sure that his decision will always be right.'

I instinctively knew what Peter would have wished to do with that money. Accordingly, I donated it to various social service organizations in his name. Today, Peter is no longer in this world. But he remains close to our heart and thanks to his donations, he is a help to the needy even after his death.

For several years after buying the motel, I continued to do my day job while managing the business at the same time. Every morning, I would get dressed in my formal clothes and catch the train to work. In the train, I would constantly be thinking about all the things to be done in the office like the meetings to attend, details about the bridge, reviewing it with the clients, meeting deadlines on particular projects and so on.

On the return journey in the train, I would be constantly thinking again, but this time it would be about things to do in the motel like mowing the lawn, repairing the TV in room no. 5 and the heater in room no. 25, etc.

It had been my decision to take up this dual responsibility, so there was no way I could complain. However tiring it was, it had to be done.

In 1974, the petrol prices increased and the US was in the grip of recession. Business was down. People lost their jobs. One day, I too got the dreaded pink slip. Normally a person who gets the pink slip is shattered but, quite frankly, I was relieved. By now, we owned two motels and we were thinking of expanding our business. So actually it was a good moment for me to give up my job and concentrate entirely on our family business.

Three months later, I was recalled by my company. I went but this time not as a regular employee, but on a contract basis. Because this time, my priority was clear. My chosen career was that of a motel owner and I had to be successful at it. I decided to take up engineering assignments from time to time in order to stay in touch with the field and not let my knowledge go waste. But I had to prove myself now essentially as a motel owner.

After buying our first motel Imperial Inn in 1970, we eventually bought several other motels. We sold some and managed some ourselves. Since Maganbhai had started working as a realtor, we bought many plots at a reasonable price and then sold them later for a good profit.

Our entire family put together—brothers, nephews, brothers-in-law and cousins, we now owned 60 odd motels. Our business was flourishing. We were all living comfortable lives. But being content with a comfortable existence is not a part of my nature. So I was itching to find a new challenge.

As luck would have it, around this time, I attended a political meeting organized by the local Congressman. There was a lot of discussion about the various issues, problems, solutions, policies to be implemented in Mansfield Township which is in New Jersey State.

After the meeting, the conversation continued informally over cups of tea. The Congressman said to me 'Mr Patel, you have now been staying in the US for the last 30 years. You are a respected and responsible citizen of this country. I think it is time you became actively involved in the social and political scenario.'

I was taken aback. I didn't know what to say 'Well, you do have a point there but...'

He guessed what I was going to say 'MrPatel, you don't have to be conscious of the fact that you are not of American origin or that you belong to a minority community here, because America is what it is today because of all the immigrants who arrived here from different lands and made it their home. And as for the fact that you are from a minority community, if someone like you doesn't participate in the local politics, how will you convey the opinions, the problems and issues of your minority group to the government and to the people?'

I was carried away by his words. 'In that case, I would love to be involved in the local politics and social organizations. But can you please suggest how I should go about it?'

He advised me, 'The elections for the school in your town are approaching. Why don't you try to get elected to the school board? That will give you a very good idea and experience of how these local institutions work.'

I couldn't get this new idea out of my head. The Congressman was right. But would it be possible for me to win the elections?

There are 5 small towns including Bordentown and Columbus in Mansfield Township. The population consists mainly of farmers out of which 99 percent are white Anglo-Saxons. There are hardly any black people or Indians or others of Asian descent. So how could I hope to win here?

I discussed the matter with Neeta and the kids at home. Chetan and Anju came up to me and said, 'Papa, you must contest in the election. We will help you with your election campaign.' When I expressed my doubts, Chetan said, 'I understand what you are trying to say, Papa. You are the first generation to migrate here from India and settle down. Even after living here for almost 30 years, you still feel a little out of place at times. But our case is different. We have been born and brought up here. Do you remember my first day at school here? I was the only dark skinned child there among all the white kids. Initially, some of them would taunt me and call out "Hey, you Indian boy." But very soon, I was accepted as one of them. Both Anju and I feel that we belong a 100 percent to this town, school, and country.'

I replied 'You are right there. But you aren't contesting the elections. I am.'

Both Chetan and Anju stuck to their guns 'Papa, you must contest the elections. We will personally meet all our school classmates and canvas for you. We are convinced you will definitely win.'

Neeta too was all for the idea. The children's enthusiasm was infectious. I decided to go for it and filled up the form for the elections. It became a hot topic of discussion in the town. 'Dalpat Patel. A man of Indian origin contesting the seat for the local school board.'

There were only 15 days left for the elections. Chetan and Anju became my campaign managers. They were all fired up about the campaign and along with their friends, they put in their 100 percent into it. We got the flyers printed. These were to be distributed among the people. We made the sign boards, to be put up on the roads ourselves. Chetan and his friends put up these boards all over the town. I started calling up people and asking them to vote for me.

We had to face quite a lot of ridicule as well. Some people made fun of our handmade sign boards while others said mockingly 'So Mr Patel. We hear that you are contesting for both the Primary and High School seats on the board. Looks like you have a lot of free time on your hand.'

But I answered each one patiently and frankly 'I was not aware that it is not customary to contest both the seats. This is the first time I am participating in an election. So there are bound to be mistakes and faux pas in my campaign but these are unintended. And I assure you of one thing: if I am elected to this post, I will do my best to fulfil the responsibilities I am entrusted with.'

There were 5 contestants for the Primary School Board out of which 3 would be elected, while of the 3 contestants for the High School Board, one would be chosen.

It was April 15, 1997, the day of the elections. When I came back after voting, I called up all my friends and acquaintances to remind them to cast their vote. There were only 30 minutes left for the voting when I called up my neighbour. 'Hey, George. Do you remember the school board elections are today? Did you vote yet?'

He cried out, 'Oh no. I had totally forgotten. But Mariam and I will go immediately. Thanks for calling.'

The voting was over and when the results were finally announced, I found out that I had been elected to the Primary School Board with a margin of only 2 votes.

What a celebration there was in the Patel household that night. The children's friends, Maganbhai and other family members, and some of our close friends all dropped in to congratulate me. It was late when everyone left. I was lying in bed, trying to sleep when it occurred to me that those two deciding votes must have been George and Mariam's. If that is the case, I won because of that last phone call I made.

I realized how important this small victory of mine was to the residents of our town on the day of the school board's first meeting. Everyone was invited. When I took my seat on the stage, I saw that the auditorium was packed.

In fact, there were many people who were standing at the back because there wasn't enough room for everyone to sit.

The board member who was sitting next to me whispered in my ear, 'This is the first time that a non-white "foreigner" is sitting up here on the stage. Everyone is here today to have a look at you and to hear what you have to say.'

This made me quite tense. But I took a deep breath and started my speech.

I began by thanking everyone for their support and then continued, 'My father was a teacher in a small village in India. In spite of having a big family and not such a large pay package, he instilled the importance of education in us. It was beyond his means, but he put me and my brother through engineering school. He would always say, "Education is a treasure that doesn't diminish because you share it with someone and that no one can take away from you." Along with the importance of education, I also firmly believe in Gandhiji's principles of truth and non-violence. My father had participated in Gandhiji's Satyagraha movement and as his children, we too are followers of Gandhiji's teachings.'

'The third and the most important point that I would like to make is that I acknowledge my debt to this town which has accepted me and my family and I will do everything in my power to repay this debt. I have been living here for the past 25 years and my family and I have got so much from this town. I now wish to work to the best of my capacity to give something back to our town.'

The thunderous applause that followed was an indication of the people's approval.

The meeting then went on until midnight and I realized that I was going to have to devote a lot of my time henceforth to the school.

I was entrusted with three responsibilities by the Primary School Board: curriculum, budget, and the new school building. All the three issues were very close to my heart so I threw myself into the work with enthusiasm.

My qualification and experience as a civil engineer proved a great help when it came to the new construction in the school building. I ensured that we got the best raw materials at the most competitive rates and I personally supervise the quality control in the construction.

Gradually, I won the trust and confidence of the other members of the Board. The very next year not only was I elected to the High School Board but I was also made the Vice President.

During a function in school, the Principal of the school spoke very highly of my contribution 'Dalpat Patel is an extremely hard working and honest man. He has fulfilled his responsibility as a member of the School Board in an excellent manner. In fact, I would not hesitate to add that if he were to become the Township Mayor he would be an excellent choice and it would prove very beneficial to our community.'

One evening, sometime after this occasion, I was all alone at home when I received an unexpected visitor. He had come on behalf of the Chairperson of the Democratic Party in our County.

He asked me 'Mr Patel, you are a supporter of the Democratic Party, isn't it?'

'Yeah, that's right.' I replied.

'On behalf of the Party, we would like to request you to consider one proposal: We would like you to contest the Township election this year as the official candidate of the Democratic Party.'

I was taken aback. It was one thing to be a part of the School Board, but quite another to participate in the Township elections. That would be jumping from social service directly into politics.

'Please give me some time to think about it. I will let you know my decision in a couple of days.'

He smiled encouragingly. 'Please take your time. But I will tell you frankly that we are expecting a positive reply.'

Even after he left, I could hardly believe it. Maganbhai dropped in a little later, so I told him all about it.

He said, 'Dalpat, has a Democratic candidate ever won a seat in the Mansfield Township election? It is true that we always vote for the Democratic candidate but our votes are in vain. It is the Republican Party which holds sway in this region and it is always white Republicans that get elected to the Township Committee.'

I knew he was right and said, 'I know it. But there are two reasons why I would like to consider this idea—one, I managed to overcome the domination of white Republicans when it came to the School Board, didn't I? '

'And the second reason is that since the Democratic Party members have themselves invited me to contest the elections, it shows that they have at least a little faith in me.'

Maganbhai shook his head 'No, no. On the contrary, I think they have not found anyone this year to contest the election and that is why you have been chosen as the scapegoat. Think very carefully before making up your mind.'

The children had been listening to our conversation. Now, Chetan put in his bit 'Magan Kaka (Uncle), you have a point. But Papa is not wrong either.'

Maganbhai started laughing 'Spoken like a true politician. Okay, Chetan out with it. What do you think about it?'

Chetan was very assertive 'I strongly feel that Papa should definitely contest this election as the Democratic Party candidate. Whether he wins or loses is not really important. But fighting this battle will be another opportunity for Papa to prove himself.'

Anju and Maya also agreed with what he was saying and assured me, 'Your campaign is our responsibility.'

Finally Maganbhai said, 'I gave you my opinion. But of course it goes without saying that if you do decide to run for the post, you have my total support. I will do everything I can to make you win and my vote will definitely go to you.'

Our informal meeting ended on this positive and heartwarming note and the very next day, I filled in the form for the elections.

The Democratic Party workers assured me of their full support and cooperation.

Chetan and his gang of friends began the campaign with enthusiasm. This time, one of my friends, Shivraj Gohil, was

145

chosen as my campaign manager. Dr Prabhakar Patel and another old friend Arthur Puglio were to be his assistants.

There was a special reason why Arthur was backing me so vehemently. He was of Italian origin. He looked like a fair-skinned European. He was living in this region and was a farmer here for the last 37 years. But he was still looked upon as a 'minority foreigner' by the white Anglo-Saxon locals. Once, he too had contested the Township elections. But everyone had come together to make sure that he didn't win. So, he had a special interest in ensuring that I win the election this time around.

There are two stages in the Township elections: the Preliminaries and the Finals.

Fortunately, there was no one to oppose me in the Preliminaries so I was elected unopposed.

The Final election was the real test. The Finals of the Township elections are held simultaneously all over the country on the second Tuesday of November. A flurry of campaigning precedes the elections.

Chetan and his friends got the flyers and posters printed. They began to personally deliver the flyers to the local residents and to put up the posters in prominent locations in the town.

To my astonishment, there was no help at all from the Democratic Party office. Finally I went to meet the Chairperson of the Democratic Party of our County. It was a lady. She told me very clearly 'Do not expect any help from me. In fact, I will not even vote for you.'

There was nothing left for me to say. 'All right, if that is your wish.'

But she wasn't done yet. As I was leaving she called out 'Mr Patel, you don't stand a chance.' and continued muttering 'Not that I am surprised. I have been living here since the last 27 years, I am white, but even then I am not yet accepted by the locals. So you have a fat chance of winning.'

I remembered Maganbhai's words at that moment. He was right. I was to be the scapegoat this time. But instead of getting angry, I was amused. And I decided that no matter what the result of the elections would be, I would do continue to do the best I could.

My opponent was Gladdock, a prosperous electrical contractor from our community. He was gearing up to ensure his win and my defeat. Not only was he rich and powerful, but he also had the support and advice of a team of experienced campaigners.

If we put up 1 poster on a road, 10 of his posters would immediately overshadow mine. Even the area around our motel was liberally covered with huge posters of him.

When he went to meet the local residents, he made it a point to tell them 'Mr Patel is a foreigner. I come from this Township. I understand the problems of our community and will be able to solve them much better.'

I kept my cool in all this and continued campaigning my way. I asked people to vote for me and assured them that I would do my best and work honestly if I was elected. But I never tried to put Gladdock down or talk about his shortcomings.

The highlight of an election in the US is always the Public Debate. It is an open meeting and the candidates have the opportunity to express their point of view. Gladdock and I came face to face three times during the course of the campaign.

An enormous amount of preparation goes into these debates.

There is a lot of research to be done: statistics and figures, popular opinion about major issues, problems and needs of the voters, etc. Once all the data is in hand, probable answers and responses to the anticipated questions have to be thoroughly prepared.

Gohil was in charge of all this preparation. During the debate, he would sit next to me to prompt me or help me out if needed.

I had to face a barrage of questions from the people:

'Mr Patel, what do you propose to do to reduce the amount of taxes that we have to pay?'

My reply was 'The Township Committee has a fixed budget and expenditure. However, I will try to reduce the expenditure and thus lessen the burden on the people as they will then have to pay lesser taxes. If elected, I will do my best to implement this.'

'Mr Patel, what measures do you have in mind to improve the security in the region?'

My answer was 'Our town is actually quite safe and quiet. The few crimes that have taken place in the area are committed by outsiders, coming from other parts of the country. I will request the police to keep a closer watch on outsiders to counter this problem and further reduce the number of crimes in our locality.

Once I was asked a question about 'Green Acre'. As I did not know a lot about it, I admitted and said frankly 'Sorry, but I do not know the details of this issue.'

A detailed account of the debates between Gladdock and me would be published in the *Trenton Times*, a prominent newspaper in the region. Once the paper featured an article on me which said: 'Mr Dalpat Patel does speak English with an Indian accent but his words are always relevant and thought provoking. Mr Patel is highly qualified and intelligent. And most important of all, he is honest and sincere. The results of our popular survey indicate that Mr Patel stands a good chance of winning, even if it is by a small margin.

This encouraging article boosted our camp's morale and we threw ourselves into the campaign with added fervour. Even if a win was not guaranteed, at least there was now a glimmer of hope.

The very next day after this article appeared in the *Trenton Times*, I had a visitor. It was a Mr Rockwell from the Democratic Party. He came straight to the point. 'Mr Patel, I am to convey a message to you from the Democratic Party. You are requested to withdraw your candidature.'

For a moment, I was stunned. But then I gathered my wits and asked 'Why? What is the reason?'

'We now have a better candidate in mind.'

I didn't know whether to laugh or be angry about it. The Party suggested my name when they were confident I would lose. But now that I stood a chance of winning, they had found a 'better' candidate? I was aware of the fickle-mindedness of politicians, but I was shocked by such blatant scheming.

I remained silent for a moment and then calmly asked 'Where was this "better" candidate of yours all this while, Mr Rockwell?'

He was taken aback and didn't know what to say.

I continued, 'I am sorry. But I am not going to withdraw now. I am the official candidate of the Party and I have won the Preliminaries. Now I will definitely contest the Finals.'

Rockwell left without a word.

I concentrated on the task in hand. As the election approached, I started making direct contact with the people. I went to their house with my supporters. We were greeted by varied reactions.

Some would take the time to listen to us.

Others would not even open the door.

A few days before the elections, we even got threatening calls, but chose to ignore them.

On the eve of the voting, the Democratic Party's Chairperson asked me to meet her at her residence. I wondered what the matter was now. When I arrived, she said, 'Mr Patel, I did nothing to help you in your campaign. But I would also like to inform you that I did nothing to harm your campaign either. I have called you here today to tell you that no matter what the others in the Party think, my family and I are going to vote for you tomorrow.'

'Thank you Madam.' I said and left.

When I related the incident to Arthur, he cautioned me 'Don't get too carried away by her words. She doesn't have a choice but to vote for you. If the Party finds out that she voted for the Republican candidate, she will be thrown out from the Party.'

But I smiled. 'Whatever her reasons, I am glad that tomorrow I will get 6 votes from that family.'

It was the day of the election. I got up early, got ready, finished my prayers and left to vote with Neeta.

There was so much excitement the whole day. My supporters were keeping a close watch on the voting process, calling up voters until the last minute to remind them and to urge them to vote.

Voting was to end at 8 o'clock and then would begin the counting.

I told Neeta, 'Please make batata vada and something sweet for everyone who will be here tonight.'

Gladdock too was making his own preparations. He was confident about his win. Since he was an electrical contractor, he had lit up his entire house and had also made arrangements for a post- election party. Drinks, food, music, everything was ready.

Late in the evening, Chetan called to say ' Papa, you are leading in two wards.'

The tension was now at fever pitch.

Finally, Chetan called after midnight and announced 'Papa, congratulations. You have won.'

The phone didn't stop ringing the entire night and people continued streaming to wish me. Neeta and Manju Bhabhi made hundreds of batata vadas. Meanwhile, Steve Gladdock's house was shrouded in darkness.

Early next morning, Arthur Puglio came in almost dancing, waving a copy of *Trenton Times*. He couldn't have been happier if he had won himself. His joy was infectious and I too smiled broadly. I took the newspaper from his hand and read the top story on the front page: 'The Democratic Party candidate, Mr Dalpat Patel, who is of Indian origin, won yesterday's Township election having secured an impressive 61 percent of the votes polled. When interviewed by our reporter, Mr Patel said, 'I am very happy that I have won the election. At the same time, I am also aware of the responsibility that I now bear. The people of Mansfield Township have placed their trust in me. I am going to do my best to prove to them that they have made the right choice.'

I showed Arthur this bit and said to him 'Now the real test begins.' Arthur shook my hand and assured me 'I have absolutely no doubt that you will soon prove them right.'

Fortunately, Arthur's words came true.

I worked very hard during my three years tenure. Of course, everything didn't always go smoothly during these three years. Two members on the Committee were openly against me and vehemently opposed anything I suggested. Once things came to such a head that one of them put in an article in the newspaper stating that Mr Patel is not trustworthy.

However, I kept my cool and did not retaliate. I calmly put forward my arguments during the meeting.

It was Arthur who was livid 'You should sue him for discrimination.' Discrimination is a serious offense in the US. However, I did not wish to pursue the matter any further. 'He will realize his mistake one day. And even if he doesn't, I will let my actions speak for themselves and prove that I had made the correct decision.'

This incident was reported in the *Trenton Times*. My policy of turning the other cheek earned me the title of 'Township Gandhi'. I was born in Gandhiji's motherland. The fact that I could implement Gandhiji's teachings in a foreign land thousands of miles away and convince others to believe in them is testimony to the greatness of Gandhiji's principles.

My faith in the convincing power of my work was proved right because in January 2001, I was elected the Township Mayor.

This time, I felt truly happy and satisfied. The headlines in the American newspapers hailed the election of the first Gujarati Mayor from the Township, while the Gujarati newspapers in India proudly declared the same news: 'Malekpore na Dalpatbhai America New Jersey ma Mayor banya hata.'

The Township Hall was packed on the day that I was to take oath as Mayor. A very learned and respected man from our community, Mr Haren Bhai Dave had come specially to administer the oath to me.

After performing a puja of Ganesha, the Hindu elephant god, Haren Bhai gave me his blessings and some valuable advice 'Always keep the ideal of Lord Ganesha in your mind. Like him, let your ears be big. That means listen carefully and patiently to everyone and gain as much of information as you can. But do not use this knowledge for spite, malice, or gossip. Always keep it a secret. Ganesha has a big stomach because he stores all the knowledge there, so that it may harm no one. Remember, knowledge has to be used at the right time and for the right reason. The elephant opens his mouth only when he needs to eat. Like him, you too must not open your mouth too much, unnecessarily. Speak little. Let your actions speak for you.'

Not just me, everyone in the Hall listening to Haren Bhai was moved and impressed by his words.

Then I put my hand on the Bhagwad Gita and took the oath for Mayor. I was now the Mayor of Mansfield Township.

As I heard the resounding ovation, I said to myself 'Come on, Dalpatbhai. You have to get down to work. From tomorrow, you have to play a new role. A new chapter in your life begins.'

Epilogue

Dalpatbhai was aware of his responsibility to the people of Mansfield Township who had bestowed their trust on him, a foreigner. They had showed confidence in him and he could not let them down. By now, be it social work or politics, he was no longer a novice at it. He had been working for three years as a member of the Township Council and this experience was invaluable for his present role.

The first matter he concentrated on was the budget. He reduced unnecessary expenses and then with the backing of the other Committee members, introduced many new schemes.

Some of the old roads in the town were modernized. He personally looked into the project and made sure that the raw material was of excellent quality and would endure for several years. New parking lots were constructed in the town. A major part of the budget was now allocated to education and sports. He ensured that schools got the best sports equipment, new sports fields, well equipped libraries etc.

Some of the problems of Mansfield Township were long standing: no public water system, no public drainage system, very few industries etc.

These had to be addressed first, for there to be progress in the region. However, any new measures were immediately opposed by the conservative farmers of the region. Finally Dalpatbhai had to give in and forego some of the modernization plans he wished to implement.

Some ideas could be put into practice. A few could not be accomplished to perfection as Dalpatbhai wished. But, he was definitely able to achieve one thing: he proved wrong the belief of the people that the elected Representative forgets all his assurances when he is elected. He stayed in constant touch with the people. He used to say 'Just because I won the election, it doesn't mean that I am the Boss. I am here to serve the people.' Everyone liked his humble and honest approach to work and Dalpatbhai set a new ideal for the people.

The Mayor, in his capacity as Police Commissioner, has the responsibility to ensure law and order in the region. This title is not in name only.

Luckily for Dalpatbhai, Mansfield County is a quiet region with a relatively low crime rate. So the police force here is not as stressed as in other parts of the country. However, there was one terrible incident during Dalpatbhai's tenure which was an exception.

It was the day of the weekly market. There were quite a large number of farmers and other locals buying things at wholesale prices. Suddenly someone started firing from a car in the parking lot.

Everyone panicked and began to run helter-skelter. One man was hit by a bullet in the melee.

The police was informed and within minutes they reached the scene. Dalpatbhai too arrived soon after. The police evacuated the area and formed a cordon around the car. The Police Chief called out to the person in the car over the megaphone.

'You are surrounded by the police. If you do anything violent, we will be forced to open fire. Throw your weapon outside the car, slowly open the door, put your hands above your head, and come out of the car. If you do so, I assure you that you will not be physically harmed in any way.'

The tension in the air was palpable. But there was no movement or sound from the car.

After a while, the Police Chief repeated his instructions and this time he added 'This is the last warning.'

Finally a weapon was thrown out of the car. A man in Army fatigues stepped out of the car with his hands over his head. Everyone heaved a sigh of relief. The policemen surged ahead to arrest him when suddenly, he pulled out a revolver from his pocket and started firing indiscriminately at the cops. They had been tricked. One policeman was already hit by then. The next moment, the Police Chief whipped out his revolver and fired at the man, who fell down, dead.

It was like a scene straight out of a Hollywood film. Hundreds of people were witness to this incident. But the story did not end there.

The case came up before the Township Court. The Courtroom was packed.

Dalpatbhai was asked to give evidence in his capacity as Mayor. 'The man opened fire on unsuspecting people and fired indiscriminately at them. The Police Chief gave him adequate warning and time to surrender. However, he only pretended to turn himself in and began firing again at the policemen. One policeman was seriously injured. Prompt action had to be taken. Otherwise more would have been injured or even killed. The Police Chief showed great presence of mind and shot the man. He did his duty admirably. I shudder to think what would have happened if the man had not been stopped in time.'

Thanks to Dalpatbhai's evidence, the Police Department was cleared of any blame in the whole matter.

Another emergency situation when Dalpatbhai was Mayor and there was a terrible snowstorm. The meteorological Department had forecast a heavy snowstorm with terrible winds. It was predicted that the town would be covered in two feet of snow.

Dalpatbhai was listening to the weather forecast on TV when his phone rang. It was the Township Manager 'Mr Mayor, What should we do? Should we close down the entire town? What do you think?'

There was no time to lose. Dalpatbhai took a decision in an instant. 'Close down the whole town,' he said.

Schools, colleges, shops, and all other business establishments and offices were asked to close immediately and everyone was asked to return home. Hence, while the storm was raging, everybody was safe at home. After the storm abated, efforts were made on a war footing to clear the snow at the earliest and only then were people allowed to leave the safety of their home.

At the end of his three years as Mayor of Mansfield County, Dalpatbhai received praise from all quarters 'Our Mayor has done a good job.' His stint as a Mayor is remembered even today by the people in the Township.

Any success story cannot be complete without a few dark clouds. Nobody ever has a smooth trouble free life.

There are always pitfalls, unexpected problems, sometimes an insurmountable mountain of obstacles, or slippery slopes on the way to success.

It was 15 years since the two brothers had bought Imperial Inn. Dalpatbhai and Maganbhai had then helped brothers, cousins and several family members to settle down in the US. Both of them were content and financially settled. But this is the time of danger for a hardcore businessman. Comfort does not agree with him. He is always on the lookout for new challenges. 'What next?' is the question foremost on his mind.

So, Dalpatbhai and Maganbhai started exploring new options. There were many pharmaceutical companies in the region. In fact, New Jersey is famous for this industry and 60 percent of America's medicines are produced here.

Dhandha

During their search for a new business venture, Dalpatbhai met Dheerubhai Solanki. He was working at a very high post in a pharmaceutical company. After a series of meetings with Dheerubhai, Maganbhai and Dalpatbhai took a decision: They would start a new company with the help of Dheerubhai.

The product was also finalized: vitamin tablets. The projected production cost was approximately $4 million. Half of this capital would be put in by the Patel brothers and the rest would be a loan from the bank. It was a new venture in a totally new terrain.

Land had to be bought, the factory had to built. Things went smoothly until they reached the most important stage: production. But luckily, even that went off without a hitch. The company began production soon after for there was a huge demand for the product.

But soon enough, a big consignment was rejected and returned to the company. After an initial reaction of shock, the team started working on finding a solution to the problem. Maganbhai tried to encourage everyone by saying, 'It's okay. It is a new field. We will face teething problems like these.'

Nobody realized that this was just the beginning of the end.

The first problem was just the tip of the iceberg. More and more problems came up, more mistakes were made. The estimated cost went for a toss and everything went spiralling out of control. The Patel brothers spent the next three years trying to salvage the business and finally came to the conclusion that it would be better to bear the loss of $4 million, rather than continue to run the company.

They sold the company to Dheerubhai Solanki. Ironically, Lady Luck seemed to smile on Dheerubhai because he was successful in turning the company around and today, his company's products are well-known the world over. Such is destiny. But this story highlights the business instincts of the Gujarati community. Where two Gujaratis had failed, a third Gujarati showed the courage to take up a failure and turn it into a success.

When I sat with Dalpatbhai for a face-to-face chat, he smiled at me and said, 'Shobha Ben, There are always ups and downs in business. This failure taught us what we should never ever do again in our business.'

Dalpatbhai and Maganbhai lived in Imperial Inn for 24 years and looked after the business and the household. Here too, like in India, they had a huge joint family setup. Even in a country as different in culture as the US, all these people were living happily together in a 3 bedroom apartment. One terrace in the motel was covered so that everyone could sit down to lunch on the floor in a row like in India. Seems strange, doesn't it?

Gradually as each person settled down, bought their own motel and house, they moved out. Finally, after seeing to it that everyone was well taken care off, Dalpatbhai and Maganbhai permitted themselves one luxury. They bought 4 huge houses for the 4 brothers.

Today Dalpatbhai's next generation has gone from motels to hotels. His elder son Chetan has already established himself as a hotelier in Washington.

What does the Generation Next have to say?

Chetan says, 'I grew up in a motel. That was our home. That was also our business. So the work to be done in a motel came as naturally to me as the household chores. All I knew while I was growing up was the motel and school. I was the first dark-skinned Indian boy in my school. All the others were white Americans. In the beginning I was scared. But slowly I was accepted as one of them.

159

Then began my dual life.

On the one hand, at home the language, the food was 100 percent Gujarati. The values and customs were 100 percent Indian. As ours was a joint family, I was used to respecting elders, adjusting with others, compromising on certain things. In fact during Navaratri, Diwali, or weddings, it felt like we were back in Gujarat, in India.

On the other hand, our world outside school was totally American. We felt a part of this world too and loved it equally. But at times, we would get confused bridging the gap between these two worlds. There were many things we were not allowed to do like our American friends. At such times, our immediate reaction was "Why not?" Sometimes, we would get an answer and sometimes the reply would be "No questions".

I have to admit that I used to get furious with the elders at moments like these. But now that I too shoulder the responsibility of a family, I understand their point of view better. The elders in our family; my parents, uncles, aunts etc all instilled good values in us.

Today, I can say with pride that everyone in my generation, who was born and brought up here, is a vegetarian. None of us drink, smoke or have any other vices. We never felt the need for it. We respect our religion, our culture. Our elders got us addicted to only one thing. Work.'

Chetan went on to graduate in Biology. He initially wanted to become a Doctor. But later, he realized that his true interest lay in the hospitality industry like his father. Chetan and his friend Amit have been successfully running their business together as partners for the past 14 years. These two young men have a completely different perspective of their profession. Earlier the objective would be to buy a small motel or hotel, run it well, and make a good profit. But this dream is no longer enough for the ambitious youth of this generation.

Their dream is to expand the business on various levels: Buy old motels or hotels, renovate them, run them successfully, and then sell them for a handsome profit; Buy new hotels, build up their reputation, and then sell them for enormous profits; or take a franchisee of a well-known hotel chain and do excellent business.

The most important thing is to appoint highly qualified professionals to do the work and not to restrict oneself to only one business. In this way, the business grows exponentially and things are easier to manage.

It is no wonder that Patels and Shahs today account for 55 percent of the Hospitality business in the US.

The second generation of Patels has great ambitions. They want to conquer the world. They are ready to take on any challenge to achieve their dream.

LIFE OF A SALESMAN

Jaydev Patel

Purnima Patel

One afternoon, as I was sipping a cup of tea and reading the latest update on the upcoming US elections, the phone rang.

'Hello, Purni?'

'Jay?'

'Will you be at home in the evening?'

'Yes, I will. Why?'

'A reporter is coming to interview me and she would like to talk to you as well.'

'Okay. But make sure you are also home on time.'

'I will be there, but before that, will you please do one thing?'

'What?'

'Will you please go over the articles that have been already published about me and compile a file for her?'

'No problem. I will keep the file ready.'

As soon as I hung up, I got down to work.

From the time Jaydev had been selected as the most successful agent of the New York Life Insurance Company, he had been consistently breaking his own records. His incredible achievements had garnered a lot of press coverage and articles on him had appeared in several leading newspapers, magazines, and journals. I, as the proud wife, had kept every one of them.

Spread out before me were articles from the *Wall Street Journal*, the *Times of India*, and so on. As I glanced at them, I couldn't stop myself from reading them once again.

The first was an article in the *Times of India*, December 11, 2006. Jay's photograph is on the front page along with a prominent write up about him:

The whole of America knows today about the Patels, a community which is synonymous with the Motel and Hotel industry in the country. But the Patels' success story does not end here. Mr Jaydev Patel has made a mark for himself in the field of Insurance. This top agent of the New York Life Insurance Company has been a member of the Million Dollar Round Table Club for the past 30 years. The company has honoured him by conferring the greatest distinction on him and appointing him as the Chairman of the Advisory Board of Directors. This is because the total worth of the policies sold by Jaydev Patel in the last 30 years is $2.5 billion.

Then there was an article with a photograph of Jay in the column 'Business People' in the *News India Times* dated October 31, 2003.

Mr Jaydev Patel has been closely associated with the New York Life Insurance Company for the past 30 years and has contributed greatly to its progress. Hence, a felicitation ceremony was organized specially in his honour.

The *New India Times* reporter wrote:

This is the Head Office of the New York Insurance Company, on Madison Avenue, in New York. Today, the lobby of this building has been decorated so beautifully that it looks as impressive as any banquet hall in a glamorous 5 star hotel: round tables covered with sparkling white tablecloths, fancy chairs, with lovely bows, exquisite flower arrangements, glittering chandeliers... A live band is playing in one corner, while the buffet table looks inviting, with a variety of Indian, Japanese, and American cuisine laid out on it. The ambience is magical.

On this occasion, Mr Seymour Sternberg, the Chairman and CEO of the Company, addressed the distinguished gathering, 'Jaydev was the number one insurance agent in this company even before I joined it, in 1983, and he still maintains the same position today. I am sure Jaydev's name will be inscribed in letters of gold in the annals of the company as the most successful agent in its history. In fact I say this with pride 'Jay Patel IS New York Life'.

A thunderous applause greeted his words.

Then, Jaydev Patel talked about his 30 year odyssey with New York Life. 'I was a chemist. When I couldn't keep a steady job is that field, I had no other option but to look for some additional part-time work. This was when I took up the opportunity offered by New York Life and started working as an insurance agent. 30 years later, I would like to say that this decision was the best and the most appropriate decision of my life.'

The President of New York Life, Frederick Sievert, gave the concluding speech. He said, 'People often wonder "What is the key to Jaydev Patel's success?"

Well, the answer is: his ability to throw himself whole heartedly into his work; his sincerity and integrity towards his work and his clients, his commitment to fulfil his responsibilities, his confidence, and of course the rapport that he builds up with people. He is a part of the family of each of his 5000 odd clients. It gives me great pleasure to say "Congratulations Jay on this incredible milestone in your life and a truly outstanding career."'

Once again, there was thunderous applause.

Several articles on Jay have also appeared in *India Abroad*, a periodical published from New York. One article states:

The name Jaydev Patel is well known to almost all the Gujaratis, if not all the Indian families, in the United States. In fact, there is a joke doing the rounds that when a child is born in a Gujarati family, the first person he is introduced to is Jaydev Patel with the words 'Hello little one. This is Jaydev who is going to take care of all your worries and tensions in the future. Make sure you remember him.'

While speaking to the journalist from India Abroad, *Jaydev says 'The work of an insurance agent does not end with the selling of a policy. In fact, I would say his real job begins then. It is his responsibility to give financial advice and guide the client when he has any problems. When there is a demise in the family, people make a condolence visit with flowers in their hand. I, as an insurance agent, meet the family with a cheque from the Insurance Company in my hand. It is extremely reassuring to the family who at least does not have to worry about financial matters and is confident that the money that they need for their day to day living, for the children's education and for future needs is provided for. At the same time, I make it a point to visit my clients during marriages or any other important and happy occasions in their household. I bond with them as a friend and give them moral support and every other kind of assistance possible during any crisis in their lives. I feel that insurance is a vocation and not a profession and requires an intense commitment to serve humanity. Today is the age of computers. Computers have taken over many of the jobs earlier done by man. Many Insurance companies sell policies through the Internet. But I firmly believe that insurance deals with a person's need for security, his financial stability and his emotions. That is why I cannot entrust this job to a machine. Even today, I travel long distances, meet people, talk to them, win over their confidence and only then sell them a policy. Quite frankly, I have to admit that I do not even know how to switch on the computer.'*

I put aside the article. I couldn't help smiling to myself. A few years ago, Jay did not know anything about computers. He believes even today that his way of working is the best. But one has to grow, change with the times. And he is ready to accept that.

When our eldest son, Sachin, started working with Jay, he was shocked to see the huge amount of files and papers in the office. He gradually persuaded Jay and convinced him of the utility of computers. Jay finally admitted that it was more convenient and easier to maintain records on the computer.

For one thing, the office looked neater and tidier. And it took much less time to locate a file or any other information.

Today, Jay takes the help of the machine to store information, work-related documents, and send and receive emails. However, till this date, he prefers direct, face-to-face contact with his clients. Even today, he travels thousands of miles for 250 days in a year for this very purpose.

India Abroad and *Garavi Gujarat* had written about another event to celebrate 20 years of his association with New York Life.

After a lot of deliberation, and with the company's assistance, I suggested that the venue should be the Museum Hall on Ellis Island. Everyone at New York Life liked the idea.

It is an age old tradition that all the immigrants who come to America with stars in their eyes and dreams in their heart first disembark at Ellis Island. Whether they come from Asia, Africa or Europe, Ellis island forms the first point of entry for them. Only then can they step into New York and begin their life in the new country. That is why I felt it was only fitting that a function to celebrate his achievements should be held on Ellis Island.

The event took place on December 4, 1993. A detailed report with photographs was published in *India Abroad*. The article said:

If Arthur Miller, the great playwright was alive today, he would have renamed his famous play 'Death of a Salesman' and instead called it 'Life of a Salesman', with the hero being, of course, Jaydev Patel.

Mr Harry Hohn, the then Chairman and CEO of New York Life, spoke about Jay in glowing terms. In his speech he said, 'I regret that we only have one Jaydev Patel in our company. If we had a 1000 more Jaydev Patels, the sky would have been the limit for our company. I am always amazed by Jaydev's sales figures. He sells policies worth hundreds of thousands of dollars and gets equally amazing commissions. But what one should see and appreciate, is the tremendous hard work and persistence that is behind this success of his.'

Garavi Gujarat, published from London and Atlanta, Georgia, also carried a big article on Jay and the felicitation ceremony on Ellis Island.

The article described in detail how Jaydev came from India to the United States and his journey towards success here; from the initial struggle to the recognition he has achieved today.

Jaydev's talent to sell insurance policies is unbelievable and worthy of praise. His incredible marketing skills are evident when you find out that he has sold a policy even to the attendant who fills gas in his car at the service station. Jaydev convinced him to purchase an insurance policy with reasonable premiums to him and the attendant is still a client of his.

It is not always that he is successful in selling a policy immediately. Sometimes he has to pursue it for months or even years. But he doesn't give up. He continues to maintain a friendly rapport with the prospective clients. More often than not, his patience is rewarded. There was one man with whom Jay was in touch for 10 years. Jay used to try and convince him of the importance of buying an insurance policy. The man would listen to him but then do nothing about it. Finally after 10 long years, he bought a policy from Jay and became his client.

Keeping Jay in mind, one could rewrite the ancient saying and change it to 'Patience, thy name is Jaydev Patel.'

Jay's achievements have been lauded in so many newspapers and magazines all over the world. It is rare that an insurance agent gets so much acclaim. At such moments, I feel so proud that Jay is my husband. And the most wonderful moment of them all was when the prestigious *Wall Street Journal* praised Jay's accomplishments in a prominent article titled 'Immigrant Saga' that appeared on January 27 in 1987. The article talked about several people of Indian origin who had made a name for themselves in various professions in the US like Dr Hargovind Khurana's Nobel Prize winning work on the genetic code and Mohan Murjani, who is the vision behind renowned international designer lifestyle brands like Gloria Vanderbilt. He associated the famous Vanderbilt name to jeans and today thousands of glamorous girls all across the globe proudly sport a Murjani Vanderbilt pair of jeans.

About Jay, the article said that he had broken all previous records as an agent in the insurance industry and that he had been consistently selected the 'Top Agent' among 9000 agents of New York Life for for the last so many years.

Names of legends like the astrophysicist Chandrasekhar Subramaniam, mathematician Narendra Karmarkar, music maestro Zubin Mehta followed.

Among the stalwarts in the fields of education, science, art, industry etc, there was also an insurance agent. Can anyone aspire for more?

In 1992, the *Wall Street Journal* conducted a detailed study of the insurance industry in the US and there was a prominent article on Jaydev Patel, the number one insurance agent in the US.

As I went through the articles which had been published about Jay, I was lost in the realms of the past.

It was the year 1983, ten years since Jay had started working with New York Life and had already established his reputation in the company. That year, Jay had been named the President of the Top Club. This is a one-time honour when you lead the company in production. Not only did he lead the company, he also broke the all-time record in production.

Even if one is consistently the top agent for several years, one can be named the President of the Top Club only once. So it was a great honour for him indeed.

The top management of the company was going to attend the event which was going to be held at Breaker's Hotel in Palm Beach, Florida, along with the top 700 agents and their families.

We invited not only our family members who were in the US, but we specially invited Jay's mother from India. It meant a lot to us because until then, she had never ever stepped out of her Sojitra village.

Her sons who were now settled in the US would often invite her but she always shrugged from the offer saying 'You come here to see me instead.'

But this time, she decided that she had to be present on this great occasion when her son would be felicitated.

Once here, she instantly fell in love with our house in Livingston. She was fascinated by all the things in the house, especially the sprinklers in the garden. When she went back to Sojitra, she used to say 'Jay's house is so beautiful. And there are so many fountains in the garden.'

I tried telling her 'Actually these are not fountains, they are only sprinklers.'

But she insisted 'How can you say they are not fountains? I have seen them with my own eyes.'

I did not have the heart to argue with her logic and left it at that.

We took her along for the event, which was a formal black tie dinner. But she was quite at ease in the 5 star ambience with men in formal suits, elegantly dressed women, the fragrance of designer perfumes, and spirited conversations in English. In fact as they say today 'she was quite cool' and eager to enjoy the new experience.

The ceremony began. Jay's performance throughout the decade was lauded by all and then the Chairman presented Jay with the biggest honour—President of the Top Club.

The applause continued for a long time and then it was time to introduce Jay's family. The first and the most important member to be introduced was of course Jay's mother. 'This is Chanchal Ben, Jaydev Patel's mother,' announced the Master of Ceremonies. Jay had already briefed his mother about this and accordingly, she got up, turned towards the audience and smiled.

The next instant, everyone was on their feet. To the little old Indian lady clad in a simple, traditional cotton sari, this was quite a surprise. When I looked at her, I saw that her face was lit up with joy and pride. What an extraordinary moment it was, for her, and for all of us present there.

After the ceremony, everyone gathered around Jay and congratulated him. The atmosphere was charged with feelings of enthusiasm and elation.

On the one hand, I was overcome with happiness and pride and on the other hand, there was a feeling of guilt at the back of my mind. I still could not forget my initial reaction 10 years ago when Jay had told me that he was going to work as an insurance agent. I had felt then that it was a step down for a man who had a Masters' Degree in Science to become an insurance agent.

According to my dogmatic sense of reasoning, I thought that anyone who was not successful in doing anything else became an insurance agent.

I had given Jay my honest opinion, 'If anyone else wishes to become an insurance agent, it is up to them. But I seriously feel that you should not take it up. Jay, you are so soft spoken and introverted. You take such a long time to open up even with friends. How will you speak to strangers and convince them to buy insurance policies from you? Please do not take any decision out of desperation. Just because you are facing problems retaining a chemist's job, doesn't mean that you take up the next thing that comes along. If you do not succeed, you will be so demoralized.'

Jay heard me out but he finally did what he felt was right and began work as an insurance agent. Today he has proved himself to the whole world and I have no qualms in admitting that I was totally wrong.

From the French windows, I could see the mountains in the distance. I stared at them unseeingly. 'Hey Purni. Where are you?' Jay asked.

I shook my head and said, 'It's nothing. Looking at all these old articles took me back into the past. I will never forget how I had not been supportive of your decision to become an insurance agent and how vehemently I had opposed it.'

Jay replied calmly, 'Everything happens for the best. Because of your opposition, I was even more determined to succeed. That is when I made up my mind that I would make it work, come what may.'

As he went into the house, I stood there thinking, 'Is it really so easy to succeed if one decides to do it? Or is it only in hindsight that things appear easier?'

Jaydev Patel

When I completed my Masters in Chemistry from Baroda University, I hadn't really thought very seriously about the future, so I took up the first job that came my way, that of a chemist in the town of Valsad with a monthly salary of 235 rupees.

A few months later, when my Nairobi-based Uncle asked me, 'Would you like to come here?', I didn't even dream of refusing.

My uncle had been in Nairobi for several years. He was a teacher and without any doubts my hero. He had been a great support to our family. It was all thanks to him that I could pursue my Masters.

So I went to Nairobi and started working as a teacher, just like him. Life was going on smoothly. I liked my job. But within me, there was a desire to see the world.

I discussed the matter with my Uncle. He was very supportive and encouraged me to pursue my dreams. Finally I decided that

I would go to Canada. It was comparatively easy to migrate to Canada. Once again, my Uncle lent a helping hand, bought me my ticket, and I arrived in Toronto, Canada.

This is when I realized it is easy to dream of going to a foreign land but the most difficult part is settling down there and standing up on your own feet.

My Masters' degree was worthless here. Maybe it was due to the recession that the country was experiencing at the time or maybe it was my bad luck.

Whatever the reason may be, I found it very difficult to get a decent job for quite some time. So, I took up any job that I got. At times, I worked as a bartender or as a salesman in a furniture shop.

I somehow got through the next ten months, and then as soon as I got my visa for the US, I hopped on to the next bus bound for New York.

It was a bitterly cold day in December, 1968. I got down from the Greyhound bus at Port Authority Bus Terminal. From there, I had to go to the YMCA (Young Men's Christian Association) where I was told I would be able to get a room at a reasonable rate. At the Port Authority Taxi Terminal, I found out that if I took the taxi from there to the YMCA, the fare was $2, but if I took the subway, it was only 25 cents. So I decided to take the subway instead.

When I reached the YMCA, I was in for a shock. Like me, there were dozens who had heard of the cheap rates at the YMCA so a never-ending queue snaked from the building right around the corner. I too stood in line, shivering in the cold.

After some time, I glanced towards the building and saw an Indian man coming out. I couldn't believe my eyes. It was Ramesh Shah who studied with me in Baroda University.

I called out, 'Ramesh!'

Dhandha

He came over, recognized me, and when he found out that I was waiting for a room, he shook his head and said, 'I don't think you will get a room here tonight. Look at the crowd. But we can do one thing.'

He took a key from his pocket and gave it to me. 'Jaydev, take this key and go to my room. I live on the third floor. You must be tired from the journey. Have a shower, freshen up, and then come down.'

'And what will you do?' I asked him.

'Don't worry. I will wait here for you. According to the YMCA rules, only one person can go up to the room at one time. You take your time. I will wait.'

I was feeling awkward but he insisted that he would wait.

I freshened up and came down. Ramesh was waiting patiently for me. I thanked him from the bottom of my heart and left.

At times like these, when someone goes out of their way to help a person in need, my belief in humanity is strengthened all the more.

Now the first thing on my agenda was to find a place for the night which was not expensive.

I walked for ages but no luck. The room rates were exorbitant.

In the evening, I had arranged to meet a friend of mine who worked in New York.

When I told him about my desperate search for a room, he burst out laughing.

'You are looking for a place to stay in New York? In Manhattan? Are you a millionaire? How much money do you have?'

When I told him the pitiful sum, he said 'Come with me to Hoboken. It is not too far away from New York. Many Indians live there. I think you will find something that suits your budget there.'

I went with him to Hoboken which was close to New York.

I thought I was really lucky. In a single day, two friends of mine had come to my rescue.

Things soon fell into place. I found a job as a chemist which allowed me to make use of my knowledge of Chemistry. The salary was $120 a week. I was thrilled. I immediately looked for a place to live and found a small one bedroom apartment nearby. The apartment was empty except for two light bulbs. I couldn't afford the luxury of furnishing the place immediately, so I used to sleep on some newspapers spread on the floor with only a thin sheet covering me.

In retrospect, I don't know how I survived through those two-three months of harsh winters in the US.

By 1971, I was quite well settled in the US. I had a furnished flat, a car, and a job. In short, in the eyes of my family, I was now marriage material. That year, on the insistence of my mother, I decided to go to India to look for a suitable life partner.

I had planned a halt in Nairobi to see my uncle. He introduced me to several girls from families that he knew, all the while pretending that it was a only a casual unexpected encounter.

He introduced me to Purnima. One look at her and I knew that she was the one for me. I decided there and then that only she would be my wife.

Purnima Patel

I too had liked Jay. There was no reason to say no to his proposal. Our families knew each other well. But I still wondered how this man had made up his mind to marry me within the first five minutes of meeting me.

It is only later when I got married to Jay and came to know him well that I realized that he always made quick decisions and then stood by them. And most of the times, his decision would be right.

Jay went on to India after informing us about his decision. On his way back, he stopped over in Nairobi, we got married, and I went with him to the US. Everything happened in a dream-like fashion.

I had not asked any questions before entering Jay's life, but when I entered his tiny one bedroom apartment, I was stunned. I had fantasized about our romantic life together in America. But there were eight to ten people already living there when I arrived. Some had arrived only a couple of days ago while there were some who had been there and would be there for months.

Jay used to invite any Gujarati person he met into his home—even if he didn't know them. 'You can live in my apartment. Please don't feel awkward about it. Make yourself at home, he would say.

Jay and I got engaged and married within two weeks and thereafter I went to the US. To my great surprise, I soon got used to this way of life and to Jay's philosophy of welcoming everyone with open arms.

One good thing was that I immediately got a job as a Secretary in a firm, with a salary of $100 per week.

Like Jay and me, everyone else living in our apartment, man or woman, did some work or the other. Some worked in a restaurant, others as cooks, petrol pump attendants, night watchmen etc.

Nobody considered any kind of work beneath their dignity.

Everyone was aware of the fact that hard work was the only way to find stability and growth in this country.

We had our meals together. Can you imagine the huge quantities of vegetables and the mountains of rotis that had to be made each day for so many people? None of us could afford to eat out every day. But as everyone pitched in, it didn't seem like a chore and everyone enjoyed eating together.

At night, some would sleep on the couch in the living room, while others slept on the floor or at times, even in the passage.

I still remember how I crossed over at least five to six people sleeping peacefully on the floor to get to the kitchen.

Those were magical days. Days full of joy, hope, and hard work. We dreamt of a fantastic future and never even realized how the days flew past.

There was only thing that troubled me: the pink slip that Jay got from time to time.

This is a way of life in the US. On Friday evening, as one gets ready to leave, with plans already made for the weekend, one is handed the pink slip which politely informs you that your services are no longer required. Being fired seems too harsh, so it is easier to accept the reality of the situation when one gets the 'pink slip'.

But whatever one may choose to call it, there is no way to escape the bitter truth and it means only one thing—you do not have a job anymore.

I failed to understand why Jay got the pink slip so often. He was clever and sincere. It is true that he did not like people bossing him around. Whatever the reason, the fact of the matter was that he could not stick to one job for a long time.

Soon it was New Year's Eve in 1972. There was excitement in the air. Shopping, gifts, preparations for a grand dinner. Our flat too was decorated to celebrate the event. The food was ready. Our friends had started coming in.

Jay entered the flat and announced 'I lost my job.'

I couldn't bear to look at his dejected face. I put on a false air of confidence and tried to console him 'Don't worry. You will get another one. Don't think of it this evening. Let us enjoy ourselves now. Tomorrow will be a new beginning.'

The party was in full swing. When I looked at Jay's face, I could see the strain behind the smile on his face.

As Jay is normally quiet and doesn't speak much, no one else except me realized that he was tense. At midnight, we wished one another Happy New Year and then somewhere around dawn, everyone left and we went to sleep.

I woke up late the next morning. When I turned, I saw that Jay was not in bed. He was already up. Or had he not slept at all? He was standing by the window, lost in his thoughts. There was a sad look on his face.

I made him a cup of tea, put it in front of him and said, 'Good morning.'

He was muttering to himself, 'What New Year gift do I get? Unemployment.'

I told him 'Jay, there are still 364 days left in this year. Anything can happen in that time.'

But he was not convinced, 'I don't think so. This was my eighth job in two years and I lost even that one.'

'Why don't you look at it this way? You managed to get eight jobs. So why won't you get a ninth job now? This time, it may be for keeps.'

Jay looked at me and said, 'You are saying this only to make me feel better, right?'

I shook my head but the tears running down my cheeks told a different story.

Jay took my hand in his and said, 'I am sorry, Purni. We had such lovely dreams for the New Year—big house, a grand welcome for the baby...'

I remembered all the plans that we had made when we had found out a few months ago about the arrival of our baby. What would happen now? All those castles that we had built in the air were now disappearing. All we felt now was apprehension about the grim reality of the present.

What a terrible beginning to the New Year.

But after a while, I took hold of my emotions and told myself, 'The world has not come to an end, has it? I still have my job. And I am sure Jay will get another opportunity soon. He is a responsible man. His self-respect will not let him keep still. Who knows. This may even turn out to be for the best.'

I got back to my usual routine. Housework, my job, preparing for the baby's arrival... I had so much to do.

Jay too started looking out for jobs. The people who were staying with us realized that our family was going to get bigger and that we would need the space now. So they all started moving out one by one.

One evening, when I came back from office, Jay was restlessly pacing in the living room. He did not even wait for me to sit down and began to speak 'Purni, you know how hard I have been trying to get a job these last few days. But I still haven't found anything worthwhile. So I have decided that I will not wait indefinitely to get a job. I am going to start doing some work part-time. And if I like the work, eventually I can take it up full-time.'

'That is a very good idea Jay. What work were you thinking of taking up? Do you have anything in mind?'

He hesitated and in a faltering voice said, 'Yeah...I mean... I saw this ad in the newspaper... I have discussed it with some people...and...I am going to work as an insurance agent.'

'What?' I didn't mean to but I almost shouted. 'Insurance agent? Are you all right?'

'What do you mean?' Jay retorted 'Do you think this is a joke?'

I realized that he was seriously thinking of taking it up. I did not like the idea at all and I said so very clearly to him. The discussion soon turned into a full-blown argument.

According to Jay, being an insurance agent did not need any capital or any other form of investment. There is hardly any chance of incurring losses. All one has to do is sell policies and earn a profit.

I was not convinced. 'Okay. But an insurance agent has to talk people into buying policies. Do you think you can do that? You hardly ever talk a lot even with your friends. How are you going to talk to perfect strangers?'

Both of us were adamant and refused to listen to the other's point of view.

Finally I said, 'If you take this up, you will fail miserably. I would prefer if you did nothing and didn't take up a job at all.'

Jay too was furious. Without saying a word, he got up and went out of the house.

I sat immobile, staring into space, feeling as if the walls were closing in on me.

Jaydev Patel
When I walked out of the flat after the heated argument with Purni, I was so angry that I couldn't think. I walked and walked, not knowing where I was headed. My mind was plagued with hundreds of doubts and questions.

What do I do? What is right? And what is wrong?

But I could find no answer. Purni had given me her honest opinion. She was my wife and she had every right to tell me what she thought. And she was not entirely wrong either. But then, why did I get so angry? And felt so hurt? Another question I didn't have an answer to.

After a long time, the haze cleared and I reasoned with myself—Purni knows me well, but I know myself even better. Should I go in for a ninth job after the eight earlier disastrous experiences? What is the harm in exploring this new option?

I had made up my mind. The very next day, I went to the New York Life Insurance Company office in New Jersey and met the Manager there. I showed him my degrees and certificates.

He smiled and said, 'Mr Patel, these will not be of any use in the field of Insurance. We have only one golden rule. Sell more, earn more. The more policies you sell, the more money you will earn. Having said that, you will need to give a test in order to get your insurance agent's license. As soon as you pass the test, you can start work here.'

I asked him a question, purely out of curiosity 'Approximately how many policies will I have to sell if I want to earn $10,000 a year?' 'About 100 policies.' I was wondering, *How am I going to sell 100 policies?*

'That would depend on the amount insured in the policy,' he replied.

I did not understand fully but I nodded my head and left the office.

Soon after this, I gave the test, cleared it, and became an agent of New York Life Insurance Company.

We began the year 1973 on a grim note, but in the end it turned out to be one of the most memorable years of our life for various reasons.

Firstly, Sachin, our son was born that year. I cannot express in words what I felt that day when I first held him in my arms and lightly kissed him on the forehead. I was overcome with emotion. I loved him so much and at the same time, I felt such a big responsibility towards him. When I looked into his bright eyes,

I promised myself 'I will be successful. Sachin, I will do everything in my power to take care of you and to give you the best. I have to succeed now, there is no other option.'

Purni was looking at me strangely, 'What are you saying to him Jay?'

I smiled, 'Nothing.'

The next day I got down to work and got the first policy of my career. Sachin's. I then began to meet my friends and relatives. In the first week itself I had sold 16 policies.

The Manager of New York Life was pleased and complimented me saying, 'Congratulations Jay. You have certainly made an excellent beginning. Your earnings for the first week is $10,000.'

I could not believe my ears. Mentally, I gave myself a pat on the shoulder and got down once again to work.

Purnima Patel

Many good things were happening in our life.

Sachin had come into our lives and Jay had started working. Jay told me that his earnings for the first week itself was $10,000. But then, why did I still feel uneasy? Two things in particular were troubling me—Jay had still not received his cheque and all the people who bought policies from Jay were our relatives or friends.

Now was the real test. Would Jay be as successful at persuading strangers to buy an insurance policy?

My mind was full of these doubts and fears. I did not have an answer to these problems but I decided one thing, I would hold on to my job, come what may.

I had been sanctioned only eight days as maternity leave. So I found a Gujarati babysitter and on the ninth day after my delivery, I was back at work.

My weekly salary was $150 and out of that I had to pay the babysitter $25.

My routine was hectic. I got up at 5 am, prepared everything for myself and Sachin, and left the flat by 6 am. I used to drop Sachin at the babysitter's at 6.30 am, from there I would take the bus up to Jersey City, and then walk the rest of the way to my office. The entire rigmarole was repeated in reverse in the evening.

When I returned home, it was usually time for Jay to leave because he had to meet most people in the evening after they came back from work.

When he returned late at night, Sachin and I used to be fast asleep and when we left in the morning, Jay would be in deep slumber.

The two of us had no time for each other, no time to give our little baby.

To add to my woes, the babysitter regularly increased her charges. So from $25, it went up to $30 and then $35 and finally $40 per week. I was feeling depressed, helpless, and suffocated.

One night, I couldn't fall asleep. I kept on tossing and turning. I was feeling so miserable that I didn't even realize when the tears started streaming down my cheek. I was afraid that Sachin would wake up so I came out into the living room and then I couldn't hold back my tears anymore and began sobbing uncontrollably. I don't know how long I sat there crying my heart out. Suddenly, Jay walked in and was shocked to me in that state. For a moment, he stood still, and then he quickly closed the door, came near me, held me close, and asked me, 'What's the matter, Purni?'

I couldn't say a thing and couldn't stop crying either. All the anxiety, fatigue, depression, and loneliness of the past few days were flowing out through my tears. Jay took my hand in his and said, 'Give me just a little time, Purni. I will never give you cause to cry ever again, I promise.'

When I heard his words, I felt ashamed of myself. Both of us were going through a rough patch. Jay had not lost his cool so why couldn't I take a hold of myself too? I wiped my eyes with the back of my hand and gave him a tearful smile 'Sorry Jay. I too will not cry again like a baby, I promise.'

But what do they say about promises being made to be broken.

Just a few days after this incident, I was in the office when the telephone rang. It was Jay. He used to call me up very rarely at work. Jay said, 'Purni, don't go to the babysitter's after work today. Come home directly.'

'Why?'

'I am going to be in that area. I will bring Sachin home. You don't need to stop by at the babysitter on your way back home. Okay? Oh, and if you come back home, don't make dinner.'

I didn't know what to make of the whole thing. But before I could say anything else, he said hurriedly 'I have to go now. See you in the evening.'

Even after I put down the phone, I couldn't get over the feeling of unease. I felt that Jay was hiding something from me, but couldn't tell what it was.

When I came home in the evening, Jay was waiting for me. 'Do you want some tea, Purni?' he asked me.

I didn't answer his question and asked him instead 'Where is Sachin? Weren't you supposed to bring him back from the babysitter?'

Jay put his arm around my shoulders and sat me down on the couch. 'Purni, listen to me carefully. Sachin is in the hospital, his arm is fractured.'

'What? Arm? Fracture? How? When?'

'I'll answer all your questions. Please calm down. Don't worry. He is fine.'

I yelled at him, 'Tell me everything now, Jay. Don't try my patience. He is only a month and a half old baby…and…'

I started to cry. Jay put his arms around me, did his best to calm me down, and told me the whole story.

Lila Ben (Sachin's Gujarati babysitter) had put him on the bed. She placed pillows all around him and went to work in the kitchen. Suddenly she heard a big thud and Sachin crying. When she rushed back into the bedroom, Sachin had fallen down from the bed and was lying on the floor, wailing in pain. She called up home. Luckily Jay had just got back. He went immediately to her place and took Sachin to the hospital. The doctors examined the baby and declared that his arm was fractured. They immediately put his arm in a plaster cast.

I could not believe what I was hearing. My entire body was trembling. I wanted to go to my baby at once.

When we reached the hospital, Sachin was sleeping peacefully. I sat next to him and gently touched his soft cheek. I was overcome with emotion. I thought to myself. 'What is happening? Why is everything going wrong? Am I not even capable of taking care of my child? Are we failures as parents?'

Jay had nothing to say when I cried. He let me pour my heart out.

Jaydev Patel

I can never forget that scene in the hospital: Sachin, his arm in a plaster cast, Purnima crying dejectedly and I, standing there silently in one corner. I was quiet but my mind was whirling with thoughts.

'Is this what my world, my family is going to be? Did I come so far away from my country and family for this?'

Mentally, I gave myself a shake. 'Everybody has their ups and downs. But it is our responsibility to overcome the problems.' I promised myself, 'I will do everything I can to change the present scenario. From now on, the only way to go is up. My family's safety and happiness is my responsibility and I am going to fulfil it.'

I took my promise very seriously and before Sachin was six-months-old, I had established myself so well in the field of Insurance that Purnima could give up her job. She now looked after Sachin and helped me out in my business.

The first policy that I had done was Sachin's. Then I bought one for me and one for Purnima. So my very first clients were members of my own family. I then sold several policies to my relatives and friends. The fact that Indians have close ties with so many people worked to my advantage.

But it was now time to meet and persuade strangers. Purnima felt that my introvert nature was one of my drawbacks in this business. I thought so too. But I decided that I had to overcome this challenge and get on with it.

It is very difficult to search for new clients. I used two techniques for this:

One is asking your clients for references. The advantage of this is that people agree to see you in the first place and at least give you a chance to talk to them.

The second was going over carefully through the telephone directories of the various cities and towns and finding out Indian and Gujarati names in them. This is a very laborious, time consuming process. But there was no other option. To begin with, I looked for names of Indians and living in New Jersey State and sent out hundreds of letters giving information about insurance policies and a free road atlas map. A few days later, replies started coming back for the free road atlas map by me. 'Mr X, did you get my letter? I would like to meet you whenever it is convenient to you.'

All the appointments had to be meticulously noted down, with all the relevant details including names, addresses, telephone numbers, dates, times etc. This is where Purnima was a great help. She took charge of all these kind of administrative work. Her experience as a secretary was a big advantage to our business.

She not only helped me to make the lists of possible clients but more importantly, she made a circular file index for all the policy holders. These were cards on which were written all the details about the policy holder. His name, address, and telephone number. In addition to this, there were also names, addresses, and contact numbers of some hotels in the vicinity. These were especially useful when I was travelling across the country.

After fixing up an appointment, I had to go and meet the possible clients. This first meeting is the most important part of my business. As they say, first impressions are often the last impressions.

When I started out during the early days, there would be times when I would meet a hundred people and not even manage to sell a single policy. At such times, I would return home feeling dejected and helpless.

But after several such disheartening experiences, I decided to find out the reason why. One day, I stood in front of the mirror, imagined myself in the role of a client, and acted the scene out:

'Hello, I am Jaydev Patel, from New York Life Insurance Company. Do you wish to buy an insurance policy?'

'No, thank you.'

There ended the conversation, with no hope of continuing it in any way. Once a person says no, it is almost impossible to convince him otherwise.

I realized that a person should not be given the chance to say no at the very outset.

I replayed the conversation in front of the mirror:

'Hello, I am Jaydev Patel. Do you know Mr X? He is a friend or relative or neighbour of mine.' If none of this was enough to establish some common link, I used other aspects like cities or towns in the US or India, a well-known institution, University or Company etc. If this still didn't work, I played the Gujarati language card, and if even that did not get a response, I tried the Indian card in case of the NRIs.

It was essential to make the conversation warm and personal, so I began the meeting with other subjects and introduced the topic of insurance only after the ice had melted. 'I am from the New York Life Insurance Company. I would like to talk to you about some life insurance options which will be beneficial to you and your family.'

Now generally in such a situation, nobody refuses to let you talk and at the very least, agrees to hear you out.

An insurance agent has to take into consideration the profession, the income, the family responsibilities of a prospective client, and then decide which policy will be the most reasonable, attractive, and beneficial for him or her. In this way we can present the client with a 'tailor made/customized' option which is right for him and makes him feel special.

An insurance agent has to first of all forget his role of a salesman and take on the role of a financial consultant. He has to put before the client, facts and figures which show him how the insurance policy will give him security and stability while helping him plan his future.

A good insurance agent should end his first meeting with the client on this note: 'I feel you should definitely give it a thought and consider the option carefully.'

Normally, no one would reply to this with 'No, I am not going to think about it.'

I am convinced that this is the first major step in winning over a client. It almost never happens that one meets a client who buys a policy in the first meeting.

One has to meet him repeatedly and win over his confidence.

It is only when the client has faith in you and you become his friend and confidant that he will probably be persuaded about the benefits of buying an insurance policy.

Purnima Patel

1973 was an eventful year for us. It was the year when Jay began his new career as an insurance agent. Many important developments also took place that year. The first one was that the US immigration policy concerning Indians was relaxed. Hence many Indians, among them a large number of Gujaratis, came to the US. The second was the exodus of many Indians, again largely Gujaratis from Uganda, following persecution by the Idi Amin regime. Most of these Indians then settled in the West, in the UK and the US.

The Gujaratis from Uganda were moneyed. Several of them realized that Gujaratis were very successful in the motel business here so they too invested in motels and the domination of Gujaratis in the hotel industry in the US increased.

Jaydev followed all these developments carefully and decided to make the most of the opportunity.

He grouped his clients into two broad categories.

One: those who were interested in buying insurance policies for the safety of their families and the second: businessmen who were mainly interested in estate planning and who needed cash periodically. Life Insurance policies met the demands of both these groups.

Jay immediately began contacting the predominant Gujarati motel owners. It was a very good opportunity for both and Jay's business soon grew in leaps and bounds. So much so, that in the very first year, Jay sold policies worth $4.25 million. It was a record for a first-year agent in the history of the company. Jay thus became a member of the 'Million Dollars Round Table' in the very first year. There was no looking back for him from that moment onwards. The only way to go was upwards.

Jay's sales figures were reaching new heights every year in New York Life. He got the tag of Number One Agent. His reputation and his aura were increasing by the moment. But I can proudly state that Jay was not affected by all this at all and remained down to earth and level headed at all times.

The only thing that was affected was his schedule. He no longer restricted himself to the State of New Jersey. He started exploring other states as well, however far away they may be. He realized the importance of spreading his network not only throughout the length and breadth of the country but even abroad.

His first destination was Toronto. As he had lived there before coming to the US, he had many friends here. His instinct was right and here too he was successful in selling many policies. The success of his business in Toronto was a very sweet victory for him because it was in this very city that he had not even been able to get a decent job years ago.

Jay literally grew wings on his feet. He toured thousands of miles by plane or road. He was rarely home. During this time, the kids and I hardly ever got to spend time with him. But I did not feel lonely or depressed as I used to earlier because once again our house was full of people. Jay's brothers, my brother, and others. The most important reason for my happiness was the fact that Jay had found his vocation and was enjoying the work he was doing. I admitted to myself that I had been wrong about his choice of career and had not realized his true potential.

It was the year 1975. One of Jay's clients had relocated to California. Jay took this opportunity to visit him there. He had the intention of extending his client base to the West of the country too. But it was not to be so easy. He did not manage to sell a single policy in his first visit there. I was disappointed but Jay was quite calm and told me not to be dishartened saying, 'Purni, the first thing that this business has taught me is perseverance. If you don't succeed, you should not be disappointed. One has to accept the fact that buying an insurance policy is never the first priority of people. It will take time to change that perspective, isn't it? So one has to accept the challenge and keep on trying even if at first one doesn't succeed.'

His words were prophetic because today he has sold more than 2000 policies in California.

Patience is one of Jay's virtues—not only in business but also in his life.

Our life changed within a year of Sachin's birth. Jay was earning excellent income and it was clear that he would settle down and succeed in this venture. But contrary to the trend here, we did not immediately buy a fancy house or car. For the next 10 years, we continued living in the same place with our family and relatives. It was only much later that we bought land in Livingston and decided to build a house there.

There is a law against discrimination of any kind in the US, be it based on race, colour etc. However, a subtle feeling of intolerance is always present and sometimes it manifests itself openly. While our house in Fawn Drive was being built, there were a couple of instances when our house was pelted with stones. We received threatening phone calls and anonymous letters.

But we didn't pay much attention to the threats. This house was our dream and we meant to see it being fulfilled. After the construction was complete, we moved into our new house. As we had lived with our extended family till then, including brothers-in-law, sisters-in-law, their children etc, we felt a little odd since it was only the four of us in this huge house. The children were not used to the American concept of having a bedroom to themselves since all this while the children had been sleeping together in one bedroom or in the living room.

Now Sachin was in the 1st grade and Seema was 2 years old. Both of them were excited and started exploring the house. 'Such a huge place?' Sachin asked.

'Yes. And this is your bedroom.' I said, showing him his room. He was thrilled. 'Wow. I love it. Pappu and I will sleep here.' (Pappu was my sister-in-law's son, his cousin)

I tried to explain 'Pappu will not live here with us.'

'Why?'

'Because this is *our* house.'

Sachin did not like this new idea very much but there wasn't much he could do about it. And nor could we. We had dinner and then went to bed. Seema was to sleep in our room as she was small but Sachin was to sleep in his own room. I went in to tuck him in and kiss him good night.

Within 5 minutes, there was a knock on our door. It was Sachin. 'Mom, Dad, I am going to sleep here with you' he said. It was the same story over the next few weeks. Finally I lost my patience and said severely to him 'Sachin, you are going to sleep in your room and there are no two ways about it.'

He had no other option but to accept the idea of sleeping alone in his own bedroom. But it still took him a long time to adapt to the big new house with only the four of us in it.

In fact when I look back, I realize that Sachin had to face a lot of difficult situations as he was the eldest child. For example, he hardly got to spend of time with his father as Jay was settling down in his career then. Due to the nuclear family system in the US, both the parents share the responsibility of bringing up the children like dropping and picking up the children from school, attending the school events, going with them for matches and other competitions to cheer for them etc. But Jay did not have the time to do all this while Sachin was growing up. He was either touring the country or catching up on the never ending paper work. There was just no time to give to the kids. The one good thing was that even though Jay was so busy, I was at home and I could give all my time to the kids. And in fact I used to talk frankly to the kids about Jay's busy schedule and why he couldn't be there even though he wanted to. That is why Sachin too understood his father's absence and never made him feel guilty about it.

The story of our life and our family would not be complete without the story of our car. Actually, Jay is not a materialist and hates any kind of show off. He does not even like to wear formal clothes when he meets his clients.

But just like one of his wishes was to build a dream house, his other ultimate fantasy was to own a Rolls Royce.

When he thought that he could afford it, he bought a Silver Spirit. We were all naturally thrilled about it. We felt grand when everyone turned around and stared when we passed by in the gleaming black car.

After the initial excitement had ebbed, Jay realized that this car was not very practical when he was visiting clients in far flung places. For someone like Jay who drove hundreds of miles daily, running this car was like maintaining a white elephant. So naturally, I was the one who had the honour of driving it. I needed the car mainly to drop and pick up the children from school, do my groceries or some other shopping, and go to the office. I found it very cumbersome to take the Rolls to these places. So I used to prefer driving my old car.

Gradually, the Rolls began to stay longer and longer in the garage. Once, some relative asked us to lend him the Rolls as there was a wedding in his family. But the Rolls had a problem starting up as it had been lying in the garage for so long. We had to call a mechanic and pay a huge sum to get it going. Once the wedding was over, it was back to the garage for the poor Rolls. It then became a custom to borrow our Rolls and all our friends and relatives asked us to lend it to them during weddings.

Once, I actually calculated how much money we had spent on maintaining the Rolls and was shocked to discover that it was so exorbitant that we could almost have bought another Rolls with that amount.

Finally I told Jay 'This white elephant is fit for the gods, not for mere mortals like us. So please let us sell this car and get something which suits us better.'

Jay had to agree with my practical reasoning and we sold our Silver Spirit (which was ironically black in colour and metaphorically speaking a white elephant).

While I heaved a sigh of relief, I think Jay probably gave a sigh of regret.

Sachin Patel

I hardly remember Dad being around when I was a child. When I would ask Mom about it, she would say, 'You father has to travel a lot for work. But don't worry, I am there for you.' I would simply nod.

Even on the rare weekend when dad was home, he was invariably buried under piles of paperwork.

Sometimes Mom would take me along to the office and then she too would be engrossed in work. I didn't mind too much because the office staff always pampered me. I think it was a good break from the monotonous routine for both me and the staff.

Anyway, I never felt lonely because there were so many people staying with us—our relatives, and their children. We kids had such a great time playing the whole day. Even at night, we used to sleep together in the living room. Our jokes and laughter would continue until one of the grownups came in, yelled at us, and turned off the light.

When I was in the first grade, we suddenly moved into a huge house in a posh locality. I loved our house but I did not like the fact that only the four of us lived in it. It took Mom a long time to help me get over this feeling. There was another major change here. When Mom went to the office, we now had a housekeeper who stayed the whole day and looked after us. Our housekeeper was so nice that I used to feel lucky that I had two mothers.

We always looked forward to the Annual Conference of the New York Life Insurance Company. The top management and the top agents went to a scenic place in the world with their families. As it was supposed to be a convention, there were a few official sessions, but the rest of the time was pure fun. Most of all, I used to be thrilled because I got to be with Dad for such a long time at a stretch.

While I was at school or college, I never thought that one day I would work with Dad. But when I had completed my undergraduate degree from the University, Dad said, 'Sachin, I would be very happy if you work with me. There are limits to how much I can do or make the business grow. If the two of us work together, the sky can be the limit for us.'

I agreed with what Dad said and I began working with him. Dad had made his business prosper with his great business sense and his experience of human behavior. Today, his knowledge and his goodwill are so useful to me. I feel lucky to be his son and to have the privilege of working with him.

Purnima Patel

People often ask Jay, 'There are thousands of insurance agents in the world but no one has even achieved the kind of success that you have. What is the secret of your phenomenal success?'

As usual Jay gives a short but precise reply, 'People trust me.'

Now the next question that comes to mind is, Why do people trust Jay? If anyone were to ask me this question, my answer would be 'It is not possible to give a short, concise, and precise reply to this question. I will first have to narrate some instances to you in detail.'

Once, Jay went to meet a client in a small remote town in the US. The client was the owner of a motel. Jay had travelled a long distance, first by plane and then taken a rent-a-car to reach this place. The motelier welcomed him, offered him hot tea, and some snacks. They chatted a bit and then got down to business. Jay gave him all the details about some insurance policies and then answered his questions and doubts.

By the time he was finished, it had turned dark. The motel owner said to Jay 'It is quite late now. You must be tired after your long journey. Why don't you stay the night here and leave in the morning?'

During the time he had been there, Jay had noticed that the motel was not well maintained. It looked old, moldy, and not very clean. The motel owner was insisting 'So, you will stay? Have breakfast with us and then leave tomorrow morning.'

Jay thanked him for his hospitality. 'You are right. I am tired and do not feel like travelling at night. I will sleep here tonight and leave tomorrow morning.'

The motel owner said, 'There is a room free in the motel. I will put you up in that.'

But Jay refused 'No, give me a blanket. I will be quite comfortable here on the couch in the living room.'

The motel owner felt awkward 'No, no, you are our guest.'

Jay replied to that 'Yes, but consider me as part of your family. I have absolutely no problem sleeping here on the couch. And secondly, if a customer arrives during the night, you can offer him that room. The customer will not have to be turned away and you won't have to forego the rent for that room.'

The motel owner appreciated Jay's simplicity and his willingness to help others.

The next morning over a cup of coffee, the owner said 'Mr Patel, I wish to buy an insurance policy. Let us complete the formalities right away so that you are then free to leave.'

As Jay was leaving, the motel owner said to Jay 'Do you want to know why I decided to buy the policy immediately? Because I liked you as a person. I will be frank with you. Yesterday another insurance agent had come to see me before you. He too had travelled quite a distance to come and see me. After our meeting, he asked me if he could make a call to his wife. During their conversation, she must have asked him if he was going to spend the night here, to which he replied "Of course not. Are you kidding? It is impossible for me to stay here. I will come back home even if it is very late."'

'He didn't care if I heard him and I felt insulted or hurt by his words. You were quite the opposite. Not only did you stay here, but you even took care to see that I did not lose out on my room rent. I trust you. I have faith in you, and I am sure that you will look after our family well.'

When he left this man's place, Jay had not just sold another policy, but more importantly, he had just added a new person to his family. And this was far more important to him than a policy.

Jay always says that 'I am not a salesman; my role is rather that of a caretaker of a family.' I would like to add that Jay does not just *play* this role, he actually lives it.

Another particular instance is of Hitesh Shah. He was a businessman whom Jay met frequently over a period of 10 years in order to convince him to buy an insurance policy. During this time, they became good friends. But Hitesh did not buy a policy. He used to assure Jay 'Whenever I buy an insurance policy Jay, it will be from you.'

One day, 10 years later, Hitesh asked Jay to come and see him. When Jay met him, Hitesh said 'I am ready. I want to buy a life insurance policy.'

Jay asked him 'Is your health okay? Have you decided to do this because of your hospitalization last year?'

Hitesh replied 'I had gone for a general check up to the hospital but all my reports were okay.'

Jay told him 'That is alright. But you will have to do a medical check up before buying the policy and submit the report.'

Hitesh completed all the formalities and bought the policy.

His premium was $600. Once he called up Jay saying, 'Jay, The premium is quite high and it is difficult for me to manage.'

Jay replied 'The premium would have been quite less if you had bought the policy ten years ago. Now your age is more and your report indicated some health problems too. That is why the premium is higher.'

Hitesh asked him 'Should I cancel the policy?'

Jay advised him 'I am telling you this as a friend. Please do not cancel the policy now. Not only will you lose money, but more importantly, you and your family will also lose the coverage the policy offers.'

Hitesh took his advice and did not cancel the policy.

Six months later, Hitesh had gone to India with his family. They had gone out shopping when he felt an acute pain in his stomach. He went to a doctor who examined him, prescribed some medicines, and told him to take rest. As he was leaving the doctor's clinic, he collapsed and died on the spot.

Jay heard the shocking news a few days later from an acquaintance. Jay dropped whatever he was doing and rushed to Hitesh's place.

When everyone had left after the funeral, Jay spoke to Hitesh's father-in-law, 'Hitesh had recently bought a life insurance policy of $1 million. I will see to it that his wife receives the cheque as soon as possible.'

The old man was overcome with emotion 'My daughter did not know anything about this policy. She was so worried about what to do and how to take care of the children's future. I am so relieved now. We have to deal with the grief of a loved one's passing away but to add to that, one is also stressed about the future. You have arrived at the darkest moment in our life and saved our family. You are nothing short of God for us'

Jay replied saying, 'I have only done my duty.'

As soon as Jay received the life insurance cheque for a tax free sum of $1 million, he handed it over to Hitesh's wife. It was a great support to the family and helped them face the future. It took care of the children's future and their education. Today Hitesh's son is a doctor.

Then there is another businessman Ashok Pandya's story. Once he suffered huge losses on the stock market and lost money to the tune of almost $1 million overnight. He called up Jay and said, 'I want to cancel my policy. I need the money very urgently.'

Jay told him it was a wrong move and tried to persuade him otherwise. 'You may get some money right now if you cancel your policy, but in the long run you will only lose much more.'

Ashok refused to change his mind. He wanted to surrender the policy right away. Finally Jay suggested another option to him 'Okay, surrender this policy now but get another one with a lesser premium. You and your family should have at least that support to fall back on.' "With a term policy, you and your family should have at least that support to fall. . ."

Ashok agreed to that. He surrendered his old term policy and got a newer one for a lesser premium. Hardly a year later, Ashok complained of chest pain and was admitted to the hospital. After a thorough check up and intensive tests, he was advised to go in for a bypass surgery. But unfortunately, only a few days later, Ashok had another massive heart attack and expired.

As the client had expired within a year of buying a new policy, New York Life Insurance Company investigated the matter thoroughly. But Jay succeeded in proving that when Ashok had taken the policy, there was no history of pre-existing illness and all the information given by Ashok then was absolutely true. New York Life gave a cheque of $1 million to Ashok's family which was a life saver for them in that situation.

Ashok's family could not thank Jay enough. They repeatedly told him that it was only because of him that Ashok bought another policy at that moment, and thanked him for taking up their cause with the company. Jay feels that the respect and admiration that this family has for him is his true reward.

Jay always stands by his client and on their behalf with the insurance company in moments like these.

Mayur Desai was another of Jay's clients. He was a young businessman in his thirties. He suffered a huge setback in his business and incurred heavy losses. He took a loan on his insurance policy. Unfortunately his business failed to recover. Neither could he repay the loan that he had taken on his policy, nor could he pay the remaining premium amount. After a while, the company cancelled his policy.

As if this was not enough, he had a paralytic stroke and four years later, he passed away. Jay went for his last rites. He was moved by the plight of Mayur's wife and children. When he returned home, he took out Mayur's old file and went over it carefully.

He realized that when Mayur had the stroke, his policy was still active. According to the company policy, handicapped persons did not have to continue to pay the premium. So Jay argued it was not correct this policy had been discontinued and Mayur was actually covered by the policy. The company approved the claim and Mayur's wife received the entire sum of the policy.

I have only described a few situations to illustrate Jay's work ethics but there are several such instances when Jay has stood by his clients and worked with the company to get them their due. There is one aspect that must be mentioned when analyzing the key to Jay's success.

Jay does all that he can to ensure that his clients get their claim. He is relentless in his efforts to get the best for his clients. There are innumerable cases where he has been successful in getting the company to pass the claims of his clients. But he is still the number one agent of the company and this is because the number of death claims for his clients is comparatively small. And he has to thank the Indian community for that. The majority of Jay's clients are Gujaratis. Even if they live in the US, most of the Gujaratis are vegetarian and their lifestyle is simple. They rarely drink alcohol or smoke. So, most of them are blessed with a long lifespan. Clients like these are a boon to an insurance company and any agent who brings in such clients is an asset to the company.

Jaydev Patel

I started off my career as a teacher and then a chemist. My third and final profession was that of an insurance agent. Some may wonder what connection there is between these varied professions.

I firmly believe that no experience goes waste and one learns something from every single thing. For instance, my teaching experience came in handy during my interactions with clients as an insurance agent. I believe that selling an insurance policy is similar to educating people.

My relationship with my clients is never limited to just a professional level. There are always emotions involved and every client of mine is close to my heart.

That is why my family and I are invited to every important occasion in my client's life, be it engagements, weddings, or christenings. And I always make it a point to be present in the sad event of a death in the family. My presence at such occasions is a moral support for the family. They are confident that I will not abandon them in this hour of need.

As I consider all my clients a part of my family, it follows that I have to be in constant touch with them and be aware of all that is happening in their lives. In order to do this, I have to spend 250 days a year travelling the length and breadth of the country.

Just as I consider my clients a part of my family, so do my clients look on me as one of their own. Why else would a person drive hundreds of miles to pick up an insurance agent from the airport?

The bonding that I share with my clients and their families is more precious to me than anything else I have earned.

I am often asked, 'Who is your Guru in this field?'

I do not know how to answer this question because I never had to learn the art of becoming an excellent salesman from anyone. I followed my instincts, used my common sense, and made my own rules which I still strictly adhere to.

To come back to the subject of my 'guru'. I did not have a 'guru' as such, but I did have an ideal to follow. It was Ben Feldman who was the top agent at New York Life before me. He was extremely popular and no one had beaten his sales record previously. When he wrote a book based on his experiences, he sent me a copy. He had written a small note on the first page:'Jay, This book was published earlier but I now know that your sales figures far outnumber mine. Congratulations.'

Epilogue

Jaydev Patel's achievements in the field of insurance are laudable but his story and indeed his portrait would not be complete if one does not mention another significant contribution of his.

It was February 2002. New York Life was entering the Indian market as Max New York Life. The top executives of the company were in India to supervise the launch and the publicity campaign of the company in Mumbai and other prominent cities in the country.

On one such occasion, Tom Flournoy, the CEO of New York Life, and Jaydev Patel were in Mumbai. As Jaydev was going to start his own office in Vadodara under the aegis of Max New York Life, the two of them visited Vadodara and from there went to Sojitra, Jaydev's village.

While they were in town, Jaydev said, 'Tom, let me show you my old school.'

Jaydev's school M.M. High School was 125 years old. Jaydev had completed his Matriculation examination from the same school in 1959. Many of the alumni of this school were now very successful in their chosen careers and were settled in different parts of the world. The school's history was impressive. However, its present state was pitiable. Jay said to Tom, 'This used to be my class room.' When they peeped in to the classroom, they were appalled at its condition. Faded damp walls, peeling plaster, deep cracks in the walls, chipped floor tiles and a leaking roof. Jay was shocked into silence to see a group of children huddled together in the dry area of the classroom. Tom and Jay went all around the school and it was the same sorry state of affairs everywhere else. There was no water in a school where 1100 students spent a major part of their day.

Tom interacted with many of the students and he was impressed by their intelligence, enthusiasm, and attitude towards life.

He said to Jaydev 'You must do something for these kids and for the school.'

Jaydev was thinking along the same lines. He replied, 'I definitely will. I will do all I can to improve the condition of this school. Come on, let us meet the Principal.'

The Principal gave them a warm welcome.

Jaydev got straight to the point 'Sir, the school is in dire need of repairs. I am ready to help. Can you give me an estimate of the costs?'

The Principal thanked Jaydev and said, 'I will call a good contractor tomorrow and let you know at the earliest.'

When Tom and Jaydev stepped out of the Principal's office, Tom said, 'Do you realize what a big responsibility you have taken up, Jay?'

Jaydev nodded his head but even he had no idea then of the enormous task he had undertaken.

He had decided that even if it cost up to 15 lakh rupees, he would personally contribute and get the repairs done.

A few days later, the Principal called Jaydev to his office. The building contractor appointed by the school was there too. He presented the details of his report: 'The state of the building is much more dangerous than it appears from the outside. Last year's terrible earthquake has damaged it a lot and the entire building is in danger of collapsing if there is even a slight tremor. At present 1100 students, teachers, and other support staff are in this building every day. God forbid, if anything happens, one cannot even imagine the consequences.'

A silence followed this grim statement. Jay then asked the contractor 'What do you propose as a solution?'

'The entire school will have to be rebuilt.'

Jay did not hesitate for even a moment 'Okay. Please give me an estimate while I am here. It is my responsibility to arrange for the funds.'

When Jaydev told Tom about the meeting and his decision, Tom was shocked 'Jay, do you realize the impossible task you are setting yourself?'

Jay replied, 'Not impossible actually. I have thought about it and this is what I propose to do: I will put in as much money as I can. And I will gather funds from other sources. I am going to contact the alumni of the school who are now settled abroad or are doing well in India and ask them to contribute and save our school.'

Tom wished Jay the best in his endeavour.

Jaydev began the Herculean task of getting the school rebuilt and started operating simultaneously on various levels.

On the one hand he visited the school and on the other he followed up on the task of raising the funds.

Jaydev did all he could to turn his dream project into reality. He had meetings with the school management, contractors, architects, and engineers. He was very clear about what he had in mind.

He told the school management about his plans and asked for a rough estimate. 'The new building must be excellent. The quality of the construction must be good, and the building should look beautiful. There should be adequate toilets and running water 24/7. There should be new benches in the classrooms for the children to sit on. The laboratories should be state of the art; the library should be well stocked. The playground should have the best sports equipment. Take into consideration all these factors and then give a final estimate.'

Keeping in mind all the above instructions, the school management submitted a budget of Rs 1 crore. 'Done. It is my responsibility to arrange for the entire funds. But I insist on one condition. I will decide all the people who will be involved in the project and I will personally supervise the construction. The school management should in no way interfere in this.'

Everyone agreed to Jaydev's condition and Jaydev immediately handed over the first cheque.

Even after returning to the US, Jaydev closely monitored the progress of the construction on a daily basis. He used all possible means of communication to stay in constant touch with Sojitra: hundreds of telephone calls, emails, letters, faxes, and flying thousands of miles to personally oversee the construction whenever possible .

The former students of M.M High School helped generously. And what was surprising and heartening was the financial support that Jaydev received from employees, including some top executives of New York Life and even some of his clients. Jaydev's own contribution was not limited to the financial level. He spent a lot of his valuable time and often visited Sojitra to keep abreast of the developments.

On one such visit, some girls from a neighbouring school came to see him. One girl who seemed bolder than the rest said to him 'Uncle, you are partial towards the boys.'

Jaydev was puzzled 'Why do you say that?'

Another girl replied a little shyly, 'Uncle, our girls school is very old too and not in a good condition.'

The bold girl continued, 'You are building a brand new school for the boys. So why don't you build a nice new school for us too? If you don't believe us, come and see our school.'

Jaydev took up the girls' invitation and went to see their school. What they were saying was true. This school too was in a sorry state. Jaydev looked at the eager faces of the school girls gathered around him and said, 'Okay. I promise your school will be rebuilt too.'

On his way back home, Jaydev also visited the primary school in the village. That evening, he called up Purnima and told her 'Purni, I have decided to help build two more schools in the village.'

Purnima couldn't believe her ears. 'What?'

'Yes, a new primary school and another new girls' school.'

'I have promised the girls…'

'Well, if you have promised them, I know you will keep to it. So tell me, when do we start collecting the funds for it?'

'Right away. I am sending you an email with some names. You draw up a list and start calling up people. When I return, we will take it from there.'

Purnima knew that the word 'tomorrow' did not figure in Jaydev's dictionary. She checked her email half an hour later and as expected, found Jaydev's mail in the inbox. She began calling up people immediately.

The construction work on the boys' school began in July 2002 and in a matter of only 7 months, the brand new building of M.M. High School was ready.

It was finally inaugurated in January 2003.

But Jaydev's work was far from over. He still had to see to the building of two new schools. The construction had to be excellent and the schools had to be ready in the projected time frame. So once again, Jaydev was immersed in figures and calculations, details of cement, stone, etc.

Sojitra village got three new schools in the space of just two years.

Today if anyone praises Jaydev's contribution to this project, Jaydev is embarrassed and interrupts the person to say, 'Sojitra is my village. I only repaid a part of its debt.'

NOT ONLY POTELS

Hasu and Hersha Shah

The September 2001 issue of the US magazine *Lodging* carried in it an article titled 'Successful succession, a tradition of success' along with a photograph of a family of four smiling into the camera: Hasu, Hersha, Jay, and Neil Shah.

There was also a photograph of the other business partners of the Hersha Group. The article said:

Hersha and Hasu Shah are a couple from Harrisburg. In 1984, their children, Jay and Neil, were studying in school. Hasu was working as a Chemical Engineer in the State Environmental Protection Department. This is when Hersha bought her first hotel. Within a year, this hotel was doing so well that Hasu gave up his job and joined his wife in her hotel business.

By 1999, Hasu had included 5 other partners in his business. The company now owned 10 hotels. This is when they took a courageous decision and formed the Hersha Hospitality Trust, an assets management trust and launched a public issue of their company. The path towards success was now more rapid. Several new companies were formed and grew beneath the umbrella of the Hersha Group: Hersha Development Corporation, Hersha Construction Services, Hersha Hospitality Management, Hersha Interiors and Supplies to name a few.

Hersha Group continues to grow at an amazing speed...

The article further went on to outline details of the present situation of the Hersha Group, the hotels owned by it, its financial statements, its future projects, etc. It ended with a special mention of Jay and Neil calling them Generation Next. Their impressive educational qualifications and their excellent work in the Hersha Group until now were highly praised. .

In the very next issue that came out in October 2001 of *Lodging*, the Editor of the magazine wrote a very frank and open letter in his editorial column 'Editor's View'.

The heading was 'Redefining the concept: American Owners.'
The letter was as follows:

This letter is for You.
You.
Someone who does not have a name, a face or an individual identity.
Someone who is a coward and runs away from everything.
Yes, I am speaking about You.
11th September 2001.
All of us were shocked, bewildered, and saddened by the terrible, inhuman attack on our country.
And then You called:
'Hello. Philip Hayward? The Editor of Lodging?'
Your tone was full of bitterness. I felt the anger even in those few words.

Not Only Potels

I had barely said 'Yes' when You lashed out venomously, 'I am going to burn the 15 copies of Lodging that I have received,' and slammed the phone down.

I did not have any trouble guessing the reason for your fury. The reason was the cover story that we had run on the Shah family, the praise that we had showered on them which You did not like at all.

Why? Do you believe that everyone whose ancestors are from anywhere beyond Europe are terrorists? Does anybody ask You where Your ancestors are from? Why then ask this question about the Shah family? But I am going to tell You the answer anyway, whether the question is asked or not.

Hasu and Hersha Shah are of Indian origin. India is the world's largest democracy and 80 percent of its population is Hindu. I need to specifically tell You this because of Your ignorance. And Your ignorance is the cause of Your extremely narrow-minded conservative ideas.

Since You buy 15 copies of our magazine every month, You must be an owner of a big hotel. How big is your hotel? 100 rooms? 150? With such a big hotel, it is evident that the number of Your employees must also be huge. These employees are most probably from different countries, of different religions, speaking different languages. If You wish to burn copies of our magazine, so be it.

But will that be enough for You? Or will the hate continue to eat You up? What will You do then? Are You going to judge and condemn your employees on the basis of their colour, origin, or religion? Are You going to persecute them? Or are You going to squeeze them financially? Or are You simply going to fire them?

While driving down the Interstate 95, at times one sees a sign on a motel or hotel 'American owner'. Are You too going to put up a sign like that on your hotel? Or have You done that already?

Actually my initial reaction was to stop the sale of our magazine to people like You. But that would not be fair to your employees. They should realize that the majority of hotel owners in the US are not as mean and petty minded as You. And for that, it is essential that our magazine reaches them.

One last and important thought before signing off: Our hotel industry and our country are great because people like You are an exception here.

Philip Hayward

The Editor received a reply to this letter in the very same month. It was written by one Tracy Kunde, who worked for the Hersha Group. In his letter, Tracy says:

Dear Mr Hayward,

I sincerely appreciate the letter addressed to a faceless and nameless individual published in your editorial in the October issue of your magazine.

September 11, 2001, is one of the darkest days in the history of America. It was a great shock to all of us and we were all devastated by it.

The Mayor of New York, Rudy Giuliani, the employees of New York Municipality, New York Police Department, the fire brigade, and thousands of volunteers worked tirelessly to help the victims of the disaster. They worked round the clock to help those whose lives had been devastated by the catastrophe. But while doing this, they did not look at the race, colour, religion, or origin of these people. There was only one thought, one sentiment prevailing—to do everything possible for the sake of humanity. Americans lent a helping hand to save the victims. This is what being American is about, this is true patriotism.

On this background, the narrow and hollow mentality of the cowardly person who made the anonymous phone call to you is even more shocking. I congratulate you for your frank and biting response to his words.

Not Only Potels

My name is Tracy Kunde. I have been working for the past several years for the Hersha Group of Industries owned by the Shah family of Indian origin. I can say with confidence that even if the Shahs are not American by birth, they are completely American in their approach to work and life.

I am American by birth. I grew up in Newcastle in the State of Wyoming. My father was in the Navy. He served his country for 20 years and did his job with dedication and honesty. He took part in the war in Vietnam. He is now retired.

I joined the Hersha Group in 1998 after having worked in the hotel industry for 18 years.

At the time, the Group owned 8 hotels. I was appointed Director of Operations. During the course of my work, I had the opportunity to interact closely with Hasu and Hersha Shah. The more I got to know them, the more my respect for them grew. I would say that Hersha and Hasu Shah are living examples of the great American Dream.

Like thousands of others, this couple came to America from India with aspirations and hope in their heart. Both of them worked tirelessly to improve their life. They did not have money to begin with. What they did have was sharp intellect, tremendous will power, and an incredible capacity for hard work.

They started with a small old motel. Today they are the owners of over 100 hotels with around 11,000 rooms in total.

These two made their business a roaring success but far more important is what they have done for the society and the country. Today, they employ over 650 people and in this way take the responsibility for all those families. They contribute generously to Red Cross and other social service organizations. They have instilled very sound values in their children who are both highly qualified and are graduates of Cornell and Harvard.

How does one define an American? Can it only be someone who is born in America? Or can it also refer to those who contribute to its glory and make this country proud? I have many unforgettable memories of the Shah family.

Take for instance my very first day in the Hersha Group. The CEO of the Group, Mr Hasu Shah, was on his way to get coffee for himself from the coffee machine. He stopped when he saw me and said 'Hello' and then very naturally continued, 'Shall I get you a cup of coffee?' It is a small example but it speaks volumes about the humane and modest approach which is typical of Hasu Shah.

This humane and caring attitude is also reflected in their professional dealings.

In 1999, when the public issue of the company was launched, all the employees were given stock option rights.

The Hersha Group has built up its formidable reputation in the American Hospitality industry due to several reasons; the most important ones being its professional approach and its dedication to service.

As I mentioned earlier, I joined the Hersha Group as Director of Operations in 1998. I am not of Indian origin but I was still given a promotion barely a year later and made Vice President of Hospitality Management. And I was also given the opportunity to become a partner in the Group.

In the Hersha Group, your dedication to your work is more important than the number of years you have been in the job. I would like to point out that I am not the first person and certainly not the only one in the Group to have been rewarded in this way.

Before concluding my letter, I would also like to categorically state that I have not written this letter because of my rapid growth in the Hersha Group or because of my current position there. I have written *it as an employee of the Hersha Group who is rightly proud of its work ethics, work culture, and work philosophy.*

Differences in the background, colour, origin, religion are respected in the Hersha Group. What is appreciated is sincerity in work. That is the key to the success of the Group and that is the reason why it has been able to fulfil the American Dream and show such phenomenal growth.

Tracy Kunde

Hasu Shah

I do not have a lot of free time but whenever I get a few moments to myself, I look back the kaleidoscope of my life and ponder for a few minutes.

Man has thousands of memories. However, there are only a few that stay with him forever because they form important milestones in your life, like the letters published in *Lodging*.

Another memory which is etched my mind is that of a journey my family and I took in 1979, when the four of us were travelling back to the US from Mumbai.

We were in the aircraft and fastening our seatbelts when I realized that I had not said a single word to anyone since we left home.

I looked at Hersha. She was talking to Jay and Neil who were seated a row in front of us, and making sure they had fastened their seatbelts, put cotton in their ears, and had sweets to chew on.

I looked out the window. In a few moments the aircraft would start taxiing down the runway and take off towards America.

The aircraft had a fixed route, a pre-decided direction, and a definite time table.

Dhandha

But what about me? What was I going to do in America now? How was I going to settle down, find a job, a house? And all this with the added responsibility of a wife and two children?

I was suddenly scared. I leant back in my seat and closed my eyes so that nobody could see the fear in them.

Hersha put her hand on mine and asked, 'What is the matter, Hasu? Why do you look so disturbed?'

My dear perceptive wife. Could I hide anything at all from her?

But I did not want to add to her tension. So I kept my eyes closed and shook my head. But she must have still guessed my feelings because she said in an assuring tone, 'Don't worry. Everything will be alright. Have faith in destiny.'

I thought to myself, *I had trusted my luck once and moved to Mumbai. But what happened? We are returning once again to the US—defeated and empty handed.*

I went to the US for the first time in 1967 to study. I had got admission to the New Mexico State University for a degree in Chemical Engineering. Bapu had allowed me to go to the US only because I had the opportunity to pursue further studies there. But he said to me, 'Dikra, India is our country. You study, work there for some years, but come back to your motherland. We will wait for you.'

I promised him that I would return one day.

The first time I arrived in the US, I only had a $100 in my pocket, but somehow that didn't scare me then. I was full of hope, curiosity, enthusiasm, and the determination to do what it takes to succeed. That is the reason why I could survive and settle down in the US and complete my education. I returned to Mumbai but only to marry Hersha and bring her back with me to the States.

Hersha and I were childhood friends and when we grew up, we fell in love. But our families were totally against it. So much so that her family had decided to get her married to someone else.

Hersha informed me of their plans and so I rushed back from the US and reached Mumbai in the nick of time like the proverbial knight in shining armour to prevent her marriage. We then got married and went back together to the US. It was a scene straight out of a Bollywood film.

Thus began our life together in the US. Both of us were working. We were caught up in our routine, bringing up the kids, and dreaming of returning one day to India. We had decided to save enough money and then go back home to India. It was not an easy task at all. But we worked round the clock. Sometimes, we even did two jobs at a time. Finally we managed to save $50,000. It was time to fulfil our dream and my promise to my father.

We both resigned from our jobs and sold our house and car.

I informed my father about our decision and left America in 1978.

I had also thought about what I would do when I returned to India. I made plans after careful consideration. Our family friend in Mumbai, Mr Diwakar Bhat, had a pharmaceutical company in Goregaon, a suburb in Mumbai. I spoke to my father and to Diwakarbhai and decided to invest money in his business and become his partner.

So even before I left the US, I had already planned my future career in Mumbai.

Our savings amounted 12 or 13 lakh Indian rupees. I decided to invest 4 lakh rupees in the business, buy a new flat for us with another 4 lakh rupees, and use the rest of the money to take care of the family expenses until I started earning. This sum seemed more than enough to tide us over until I started getting returns from the business.

Hersha, the kids, and I returned home to Mumbai. The entire family was very pleased but most of all was my father. He used to tell everyone with pride, 'See. Didn't I say my Hasu will definitely come back?'

When I saw the happiness on his face, I felt that I had taken the right decision. I had done the right thing by keeping my promise to my father and returning to India.

After coming back, the first couple of days whizzed past before we even realized where we were. But then I immediately got down to work. On the one hand I was busy visiting the factory in Goregaon, having long meetings with Diwakarbhai, and on the other I was running around looking for a flat. Once things could be settled the way I had planned it, I would feel at ease. So I quickly drew up the necessary legal documents to invest money in Diwakarbhai's business.

Hersha and I went house-hunting every day.

It was now two weeks since we had come back. And then our entire world turned upside down. My father had a massive heart attack and passed away. We could not believe what had happened. Everything seemed dark and dismal. For a few days, I could not come to terms with the situation. My mind was beset with questions—What had happened to my plans? How did this happen?

Why? What now?

Finally I took hold of myself. I had no other choice. Now the responsibility of the entire family lied on my shoulders.

I started going to the factory in Goregaon once again and looking into the business.

A few days passed by. I was trying my level best to cope with the situation on hand. But I don't know what the matter was. Nothing was going the way I had planned it. Things were not exactly perfect in the company. I did not agree with the way many things were done and the profits were also less than I had estimated. My discussions with Diwakarbhai ended more often than not in full-blown arguments.

There were problems on the home front too. The children were not too happy in India. It was different coming to India for a holiday and totally different living here. Adults learn to make a few adjustments, but the kids were too young to understand that. To make matters worse, Neil had an asthma attack twice and had to be hospitalized. Neil's health had always been a little delicate. He used to suffer from asthma even in the US but here it was aggravated. The Doctor was of the opinion that Mumbai's humid weather did not suit him. We were worried. We did not know what to do. At times we felt that we should just go back to the US. But then I remembered my promise to my father. It had been his wish that I return to India for the sake of my family and my country. Even if he was no longer with us or may be more so because of it, I had to stick to my decision. There was another reason which prevented me from going back to the US: my ego.

Going back now would amount to admitting that I had lost. And I was not ready to do that.

I used to pour my heart out to Hersha. She would reassure me saying, 'Hasu, I never wanted to go to the US in the first place. I am not fascinated by big cars or houses. I grew up in luxury here. I had everything I ever wanted, had a chauffeur driven car since the time I remember. I went to the US only to be with you. I will be with you wherever you choose to be. I will stand by the decision you make, whatever it may be. But don't make any emotional decisions or decisions in haste. Think about everything calmly and objectively and then decide what you have to do.'

I decided to wait for some more time and try my level best to make things work here. My first experience with business was not a success so I thought I should look for a job instead.

Dhandha

It was now four months since we had come back to India. Once when I was talking to a friend of mine, he said, 'Hasu, you were working in the field of environment in the US. Why don't you look for a job in the same field here? There might be a suitable opening in the Environmental Protection Department of our Central Government.'

What he was saying was interesting but I had heard that in India one needed contacts and influence to land a government job.

My friend laughed when he heard my doubts. 'Which contact do you want? Will the Prime Minister of India be good enough?'

I replied glumly, 'Yes, you too make fun of me now.'

My friend smiled and said, 'No yaar, I am serious. Do you know Haku Bhai Kapadia?'

'Yes of course. I have known him for a long time.'

'Arrey baba. Hakubhai and his brother have a huge textile industry 'Hakoba'. He has a lot of clout in the industrial world. The most important thing is that Morarjibhai Desai, our Prime Minister, is his close friend. Now do you see?'

I finally understood what he was getting at. I decided to meet Hakubhai at the earliest who spoke to Morarjibhai on my behalf.

And that is how I was asked by the Prime Minister of India himself to come and see him in New Delhi.

I went to New Delhi and met Morarjibhai. He spoke to me very warmly and asked me a lot of questions. Finally I said to him, 'I am interested in working for the Environmental Protection Department of our Central Government.'

There was a moment's silence and then Morarjibhai gave me a piercing look before saying, 'You will definitely get a job in the Environmental Protection Department here. You have ten years of experience in the same field in the US. But have you thought about the difference in your salary there and the salary that you will get here?

Another very important point: you are from the business-oriented Baniya community. Why do you want to do a job? You should be doing business instead. Do it here or in the US, but start a business of your own. That is my advice to you. I wish you all the best.'

And with that the meeting was over. By the time I returned from Delhi, I had made up my mind. I would go back to the US and start my own business there.

Hersha as usual supported me completely and we began to prepare for our return to the US. I had visited Mumbai and returned to the US many times before this, but the situation was completely different now.

I was back to square one and had to start all over again.

The aircraft took off. I tried to hide my anxiety and looked at Hersha. Her eyes were closed and she was sleeping peacefully, her head resting against my shoulder.

Hersha Shah

We had travelled between Mumbai-New York and New York-Mumbai several times since we had settled in the US. Each time we reached our destination, we would feel happy to finally arrive after the long 18 hour journey.

This time around though, my heart was not full of enthusiasm like usual.

After living in the US for 10 years, we had sold off our house and car there and gone back to India 4 months ago, full of hope and dreams.

But nothing had gone the way we had planned. So here we were, back in the US to rebuild a life for ourselves. What did the future have in store for us this time?

The first time I came to the US was as a new bride. Then too my heart was full of regret at leaving my family behind and I held a lot of apprehensions about the new place. But at the same time, there was curiosity about my life here, and happiness that Hasu and I were together.

I soon realized that in America life is full of luxuries but in order to achieve that lifestyle, one has to be prepared to work very hard indeed.

Our first home was in Trenton in New Jersey State. Hasu was working at a chemist in the New Jersey Police Department.

I still remember those initial magical days when I had just arrived from India.

And I remember the universal dilemma that women like me who were new to the country faced—what to cook when they entered the kitchen. In 1968, none of the Indian ingredients were available: no pulses, vegetables, lentils, flours; nothing. So we came up with innovative preparations like dal made of dried peas, kadhi made of pancake batter, and rotis made of plain flour.

I had just about started getting used to life here when Hasu announced 'Hersha, one day we will definitely go back to India. I have promised Bapu that I will.'

I thought for only a moment and then said, 'Okay. I don't mind at all.'

Hasu smiled and added, 'But we will have to save a lot of money for that. I have calculated and I feel that we need to have at least $50,000 before we can think of going to India for good.'

I agreed and suggested to him that in such a case, we should look out for a job for me as well. I told him, 'We will not be able to manage the household expenses and also save money with your salary alone.'

Hasu liked the idea. As luck would have it, or perhaps it was Hasu's recommendation that did it, I got a job in Hasu's department itself.

I had completed my Inter Science in Mumbai and had studied microbiology for a year. The New Jersey Police Department must have felt that my qualification was enough and I landed a job in the Forensic Lab.

I had to test the blood samples of criminals against whom were charges of rape, drug abuse, etc.

Both of us were working but our responsibilities were also increasing with each passing day so we were finding it really difficult to put money aside in the bank for our return trip to India. We gave it a lot of thought. Finally Hasu came up with an idea. 'Hersha, why don't we buy an old house and renovate it? Then we either give it out on rent or resell it at a higher price. So what do you think of my idea?'

'Brilliant,' I said. 'But I have only one doubt. We will have to spend quite a lot of money on repairing the house, so how much will we be able to earn from it?'

Hasu had an answer to that as well. 'We only spend on the raw materials that we will need but we can save on the labour cost.'

'What do you mean? I don't understand.'

'I mean that you and I, we will do the repairs ourselves.'

I couldn't believe what he was saying. 'Hasu, painting, plumbing, carpentry, masonry, electrical work... Are you serious? All these things are not as easy as they look.'

'It is not easy but it is not impossible either. We can do it. I will teach you.'

I could think of no other arguments so I agreed.

The very next day, we started looking at the classified advertisements in the newspapers.

This is how we bought our first house, restored it, and sold it at a good profit. This new business of ours was working out quite well. I had to admit that Hasu had a sound business sense.

Around this time, Hasu began working in the Environmental Protection Department.

Life was going ahead at breakneck speed. Job, home, kids, renovation, and resale of old houses: it was an unending cycle.

But there was one thing which kept us going: our increasing bank balance.

Slowly but steadily we were inching towards our goal.

One day Hasu came back from office and announced, 'Ba and Bapu are coming here. They will be with us for two months.'

I didn't know how to react. Both his parents and mine had been totally opposed to our marriage.

Actually our families lived opposite each other's in Mumbai. Both were from the Baniya community. Both knew each other really well. But the bone of contention was that we hailed from different regions of Gujarat—I from Saurashtra and Hasu from Kutch.

Hasu and I had gone against our elders' wishes and married each other. After our marriage, we visited Mumbai regularly and gradually our families came to terms with the situation. Hasu's father began to speak to me and finally accepted me as his daughter-in-law. But Hasu's mother had still not come to terms with our marriage. She had not yet forgiven me and still did not speak to me. Given these circumstances, I was naturally tense when I heard that they would be staying here for two months.

Hasu reassured me and said, 'Hersha, look at it this way. This is your last opportunity to win over your in-laws.'

I decided to do precisely that. Luckily at that moment, I used to be at home because Neil, our younger son, was still small and had to be taken care of. Hasu was looking after everything on the business front. So I had the time to welcome my in-laws and do my best to break the ice with them.

When Ba and Bapu came home, I was wearing a sari the traditional way, with one end covering my head. I touched their feet as soon as they entered. All the time that they stayed with us, I wore a sari. I had decided to do everything the way they liked it for the two months that they were here.

I cooked elaborate meals, including breakfast, lunch, and dinner. And I took them around the city, sometimes to visit their relatives or at times for sight-seeing or shopping. Somewhere along the way, Ba's antagonism towards me melted away only to be replaced with respect and love. I saw her loving and caring side and all misunderstandings between us disappeared, and a new bond was formed between us which strengthened with each passing day.

Hasu was thrilled with this development and I was even happier because I knew it was the love of our near and dear ones which was the most important.

There were many funny moments while I played the role of the 'ideal daughter-in-law'. Ba and Bapu were both very fond of ice-cream so I would often take them to an ice-cream parlour. Once when we had gone there, there was a big queue so I stood in line for my turn to come. Most of the people in the line were Americans and there were two Indian girls. When they saw me, they started making fun of me saying, 'Look at her. A traditional cotton sari covering her head. What is this Mani Ben doing in America?' and they both burst out laughing. I pretended I hadn't understood or heard what they were saying.

A couple of days later, we had all gone for a programme organized by the local Indian community. While we were chatting with the people around, I saw the two girls who had made fun of me at the ice-cream parlour. I went up to them, smiled, and said, 'Hi. I am Hersha.'

'Hi. I am Pradnya,' one of them replied.

'And I am Maya.'

They clearly didn't remember me. I then reminded them of my meeting, 'By the way, my name is not "Mani Ben". You thought I was Mani Ben when we met at the ice-cream parlour, remember?'

They were both taken aback and embarrassed. I smiled and said, 'Don't worry. I didn't mean to embarrass you. In fact, I was quite amused by your comment. But do you know something? It is thanks to the 'Mani Ban' attire that I could win over my in-laws.'

The two of them laughed with me now. We chatted for a long time after that and till today they are quite good friends of mine.

My mother-in-law was so impressed with me that she started saying, 'Hersha is an ideal daughter-in-law. I feel she is closer to me than my own daughter now.'

In fact, when we all went out together, my mother-in-law would say, 'Hersha, you drive the car. I feel very safe with you. Hasu drives very rashly.' The expression on Hasu's face would be worth seeing.

'Ladies and Gentlemen, you are requested to kindly fasten your seatbelts. We will be landing shortly at the JFK International Airport in New York,' the airhostess announced.

Hasu and I looked at each other. As soon as I looked into his eyes, my doubts and fears melted away, and I saw instead a small ray of hope.

'We are together, aren't we? That is all that matters. Together we can face the world and make anything happen. And we will win.'

When we returned to the US in 1979, I was a little apprehensive about the future. But we had one bit of good news immediately after we got back. Hasu got back his old job in the Environmental Protection Department. So we hardly had any trouble re-establishing ourselves: house, car, the children's schools, everything was taken care of and we settled down into our familiar routine before we knew it.

One evening, Hasu came back home from work, excitedly waving a newspaper clipping. 'Hersha, look at this ad.'

I saw: Motel for sale.

The owner of Starlite, an 11 room motel located near Harrisburg, had put it up for sale.

I was puzzled. 'What does this ad have to do with us?' I asked.

'It certainly does,' said Hasu. 'I was on the lookout for precisely such kind of an opportunity. This motel has 11 rooms, so it is not too big and quite close to our house. So if it is within our budget, let's buy it.'

'What?' I was shocked.

Hasu began to explain. 'Look Hersha, we had decided when we returned here that we should go in to some business. I am doing a job only as a stop gap arrangement, right?'

'Right. You have often said that you would like to have your own enterprize. But I always thought that you would go into a business that had something to do with your education or with your experience in the field of environment. Why are you suddenly interested in owning and running a motel now?'

Hasu smiled mischievously. 'Not me. You. You are going to buy the motel and you are going to run it. I will only be a partner.'

'Stop joking, Hasu.'

'But I am serious. See, I believe that the most important aspect of any business is the profit. The profits in the motel industry are huge. Some Gujarati families in the West, in Los Angeles and San Francisco, have been successfully running motels since many years. Since the last few years, some Gujaratis have bought motels in the East and are very successful. Some of them had been already living here and some were from Uganda or Kenya. What is to be noted is that all of them were successful in this business.'

'I accept what you are saying. But Hasu, you want me to take charge of the business and I know next to nothing about it.'

'Hersha Ben, if you are prepared to learn, nothing is impossible. Now, tell me, a few years ago, did you know how to fix a leak in a tap? Did you know how to change and repair electric fittings? Did you know how to repair a television? Didn't you learn all these things? Be prepared to do the same thing now.'

My husband had an answer to each of my question. Finally all I could say was, 'Let us have a look at Starlite motel before deciding on anything.'

'This is it. Starlite motel,' Hasu said, getting down from the car. I looked at the motel and was speechless. My initial reaction was one of shock.

Before I could say anything, the owner came up to us, welcomed us, and took us inside. The motel was as run down and dirty on the inside as it was on the outside.

After seeing the place, we said goodbye to Mr Brown, the owner, and left.

'So, how did you like the property?' Hasu asked.

'Hasu, are you seriously planning to buy this place? It gives me the creeps. It is like a haunted house.'

'You are right. Right now, it is like a haunted house. But we are going to renovate it. We will change the wiring, plumbing, electrical fittings. We will paint it and clean up the rooms, put in new carpets, curtains and upholstery, covers, bedspreads, cushions. Can you picture it now? It doesn't look like a haunted house now, right? It looks like a spanking new, beautiful motel, doesn't it?'

'Oh. So we will have to put in all that effort?'

'Naturally, if we want to turn it around, there is no other way. Madam, it is precisely because it is in such a pathetic state that we are getting it so cheap. $80,000.'

'$80,000.'

'Yeah. $50,000 as down payment and the rest we can take a mortgage loan and repay the bank in installments. I am sure we can easily do it.'

I was quiet. This was a major decision of our life. We had saved $50,000 to begin a new life in India. We had not spent all that money there. We had not been able to set up and run a business successfully there. But at least we had not lost the money. We had got it back with us when we came back.'

Now, Hasu was thinking of putting in the entire amount we had saved over the last ten years into this venture. And take a loan for $30,000 over and above that.

What should we do? I was very tense. I looked at Hasu. He was calm and confident. His self-assurance communicated itself to me too.

Hasu was saying, 'If we do not take some risk, we will never be able to start our own business and never know the joy and pride of becoming successful entrepreneurs.'

Finally, the business oriented Baniya blood in me took over. I put my hand on his and said, 'Okay Hasu. Let's buy Starlite and make a success of it.'

Once the challenge was taken, there was no looking back. We made the down payment for Starlite and at the same time also arranged for the mortgage and fixed the amount for the installment.

As soon as all the formalities were over, we got down to transforming the place. Just like Hasu had predicted, Starlite soon started to look like a bright, clean, and lovely motel.

We also had several discussions about how to run the place. The motel did not have a separate apartment for the owner. So we decided that we would continue to stay at our house and run the motel. I was to manage everything during the daytime. Hasu would come directly to the motel from his office and then take charge for the next few hours until he returned home late at night.

We had employed a young couple who would look after the reception during the night and do the cleaning during the daytime. In this way, we were able to ensure that the motel was operative 24/7.

In the morning, after the children left for school, Hasu would go to his office and I would go to the motel. I would supervise the cleaning and other maintenance work there and take the cash to the bank to deposit. I would then manage the front desk for the rest of the day until Hasu came from office and took over.

I now began to think of ways to increase the clientele of the motel. There was a heavy vehicle driving school close to the motel. I went and talked to the Director and signed a contract with him. All the students who enrolled in the driving school had to stay in Harrisburg for four months. It was agreed that those who were in need of accommodation would stay at Starlite Motel. In return, I would look after the driving school's register at the time of new enrollments, which was once every two months. Earlier, the driving school had to hire someone for that period to maintain the register. Now I did this for them without charging a penny.

Our motel was also constantly occupied thanks to the students of the driving school. It was a profitable arrangement for all—the motel, the driving school as well as the students.

We realized within a month of taking over the running of Starlite that there was a lot of potential and huge profits to be made in this field. Even after paying off all the overhead costs and the salary of the couple we had employed, we still had a tidy profit left over each night.

Both Hasu and I were so happy. We had started thinking of ways of growing and expanding when there was an unexpected crisis.

There was an island called Three Mile Island very close to Starlite Motel. There was a nuclear generating station on that island.

Just as our motel was getting off to a good start, there was an accident in this generating station.

Something went wrong while some tests were being conducted there. There were no details given, but suddenly all the residents of that area were evacuated and all industries in the region were asked to close down until further notice.

We didn't know what had hit us.

Even though our motel was shut, the installments to the bank had to go on and the salaries of our employees had to be paid. It was a catch 22 situation.

We were literally counting the days. There was a terrible fear looming in front of us. Was this motel going to wipe us out?

And then as suddenly as they had appeared, the clouds disappeared. There was a directive from the Government permitting the industries in the region to begin work. Everything went back to normal including our motel. Hasu and I heaved a sigh of relief.

It was now six months since we had started managing the motel. One day, Hasu and I reviewed our accounts for the past six months.

Hasu said 'Our profits in terms of dollars are very good. But there is another thing we have gained which is far more important.'

'What is that, Hasu? I don't understand.'

'We made this business a success without any prior experience in the field. We have gained so much of confidence and self-esteem, haven't we?'

'You are absolutely right about that, Hasu. This confidence is something to be treasured and which will last us a lifetime. I still remember how nervous I was when you said that I will be running this motel. But everything started falling into place once I had made up my mind to do it.'

'Definitely the major part of the credit for the success is yours Hersha. I was there only for a few hours every day after work. But you were the one who took care of the front desk, maintenance, cleaning, banking operations, and public relations all by yourself. I am so proud of you.'

These words of praise made my day. Seeing the look of contentment on my face, Hasu said, 'We can now expand the business even further.'

I came down from the clouds with a thud. 'I see. All those sweet words were only a precursor to what you really wanted to say, isn't it?'

'Not at all. I sincerely meant every word of praise. But are we going to be content with what we have achieved so far and stop at that? We have climbed one small ladder. Now we have a bigger one to climb.'

This was a new Hasu I was seeing. A true businessman.

'Well Hersha Madam. What are you thinking?'

'I'm thinking about what you said. The ladders, peaks etc. But what exactly are we going to do about them?'

'I have big dreams but I will tell you about those at the right time. For now, I was thinking of increasing six rooms at the Starlite to begin with. It will give a boost to our business.'

I nodded in agreement.

The very next day, we started playing several roles simultaneously: carpenter, mason, painter, plumber, electrician, construction worker etc…

The couple who helped us with the night shift also pitched in. Within a matter of 45 days, we managed to build, decorate, and open six more rooms.

Once the 17 room Starlite motel started doing well, I began wondering what Hasu's next step would be. I didn't have to wait for long.

One weekend Hasu said, 'Tomorrow morning we will go to Elizabethtown. We will take the kids along.'

'Why?'

'There is a motel up for sale there: Red Rose. Let's go have a look.'

As soon as I saw Red Rose, it was love at first sight. The surroundings were green and tranquil.

The horse shoe shaped motel nestled in these peaceful surroundings. The motel was clean and pretty. There were two things we loved above all: one was the swimming pool and the second was the furnished two bedroom apartment meant for the owner.

We finished discussing all the financial details with the owner Mr Hoover. The deal was affordable and manageable.

Mr Hoover made one point clear—'You are buying the motel. But I will not be selling the restaurant next to it. I will run it myself.'

We agreed.

When we came back home, Hasu and I discussed the financial aspects of the deal. I said, 'If we put in a little money and add to what we will get from selling Starlite, we will be able to manage it easily.'

Hasu shook his head and said, 'No, no. Why sell Starlite? We have put in so much of effort to make it successful. Why give it up now? We can manage the down payment for Red Rose and will arrange for a mortgage loan once again from the bank. We can repay the bank in installments. What do you think?'

This was unexpected and once again, it was difficult for me to accept the idea. But it fitted in perfectly with Hasu's vision for the future which I was only just beginning to understand.

I had complete faith in him and his business acumen so I said, 'Okay. I would love to be the owner of two motels.'

Hasu Shah

I was very pleased that Hersha agreed to go ahead with my idea but at the same time I had a feeling of regret too. Hersha was born with a silver spoon in her mouth. She had led a very pampered childhood. She had always had maids to do her work. She never went out without a chauffeur-driven car. She had come to the US only because of me. She had worked so hard and had not been scared to face any challenge.

She had done her best to support me in every situation. Whether it was in my business or winning over my parents, she had always stood by me, ready to put in all the hard work required. But even now she had not been able to enjoy a luxurious lifestyle in America.

I always had a dream to provide her with all that her heart desired and was ready to work to the bone and save money for it. Hersha had never complained. On the contrary, she had always held my hand and shared every moment, bitter or sweet, with me.

I had never voiced these thoughts but decided that one day I would definitely give her all the comforts and luxuries that she deserved.

To come back to Red Rose, we put in a part of the money, arranged a mortgage for the rest, and bought Red Rose like we had done in the case of Starlite, but this time, we moved into the motel too.

There was now a drastic change in our lives because for the first time we really felt like we were the owners of a motel. Red Rose became our universe.

The motel was at a distance of only about 16 miles from Harrisburg. I still continued to do my job in the Environmental Protection Department. But now, from the time I came home in the evening to the time I left for work the next day morning, the front desk became my responsibility.

The American owners often put up a 'No Vacancy' sign in front of the motel at night. However, we could not afford such a luxury. I cannot remember a day in those five years when I actually found time to change into my night clothes before sleeping. I used to sleep in the formal clothes like the ones I wore through the day, so if there was a guest who came in even as early as 2 am, I was ready to welcome him. At times, a student from the driving school who had just arrived from his hometown would ring up at an unearthly hour. I then had to get the car out and go and fetch him.

In the five years that we spent at Red Rose, it would not be an exaggeration to say that I was on duty 24/7.

Hersha and the children too chipped in and helped in every possible way.

After the children and I had left in the morning, Hersha would first make a visit to Starlite, which was at a distance of 8.5 miles from Red Rose.

Once there, she would go over the register, supervise the cleaning of the rooms and other maintenance jobs, and then take the cash to deposit in the bank.

After this, she would return to Red Rose where she once again had to supervise the cleaning and check the register. Since Red Rose was bigger, we had hired four girls to do the cleaning, but the role of maintenance was solely Hersha's. And in addition to all this, she was in charge of the front desk at Red Rose throughout the day.

Hersha Shah

My workload doubled when we bought Red Rose, but gradually I learnt to manage both properties simultaneously.

It goes without saying that however well you may plan things out, there are always things that go wrong or unforeseen difficulties that crop up.

We had one golden rule that we followed in the motel: we did not give rooms to people who were under the influence of alcohol or drugs. Most of the people went away when they were told there was no room available. But there were some who insisted they be be given rooms and argued when told otherwise. At such times, it was really difficult to handle these people, not lose one's cool, and avoid creating an unpleasant scene. There have been instances where we have had to even call the police for we had no other alternative.

Another common problem in the motel industry is theft. We had put in place a number of measures to prevent theft but there would be an occasional slip here and there.

Once we were really duped. One evening, a couple came in a sleek Cadillac and booked a room for a day. The next morning when the housekeeping girl went in to clean the room, she saw the door wide open. Suspecting something wrong, she cautiously peeped in the room and was shocked to find that it had been totally cleaned out. The thieves had taken everything: AC, TV, microwave, pillows, bed sheets, blankets, towels, even the soaps in the bathroom— everything was gone.

We later came to know that the couple had quietly sneaked out in the middle of the night and no one had suspected a thing till morning.

In the motel industry, one also gets to meet many different kinds of people and have varied experiences.

Once a customer called on the Intercom and said that his TV was not working properly. I went to his room with the repair kit. The man was stretched out on the bed. He pointed to the TV which was fixed at a little height. I climbed up on to the chair and began to check the TV. Suddenly I realized that the man on the bed was staring at me. I was furious and scared at the same time. I could not leave until the problem with the TV had been attended to. I decided that if he tried anything, I would use the screw driver as a weapon. Luckily it did not come to that. The man did not do anything more than stare.

Along with the bitter experiences, there are also some great ones. One person I cannot fail to mention is the former owner of the motel, Mr Hoover. After selling us the motel, he used to manage the restaurant beside the motel. But he used to do so much more than that. He would give us invaluable tips on how to run the motel successfully—from maintaining a register to greeting the customers, and lots more. If I could not manage a particularly difficult job, I would call him and ask, 'Mr Hoover, can you help me, please?'

And he would literally put down whatever he was doing and rush to help me.

The students of the driving school too lent me a helping hand at times. There were some repair jobs where physical strength was needed and at such times, the students willingly helped me out.

I believe in the inherent goodness of human beings and in the proverb 'As you sow so shall you reap'.

Take the example of these students. Sometimes, they would come back really late from the school to grab a bite at Mr Hoover's restaurant which would unfortunately be closed by then. The motel was far from the city so there was nowhere they could go and eat. At such times, I would make upma, or poha or sandwiches for them. They used to be so thankful and devour not only the sandwiches but also our traditional Indian snacks.

They would thank me profusely for the meal and I would say, 'I didn't do anything much. I only followed the age-old Indian tradition of hospitality and did whatever I could in my capacity as a host.'

Anyway, the point is that these little gestures made them feel like they were a part of the family, so much so that they would help out whenever required.

Red Rose motel was now our home. Hasu's workload and mine had doubled, and Hasu had to commute a longer distance to get to office. But the biggest changes came in the lives of the children. For them, there was no one at the motel of their age to play with after school.

The other change was that there was no demarcation between home and business. So it was business talk all the time, even at home.

A third change which Jay had to face was the change in the school environment. Elizabethtown was essentially a white American farmers' town. So naturally, almost all the kids at school were white Americans. Jay was the first child of Indian origin to join the school, and that too directly in the 5th Grade. Initially, the other kids would exclude him from all the activities, behave rudely, and make fun of him incessantly. It must have been a very difficult period for Jay but he never once complained or blamed us for the change in his life.

Since Neil was only five years old, he was not aware of these undercurrents and adjusted more easily to the change in his surroundings.

Once when Hasu and I were talking, I said, 'Hasu, the children are very lonely here. What can we do?'

Hasu thought for a moment and then said, 'Hersha, we can call our friends and their kids here for the weekend. That way the kids will have company their same age.'

I liked the idea.

As decided, the very next weekend we called all our friends who came over along with their kids. What a great time we had. The adults chatted, played cards, and spent hours in the swimming pool. The kids too had a blast; running around the place, chasing one another, dancing, swimming... Nobody realized how the weekend flew past.

Jay and Neil were thrilled.

Weekends at Red Rose then became a ritual for our friends and their families. Every weekend, our home was filled with people. To tell you the truth, these weekends were terribly hectic for Hasu and me because we had to work round the clock to take care of all our guests, but one look at Jay and Neil's face was enough to drive away our fatigue. I still remember an instance when we planned to make pani-puris duing one such weekend. I would spend hours the previous night preparing almost 300 to 400 puris.

Everyone who has migrated to a foreign country always has this fear in the back of their minds if the new country will take their children away from them. What if they forget their roots? Their origin?

We had come here, worked, settled down, learnt a foreign language, picked up a little of the foreign culture, but essentially we were still Indian at heart. Our roots were still in India. But it was not the same for the children. They had been born and brought up in this country.

There were only around 100 Indian families in Harrisburg. But we got together all the same, discussed the matter at hand, and decided to start an Indian culture club. Here the children had the occasion to meet other children of Indian origin. They learnt about Indian culture and traditions.

They learnt and spoke Indian languages. And most importantly, they learnt about their roots and understood more about where they came from.

Since relocating to Red Rose, Jay and Neil had not been able to attend these Indian culture sessions. So hosting these weekend parties was very important from our point of view because it gave the children an opportunity to be with other Indian families, interact with them, speak our Indian language, and imbibe the essential elements of Indian culture.

Jay Shah

When we moved to Red Rose, Neil was 5 years old and I was 12. I was at an awkward age and it took me a long time to adjust to the new school. Though I did not have a single friend to play with after school, I would keep myself occupied by helping with small chores at the motel like mowing the lawn, gardening, cleaning the swimming pool, taking the customers' luggage to their room, etc. I did everything that I could. At times, I even managed the front desk to help out Mom.

Sometimes I did feel sad when I saw other kids my age playing or watching TV or going for some hobby class after school for I couldn't do any of these things. But then I would console myself by saying that I was helping my family in our business and that was equally important and satisfying. A business can grow only if the entire family contributes to it. This motel was just the beginning. In my heart I knew I was going to go much ahead from here in the future.

Mom and Dad soon realized that our life was monotonous and there was no fun in it. So they gave us as much time as possible. And then there were the weekend parties which Neil and I looked forward to.

Our life in Red Rose can be summed up in just a few words: 'Hard Days… Happy Times.'

One day, Dad came up to me and said, 'Jay, from today, you are going to manage the Coca Cola vending machine.'

'Manage? What do you mean?'

'You will be the one buying the bottles, filling them in the vending machine, and you will be the one who gets to keep the profit.'

I suddenly felt all grown up. I asked eagerly, 'Dad, are you giving me a business proposal? Is it going to be my own business?'

'Of course, son. I am sure you will be great at it.'

From the very next day, I began searching the classifieds in the newspapers. After four days, my patience was rewarded and I found the ad that I had been looking for.

It was an ad given by a supermarket saying: 'Coca Cola bottles at incredibly low prices if bought in bulk.'

I showed the advertisement to Dad and asked, 'Will you come with me tomorrow?'

Dad agreed and since I was too young to drive on my own, he drove me there.

He even gave the money to buy those crates of coke. He said, tongue in cheek, 'Jay, consider this a loan from me for your first business venture.'

I nodded my head.

As soon as we got back to the motel, I filled the vending machine with the bottles of coke. The customers who stayed in the motel would put coins and take the bottles whenever they needed.

The machine was empty in four days. All the bottles of coke I had bought had been sold. I did the accounts, returned Dad's 'loan' and literally danced with joy. I had made quite a good profit on this first business venture.

More important was what this experience had taught me. I now understood the meaning and importance of words like 'purchase', 'sale', and 'profit'.

I had taken the plunge for the first time, even if it was in a small pond, and had learnt to swim. I had also learnt that I could keep afloat and had gained the confidence to jump into even deeper waters.

Hasu Shah
It was the end of January in 1984. It was biting cold and had been snowing since the last two days.

When I woke up this morning and looked out from the window, I saw that a 1 foot thick layer of snow had covered the driveway of Red Rose.

I thought to myself, *Oh my God. It's going to be terrible today. I must clear the snow from the driveway at least or I will not be able to go to office today.* Suddenly, the phone rang. It was my colleague calling from Harrisburg.

'Hasu. There was a major accident last night on the highway near the junction. About two to three roads coming in to Harrisburg are closed.'

I thought about it and decided that I would not go to office today. I could finish some pending jobs at the motel instead.

I started going over the registers and other files. Hersha came in with a cup of tea. 'Red Rose and Starlite are doing fine now. The business and the profits are good.'

Hersha started laughing. 'Hasu, why are you telling me this?'

'I know my dear wife, that you know more about the present situation of the motels than me, but my reason for saying this right now is becasue I think it is now time to move on.'

'Another motel?'

I shook my head. 'Not exactly. This time I think we should go in for a bigger property, maybe a big hotel, located in the city.'

'Hasu, I think that is quite a jump. Will we be able to afford a place in the city?'

'We will sell Red Rose and Starlite if need be, but no motels for us from now on. We have to buy a hotel, and a big one at that.'

Hersha did not say a word and we left it at that for the time being. . .

Many days passed. I had spoken to a couple of agents and was on the lookout for a suitable advertisement in the newspapers. But there was nothing interesting.

This was when we heard that 'Nationwide'—a hotel on the river bank, was up for sale. I went to see the place with Hersha and the kids.

The location of the hotel was excellent; the river at the back, the main road in the front. But the hotel itself was not in a very good condition.

Hersha whispered, 'Hasu, we will have to do the painting, plumbing, electrical fittings, and decoration once again.'

But what was worse than its appearance was the bad reputation the hotel had earned over time. It was known as a 'drug hangout'.

Some people were even of the opinion that the drugs were supplied by the hotel staff themselves.

In spite of this, we decided to go ahead and buy the hotel. For one thing, we were getting it at a reasonable price and had managed to find buyers for both Red Rose and Starlite for a good price too.

We had bought Starlite for $80,000. We were now getting $1,55,000 for it. As for Red Rose, we had bought it for $1,56,000 and we now had a buyer who was ready to pay $2,62,000 for it. Selling both the motels would give us an almost 100 percent profit.

I did a lot of calculations. We were getting $4,17,000 for the two motels. But it was still not enough to buy the hotel. We would still need to get a loan from the bank. We began work on the mortgage loan but this time, not a single bank was ready to offer us the loan. Some refused when they heard the name of the hotel, while others were not too keen on giving loans to someone of Indian origin.

But I had made up my mind. 'I will buy this hotel against all odds. I will turn it around and make it a success.'

Finally, the Horizon Bank from California agreed to give us the loan on a mortgage. They were charging a hefty 15 percent interest on it, but I accepted it nevertheless. I didn't have a choice and I was also confident that like the last two times, I would be easily able to pay the installments once the hotel began to do well.

I was worried about the money and was constantly thinking about the figures whereas Hersha was tense due to another reason altogether.

'Hasu, will I have to manage this hotel all alone?'

'Alone? I am there with you.'

'You will be here only after office hours but I will be on my own the rest of the time, isn't it?'

'Yes, but why are you worried? You have successfully managed two motels all by yourself before this.'

'Hasu, running a motel is totally different. There we were only giving rooms on rent. But now we are buying a big hotel, with 125 rooms, a restaurant, and a bar lounge to manage. I don't have any experience in any of this.'

'I am confident you will do just fine, Hersha. We will employ experienced staff to help you. You have always been good at picking up new things. Be ready to do the same here. I am sure you can do it.'

I tried to reassure Hersha and so did the kids. 'Don't worry, Mom, we will help you as much as we can.'

The paperwork was done and finally Hersha became the owner of the hotel.

This was only the first small step towards the beginning of our future empire.

Hersha Shah

Looking back, Hasu says this was just a small step towards our final goal.

But at the time, running that 125 room hotel seemed like an enormous challenge to me. My mind was beset with fear and doubts. But I decided to take up the challenge and do my best.

One good thing was that we relocated once again to Harrisburg. Hasu's office and the children's school were nearby and they could devote more time to the hotel.

After buying the hotel, the first job we undertook was the cleaning, or in other words, 'cleansing' of the hotel. We got rid of all the old staff except for two front desk managers and two employees from the housekeeping department. We had two reasons for doing this: the first one was that we knew business would be slow initially and we would not need so many staff members and the second was that if any of the old staff was really involved in the drugs racket, we did not want them there.

The cleaning job also included painting, renovating, etc.

With all the other changes, we also decided to rename the hotel: it was now called River Front Inn.

We refurbished the restaurant and the bar lounge and appointed new staff for them. The hotel had a new look, it was attractive, neat, and clean. People on the streets began to stop to give it an appreciative look.

I decided that it was now time to improve our public relations and to begin marketing the hotel.

I met all the prominent business houses in Harrisburg and extended a warm invitation to them.

'Our hotel River Front Inn is operational now. Please do visit. And your guests are most welcome to visit or stay there. River Front Inn is also well equipped to host business meetings and conventions.'

Gradually people were convinced and began to visit the hotel.

Their experience was generally so good that they almost always returned and soon River Front Inn turned popular.

As the business at River Front Inn picked up, we first paid off the bank loan and then decided to reinvest the profits back into the hotel itself. Everything in the hotel—including carpets, curtains, furniture, and linen—was now brand new and this changed the entire look of the hotel.

Hasu and the children kept their promise and helped me as much they could in the management of the hotel. Hasu was not very interested in the day to day operations of the hotel. His forte was finance and future planning and he did this in an excellent manner. Neil and Jay would come to the hotel directly from school. Neil was now 11 years old while Jay was in his final year at High School. They used to take care of several things like keeping the parking lot clean, mowing the lawn, gardening, small maintenance jobs, etc.

Neil waited the tables during his summer holidays. He earned $127 in tips. This was his first earning and he was over the moon about it. He bought himself a Sony Walkman with the money.

I can never forget the look of pride on Neil's face as he walked about listening to music on his Walkman.

Just as Riverfront began to do well and we heaved a sigh of relief, tragedy struck in the form of monsoons. The heavy rains seemed to intensify with each passing moment. The river flooded, the waters kept on rising, passed the danger level, and began to overrun the banks, submerging everything in their wake. The ground floor of Riverfront was under water. The property was being damaged but there was nothing we could do about it.

When the rain stopped and the water receded, we took stock of the situation. The restaurant on the ground floor had been completely washed out. The cars in the parking lot were floating and the hotel grounds were a total mess. We decided to close the hotel for a week and undertake a massive clean-up campaign. We got the restaurant cleaned and bright as new and then opened it to the public. But we had lost thousands of dollars in the bargain. We consoled ourselves by saying that it could have been much worse.

However, the floods seemed to have turned the tide. After the monsoons, things suddenly started to happen for the better. I signed a big contract with Conrail. Thanks to the Railway employees, our hotel was now full to capacity every day.

At the end of the first year, the hotel showed a huge profit. Thanks to the excellent figures, the world renowned hotel chain 'Holiday Inn' offered us the opportunity to become their franchisee.

This was an honor indeed and a recognition of our hard work and success.

Hasu now gave up his job and gave free rein to the pursuing of his dreams which only got bigger and more ambitious with every successful venture.

Hasu Shah
River front Inn was now running under the name of Holiday Inn. It was time for me to give up my job and throw myself entirely into the business.

Our hotel had seen a lot of ups and downs and faced many problems, but these problems were behind us now and we were doing well.

However, profits and money were not the only things I was interested in. I was getting restless once again and was ready take on a new challenge. 'Now what?' was the question constantly on my mind.

Around the same time, I met an old friend of mine, Bharat Mehta. He was a Chemical Engineer like me and had completed his Masters from the Pennsylvania University. At the time I met him, he was holding a very high position in a multinational company 'Lever Brothers'. While talking to him, I realized that he didn't seem happy with his job. When I asked him the reason for it, he said, 'A well-paid job in a big company doesn't necessarily translate into happiness. At least I don't think so. Every few months, I am sent to a new city in my role as a "trouble shooter". I am now tired of this gypsy like existence. I cannot take my family along every time. So I often find myself living alone with no one for company.'

When I tried to calm him down, he exploded. 'Hasu, it is impossible for you to understand. You have your own business. You take your decisions yourself. I would love to do something like that. But…'

I kept his words in mind.

After coming back home, I narrated the incident to Hersha and told her what had crossed my mind. 'Hersha, let's ask Bharat to join us as a business partner.'

Hersha looked at me with surprise. 'Partner? Why? We are doing pretty well on our own.'

'It is evident that if we have to expand the business any further now, we need huge investments and we will need to have partners for that.'

'Agreed, but most of the people we know have asked their family members or close relatives to become partners.'

'No, I am very firm about that. I feel that business and relations are not to be mixed and should be kept separate. Otherwise, very often both are ruined.'

She thought for a moment and then said, 'Yes Hasu, you are absolutely right. I have heard of families that have been separated because of business tensions. In fact, to tell you the truth, I sincerely feel that even our children should do something on their own and not join the family business.'

Trust Hersha to take a thought to the other extreme. When I told her as much, she did not agree. 'I am not going to the extreme. What is true of relatives is also true of children.'

'How is that?'

'See, right now we get along fine with the kids. We are very open with them and they too consider us their friends. But if we get into business together, we may differ in our thinking. There may be conflicts because of the generation gap. And you know how hot-tempered you are. You may say something and might hurt their feelings and spoil our relations with them.'

'So now everything becomes my fault, does it?'

'I didn't say that, but tell me frankly, did I say something wrong?'

I employed the usual tactics of a cornered person and parried her question with another question.

'But we were talking about Bharat Mehta, what do you think of that?'

'I agree with your idea of taking on a partner. Talk to Bharat and decide.'

A couple of days later, I spoke to Bharat. We had a detailed discussion about business and other matters and finally Bharat Mehta officially became a partner of Hersha Enterprises.

Jay Shah

I have been closely observing our family business since the age of 12 and whenever possible, I have contributed as much as I could to it.

I confess that I did not always do the work willingly. There would be times when I was so tired. I would have preferred to watch TV or catch a play. At these times, I would look at the other kids my age and wonder why my parents could not have been doing ordinary jobs like everyone else.

Like they say 'the grass is greener on the other side'.

But these thoughts were rare. Generally I thought the world of my parents and saw the enormous hard work they both put in. I felt that if I helped them out, their burden will be lighter, so I pitched in whenever I could. The idea that I was helping my family was the most important according to me.

As I grew up in a business family, I had seen the pros and cons from up close and had made up my mind. 'I will not get tied down to the family business. I am going to study and choose my own path, my own field of interest.'

Luckily, Mom understood my feelings completely and both she and Dad never enforced their views and opinions on us.

After graduating from High School, I went to Cornell University. I had decided to focus on my studies, get excellent grades, and later study Law. I was a very serious student and hardly ever did the crazy things that one does in college.

Here too, I found a way to earn my own pocket money. Since the time Dad had entrusted me with the vending machine business, I had always done something or the other to earn my own money.

I was on the lookout for such an opportunity at the University too. The advantage of growing up in a business family is that one can see a business opportunity where others cannot.

The very first year, I had an excellent idea. There are often elections in college and these are as closely contested as any political elections in the country. The candidates address meetings, arrange rallies, and put up a few posters as part of their campaign. I thought *What if one increased the number of posters?*

I did a detailed survey of the campus and identified 250 possible locations for putting up the posters. All these locations were highly frequented by the student community.

I then met the students' agencies and persuaded them that their campaigns would be much more effective if 250 posters were displayed in those places as the candidates would get more exposure and publicity.

They liked the idea and gave me the job of putting up the posters. The first thing I did was get permission from the University authorities.

I then arranged to have the posters printed and employed four boys who were to be paid on an hourly basis. I bought some thick cotton bags cheap from the Army Navy store on campus and then I was ready to roll. Each boy was assigned a certain area of the campus and it was his job to put up the maximum number of posters there in a limited amount of time. The boys finished their work in 4 hours, exactly as I had calculated, and after giving them their money, I was left with a good profit. There were always some elections or the other at the University so this became a regular source of income for me.

In addition to this, I also got the post of 'teacher assistant' in the Departments of Communication and Management.

In short, my routine of studies and work continued in much the same way at University as it had in school.

I used to do odd jobs in our hotel during the summer holidays; sometimes in the housekeeping section and sometimes in the maintenance department.

I used to get the same salary as the others in the same position. I did not get, and I did not expect, any extra concessions as the owner's son.

One summer holiday, I came up with a new idea: our hotel should have a separate sales office.

Dad and Mom both liked the idea very much and the responsibility of setting it up was given to me.

Harrisburg is the capital of Pennsylvania State so several large organizations have their offices here—the Pennsylvania Teachers' Association and the Association of Engineers to name a few. I researched these and other organizations and then started meeting their officials.

After giving them all the information about our hotel, I would end by saying 'Please arrange your meetings or seminars in our hotel. Your outstation guests can be accommodated comfortably here. We will also offer you good discounts. Before you decide, I invite you to visit our hotel and judge it's quality for yourselves.'

Many of the officials took me up on the invitation and visited the hotel and were pleased with the ambiance, the facilities, and the service.

This satisfaction was reflected in the increased business of the hotel.

When I returned to University after the vacations, we appointed our first employee for the sales office. Today our Sales office—which was started by one person on zero budget—employs a staff of 75 persons with a budget of $35 million.

Hersha Shah

Our business was flourishing. Buying the 125 room Riverfront Hotel, running it successfully as a franchisee of the famous Holiday Inn chain, all these were important milestones in the path of the success of our enterprise.

From 1985, Hasu gave his entire time to our business. Jay, who was away at University, helped a lot when he was home and would come up with innovative ideas to expand the business.

Naturally, my load lightened. For the past several years, I had been battling on so many fronts single-handedly. Now we employed new personnel to take over many of the responsibilities. All of them were highly qualified, experienced, and professional.

Hasu's idea of taking partners and expanding the business worked extremely well. By 1990, three new partners had joined the Hersha Group of Companies. Once I asked Hasu, 'How do you choose a partner? What do you look for in a partner in our Group?'

Hasu replied, 'Today many people are willing to join the Hersha Group because everyone wants to work with successful entrepreneurs and be a part of their success. And that is precisely why I am doubly careful while taking on partners. The person has to be well educated, intelligent, honest, and hardworking. It is not necessary that he should be from the hotel industry. But he should be at the top level of his chosen field because such people always strive to remain at the top and to succeed in whatever they do. They should be theists like us. I firmly believe that those who believe in God will not resort to unscrupulous means. And of course, work should also be a religion for them.'

'I have to admit Hasu that your decisions about our partners are always correct and this is confirmed by the rapid growth of our business in the past few years.'

'Thanks for the praise, but the entire credit does not go to me alone. Our partners Bharat Mehta, Rajendra Gandhi, and K.D. Patel had faith in us, agreed to our terms and conditions, and contributed actively to the growth of our business. That is why our partnership is so successful.'

Putting an end to our conversation, Hasu asked, 'Well, if my interview is over, could I please get a cup of tea now? Piping hot and strong?'

I got up to get him a cup of tea but I could not stop thinking about what we had discussed. I remembered how Hasu had told Bharat, 'Bharat, you will have to resign from your job before joining Hersha Enterprises as a partner. I don't want a partner who contributes only the capital. I want someone who will contribute actively in every way possible to the growth of the business. In Lever Brothers, your salary was $75,000. Here you will get only $35,000. But if you have a look at the financial records of the company, you will realize that your share of the profits will ensure that you earn much more than your present salary.'

Bharat accepted all the conditions that Hasu had laid down and became a partner in the Hersha Group. Immediately after this, Hasu bought another property along with our partner. This was the Sheraton Hotel near State College.

In 1986, Rajendra Gandhi joined the Group and then K.D. Patel in 1989. We acquired a new hotel with the entry of every new partner.

Hersha Enterprises now owned 4 big hotels and the Group had undertaken the construction of 3 more new hotels.

Thanks to the grace of God, our business had prospered so much that for the very first time, Hasu and I indulged ourselves in true American style. We bought a Rolls Royce and even an airplane. Our days of cutting corners were finally behind us. Our dreams continued to get bigger and better.

Some of the biggest problems of the hotel industry are theft, accidents, natural calamity, or lawsuits. As the business grows bigger, the number of problems too increases proportionately. This is because the number of people—guests, staff—is more and it is almost impossible to keep an eye on everyone all the time.

I remember so many unpleasant scenes in this context.

Purchase of food items and ingredients is done on a very large scale in a hotel. So theft is common here. If the thief is caught red-handed, he is punished immediately but sometimes, even if one knows that something has been pilfered, it is advisable to turn a blind eye.

However, stealing of cash is a serious offense and should never be overlooked. It was a rule in our hotel that as soon as there was more than $500 in the cash register, it had to be transferred to the safe deposit vault. In so many years, there have been only a couple of managers who deliberately made wrong entries in the register and stole cash. When their crime was discovered, we immediately sacked them.

Usually the hotel is very busy on the weekends and as the bank is closed then, the cash is collected from Friday to Monday. One Monday morning, we received a panic call from our manager. 'I was about to leave for the bank to deposit the cash when an armed robber showed me a weapon and ran away with the entire amount.'

This incident occurred when we had just started Riverfront and there were no cameras installed in the hotel. So there was no other option but to take the manager's word for it as nothing could be proven.

But we learnt a lesson from this incident and installed cameras in the hotel. Now the number of petty thefts reduced because people were more scared of being caught on camera.

We too relaxed a little. And then one night there was a bizarre robbery. All the computers in the office were stolen. The robbers were probably aware of the cameras because they placed the computers on chairs and hid their faces behind the computer monitors. So it was impossible to identify them. However, what we did spot was that as the robbers passed the front desk, the night duty manager was fast asleep. The robbers could not be apprehended but the night duty manager was asked to resign immediately. Losing our computers did not just mean a monetary loss, all the invaluable data stored in them was lost too. We had to spend the next few days getting everything back on track.

Accidents like someone slipping down the stairs are a common thing in India but here in the US, the hotel is invariably sued and has to give out a hefty compensation to the person. So great care is taken to avoid any kind of mishap in the hotel premises.

But there is a limit to the precautions that one can take and accidents do happen.

Once, a guest who was completely drunk was lying down on the bed and smoking a cigarette. He did not even realize when the cigarette fell from his hand onto the carpet and the carpet caught fire. He had passed out. The fire spread to the rest of the room. As soon the staff realized what was happening, the fire brigade was alerted. They came immediately, got the man out safe, but the room was totally charred. Refurbishing the room was a big expense but we did not mind it at all because the loss for the hotel could have been far more if anything had happened to the customer. We thanked our stars that the guest was safe and we were spared at least that trauma. In such circumstances, it is better to blame it on bad luck and move on. As long as the profits are more than the losses, it is okay.

In spite of such setbacks, Hersha Enterprises was growing at an incredible speed and by 1990 our profits were reaching new heights. We were all very happy and were making grand plans for even more spectacular growth in the future when suddenly the country was gripped in a wave of recession.

We almost drowned in this terrible wave. The first business to be affected in times of recession is almost always the hotel industry because staying in a hotel is considered a form of luxury which can be dispensed with in times of a crisis. Before we realized what was happening, our business diminished so much that we could not even recover the overheads of maintaining the hotels. At the same time, our debts were increasing. The most severe crunch was with the cash flow. We had recently begun the construction of three new hotels and all the partners had invested heavily in them. To top it all, we had the burden of the bank loans to be repaid. The income from the existing hotels had decreased at an alarming rate and the expenses for the new hotels only kept increasing. The situation was frightening.

One day Hasu said, 'We are losing $50,000 per day.'

I almost blacked out when I heard the horrific figure.

'Well, what can we do now?'

Hasu too must have been shell-shocked but he put on a brave front for my sake and said, 'We have to sell off as many personal assets as we can and raise some money. We will sell the house, cars etc but we have to have cash in hand.'

There were tears in my eyes. But Hasu tried to reassure me saying, 'Hersha, there are ups and downs in business.'

'I understand Hasu. And I didn't actually want to cry but then I thought of the children. It is Neil's final year in High School and Jay is still studying at University...'

'It's okay. We are doing all we can. Everything will be alright.'

Even though I wiped away the tears, I could not erase the turmoil in my mind. After this, we put up a desperate fight for survival.

The first thing to go was the plane, then the Rolls, until finally we decided to put up the Holiday Inn hotel for sale. Unfortunately because of the recession there were no buyers.

Our daily routine continued as usual. We had to mask our fears with a false smile and get through the terrible days. In fact, it was the strain of putting on an act during these days that was the reason for the beginning of my migraine attacks.

The children realized that the situation was bad and asked us a million questions about the situation. As always, we gave them truthful answers and told them of the gravity of the problem.

One day Jay said to us, 'Mom, Dad. I can't bear to see the stress you are going through. You are making sure my fees are paid even in this situation. I feel guilty about it. I think I should quit college and get a job.'

We were touched by his concern but Hasu patted him on the shoulder and firmly said, 'No, Jay. You need to complete your course. Don't worry about the situation at home. Your Mom and I will do two jobs if needed but make sure that both of you get the best education. Okay?'

The recession gradually receded and our hotels started doing business as usual. We were especially pleased because we had recently inaugurated one of our new hotels and it had started gaining popularity.

We heaved a sigh of relief. It had come to a point when we had almost gone under the pressure but had managed to emerge safe. Once again Hasu and other partners began making ambitious plans for expansion. I had only one prayer, 'Dear God, we have managed to emerge safe from this test of fire. But please do not put us through such torment once again.'

Jay Shah

I completed a course in Hotel Management from Cornell University and then pursued an MBA from Temple University and also studied Law there. All this while, I closely observed our family business and experienced its highs and lows. It further strengthened my resolve not to join the family business. It was not a decision I had made out of selfishness. If Mom and Dad ever had to undergo a crisis like that once again, I would have done everything possible to help them. I just felt that it was better if members of a household had different professions. So even if there was a problem on someone's work front, the rest of the family did not have to suffer.

Gradually our family business became stronger. Dad took on two new partners, David Desfor and Kiran Patel. David had a lot of experience having worked in the Hospitality industry since 1982. Kiran Patel was a mechanical engineer. He had finished his Masters in Industrial Engineering in the USA and was a senior manager in a big firm.

Hersha Group's tradition of getting new partners and new hotels continued and the Group now owned 8 hotels in total. It had come a long way from its inception in 1978 but Neil and I were of the opinion that our growth was cautious and slower than what it could have been.

Neil was the youngest of the family and was studying at the Pennsylvania University. He too had seen the business from close quarters while growing up and we often had discussions about how the business was shaping up. Once Neil said, 'Jay, Hersha Group was begun on a 'Mom and Pop' kind of small scale level. We now have 8 hotels. This means that Mom and Dad have definitely been successful in expanding it. But our Group is quite conservative and cautious in its approach as compared to the rapid growth of the other modern business houses. Do you agree? Taking on a new partner and acquiring a new hotel, this is growth at a snail's pace. At this rate, I doubt if the Group will even have 60 hotels by the time we are 60.'

Neil had a point. Today big businesses need big risks, huge leaps, and an aggressive strategy. The reputed names in the Hotel industry are involved in buying, developing or constructing several hotels simultaneously. That is the reason for their spectacular growth. I replied saying, 'Neil, you have to understand. The present administration of the Hersha Group belongs to an earlier generation. They have their own way of thinking. We could have changed it if we were a part of it. But the point is that we are not a part of the Hersha Group at the moment and may never be. So what is the use of speculating on it?'

Neil sighed. 'Yeah, I understand Jay. But at times, I am dying to introduce changes, put into practice new ideas… But what you say is correct. Let them do things their way and we will go our way.'

But Destiny willed otherwise. Both Neil and I did not have a clue of what was about to happen. If only we could have foreseen the future.

When I completed the Law Degree at Temple University, I had degrees in 3 subjects: Hotel Management, Business Administration, and Law.

I decided to pursue a career in law and was lucky to get a job in the prestigious law firm, Coopers and Lybrand. This was the beginning and led to many other opportunities. Thanks to Senator John Haynes, I was introduced to the world of politics, politicians, and Capitol Hill. I also worked in another reputed law firm and in the District Attorney's office in Philadelphia. I was in the field of law for 5 years. I was doing well and had succeeded in climbing up the ladder. Then one day, I reviewed my life and asked myself some questions—'What am I doing exactly? Am I happy?' I compared my last five years in the field of law and all the years since my childhood spent in the family business environment. I had many ambitions and many things that I wanted to do. But I did not have the freedom to make my own decisions in my job. There was always a boss who decided my line of action and I was happy just doing that job well. But nobody took risks here. Life was well ordered, planned. I would be doing the same thing for the next 25 years that I had been doing for the past 5 years. Very boring.

It is not at all like that in business. Here you are taking a risk every moment. You can become successful beyond your wildest dreams but if you fail, you have to pay the price for it yourself. In that case, you begin all over again.

I realized that it was time to take a major decision. This could be the turning point of my life. My heart was leaning towards our business and the one thought was running constantly through my mind was, 'If I do have to get into business, it would be best to join the family business which I have seen from such close quarters since childhood.'

Once again, I spoke to Mom and Dad. Mom was surprised to hear about my change of heart. She was still of the opinion that I should not join the Hersha Group and follow a career of my own.

She gave me many reasons to support her point of view while Dad told me that he would stand by my decision, whatever it may be. Mom had put forward the argument about the generation gap. This seemed a very important issue to me. For the last few years, I had been away from home, initially for my studies and then because of my job. But wherever I was, I had followed the business closely and kept in touch with the latest developments and news in our business. Sometimes when I was home for the holidays, I would have discussions with Dad and the other partners about business matters. They used to listen to my thoughts and opinions and our discussions were always be very frank and open. For example, everyone liked my idea of centralization and they took immediate action to ensure that it was implemented. Thanks to this, the operations of Hersha Development Corporation were streamlined and became more efficient.

Instead of the old system of each partner being responsible for a couple of properties, there was now a more widespread distribution of work and responsibilities. Different companies were formed specifically to manage the different aspects of the business like Hersha Construction Company, Hersha Interiors and Supplies Company and so on.

Although all these companies did work mainly for the Hersha Group, they could also accept external jobs which increased the operations and turnover of the entire Hersha Group considerably.

Dad and his partners would patiently listen to what Neil and I had to say, discuss the issue frankly, and if they were convinced, accept our suggestions and implement them immediately.

That is why after giving the matter a lot of thought, I decided to join the Hersha Group.

Dad gave his reaction in just two words, 'Congratulations and welcome.'

Hersha Shah

Jay joined the Hersha Group in 1997 as Managing Director.

Neil, who was studying at the Harvard Business School, came home for the weekend one day. He asked Jay, 'So brother? Any new plans?'

Jay replied, 'There are several new plans. But the first thing we have to do is to get out of this small place and go to a big city.'

I was confused. 'Why? What is wrong with our home in Harrisburg?'

Jay laughed and said, 'Mom, I wasn't talking about our home, I was talking about our business. Yes… I know that you do not like shop talk at the dining table but we have already finished eating so can we please go to the TV room and talk? And Mom, I want you to be there and give your opinion.'

I said, 'Okay, you go ahead. I will bring the dessert and join you.'

Jay gave us an outline of his plan, 'Dad, Mom, we have been in the hotel industry for the last 19 years. Our Group now has 10 hotels. But all these hotels are located in small towns or small cities like Harrisburg. I feel that we should enter the metropolitan cities like Philadelphia and New York and establish ourselves there. We will get recognition and our business will grow tremendously.'

Neil liked the idea and supported Jay, whereas Hasu and I were a little cautious. Hasu said, 'Jay, buying a property in a city like New York is not easy. What if we take such a big jump and fall flat on our faces? We also have to consider the intense competition in the big cities. What if we cannot survive?'

Jay tried to explain. 'Dad, a business house has to constantly increase its strength. We have a solid foundation now. Haven't we grown from just 11 rooms to owning 10 hotels now? We will continue to grow in the same way. The only thing is that we have to increase the speed of our growth and incorporate the latest changes in our work style.'

After a long discussion, Hasu and I accepted Jay's suggestion.

Jay then called for a meeting with all the partners. He presented his plan to them, put forward his arguments, and succeeded in convincing them.

As luck would have it, a reputed 96 room hotel in Philadelphia came up for sale soon after. Hersha Group submitted a tender and became the owner of 'Clarion Suites'.

This was our first step towards establishing our hold in a big city.

The business was expanding rapidly. Hasu, his 5 partners, and now Jay were looking after everything. I had the responsibility of only one department now; Interiors and Supplies.

Decoration, whether it is of our home or our hotel, is my passion. People often ask, 'We love the décor of your hotel. Could you please do the same for us?'

At such times, I feel happy and proud.

Since I was now in charge of only one thing, I had more spare time to pursue my interests and hobbies.

At present I am not involved in the day to day functioning of the Hersha Group but I keep a close eye on all the important developments and I am interested in knowing the latest.

Jay stormed into the Hersha Group like a whirlwind and brought about a series of innovative changes in its style of functioning. He believes that in order to achieve the dream of an ever expanding enterprise, the Group should have a huge amount of capital.

With the approval of everyone concerned, he succeeded in putting this idea into practice. The Group sold four of its excellent and well performing hotels. With the help of the capital that was thus raised, the Group began developing 10 new hotels.

Each new idea of Jay's—from the sales office to centralization to moving to big cities—showed great results and enhanced the power and reputation of the Group.

Now he put forward another proposal: register the company on the Stock Exchange and come out with a public issue to raise the capital.

Until now Jay's innovative ideas had always worked and proved beneficial to the company. But this was a very daring idea indeed. Making the company a Public Limited one meant opening the doors of the business which were closed until now, and inviting the people to look into our business and invest in it if they liked the set-up and become a part of the family. This was perhaps the need of the day and everyone accepted that but they were a little apprehensive too. If it did not work, it would be publicly inviting ridicule, and could also prove potentially dangerous. These were the thoughts running through the partners' minds.

There was also a technical hitch in listing the company on the stock exchange. According to the rule, a company registered on the Stock exchange cannot run the hotel and has to hand over the administration of the hotel to another company.

In short, it was not an easy decision as there were so many aspects involved that it took us not a few days but an entire year of detailed discussions to arrive at a conclusion.

Jay's persistence during this time is worthy of appreciation. He patiently answered all queries, provided a solution to every anticipated problem, and did his best to clear all doubts. Finally in 1999, with the approval of all the partners, we decided to make our company a Public Limited Company.

However, destiny plays strange games. There was another wave of recession in 1999. We had not forgotten the horror of the earlier recession. Jay too had seen its impact. But he was a college student then and today he was an experienced businessman.

He reasoned with everyone saying, 'Recession and growth are both inherent parts of business. If our foundation is strong, we do not need to fear recession. Similarly we should not take unnecessary leaps just because business is booming. If our calculations are right and our work is perfect, we can tide over the recession and enjoy the benefits of the industrial boom.'

Finally in 1999, our new company, Hersha Hospitality Trust, which owned 10 hotels, was registered on the Stock Exchange. Hersha Group now consisted of 5 companies along with Hersha Hospitality Management, Hersha Development Corporation, Hersha Construction Services, Hersha Interiors and Supply, and now Hersha Hospitality Trust.

As projected, our public issue was launched in 1999. However, apart from the $15 million which had been underwritten, the issue was a complete failure. The public ignored it completely, so much so that until 2003, shares worth only $10,000 had been sold.

It seemed as if Jay's plan to raise capital through a public issue had failed.

The good thing that came out of the debacle was the unflinching support of all the partners. Everyone kept their cool and hoped for a brighter tomorrow. Nobody played the blame game. Everyone was sure that even if the scales seemed tipped against us, they would swing back up.

In 2000, while the recession still gripped the country, Neil gave up his well-paid job and joined the Hersha Group following in the footsteps of his elder brother. Now two youngsters full of life and ambition together with 6 experienced men were at the helm of Hersha Group. The team spirit was incredible. New ideas were being introduced, new plans being put into action; in short,

Hersha Group became the breeding ground for innovation. We then made the major decision to sell the 8 hotels that the Group owned then. This money was added to the $15 million received from underwriting the public issue and the Group purchased 18 new properties. Some of the people from whom we bought the hotels were paid with company shares instead of cash.

Finally by 2003, Hersha Group had 20 hotels. Around this time, the effects of recession also started diminishing. We all heaved a sigh of relief. The hotel industry began to prosper once again. The stock market too started to boom.

Jay and Neil decided to expand the Group. They used the latest marketing strategies and introduced modern work practices to breathe new life into the company.

Within a matter of just 3 years, the worth of the company leaped from $50 million to $150 million, almost a three-fold increase. By 2006 the number of hotels owned by the company more than trebled. Hersha Group now owned 70 hotels. The majority of these hotels were in big cities like New York, Philadelphia, Washington D.C. and Boston.

I was observing these huge strides in the business with wonder, amazement, and pride. What else could a mother hope for than to see her children succeed?

Jay Shah
Our journey from an 11–room motel in a small town to owning over 11,000 rooms: that is the story of the rise of the Hersha Group.

Today Hersha Group manages over 100 hotels including world famous 5 star hotels like Hilton, Marriot, Holiday Inn etc.

From small places like Edison, Hartford, Harrisburg, Wilmington, Delaware to metropolitan cities like New York, Washington,

Philadelphia, Boston, Atlanta; from the East Coast to the West, Hersha Group has established its presence all over the country.

Some may call it a success story or a miraculous journey. All this is immaterial to me. What I want more than anything is to take the Group to even greater heights. Our customers should have the confidence that Hersha Group stands for excellence in the quality of hotels and service. Even when Dad, Mom, Neil, and I are no longer around, the name of Hersha Hotels should evoke the same feeling of confidence and trust in the customers. That according to me would be the true success story of the Hersha Group.

Now when I look back at the past, I am amused. Neil had joined the Group only recently. I had some experience but I was not yet a seasoned player. Both of us were introducing new ideas and initiating change in the Group. At the same time, we were also observing the other more experienced persons and learning from them.

There are several Associations of hotel owners in the USA. The AAHOA (The Asian American Hotel Owners Association) consists mainly of hotel owners of Indian origin. Each year, the AAHOA organizes an annual convention for its members. There are seminar and speeches during the convention. The main objective of the convention is to provide an opportunity for the Indian hotel owners to get to know one another, interact and exchange ideas in a cordial environment.

Neil and I made it a point to attend these meetings. We knew very few people and almost nobody knew us. We used to wait in the hotel lobby. If we saw a member of the Association walking past, we would introduce ourselves saying, 'Hi, I am Jay Shah and this is my brother Neil. We are from the Hersha Group.' We felt a little nervous and overawed when we talked to famous Indian hotel owners who had become legends in the industry. We pretended to seem confident but actually heaved a sigh of relief when the conversation was over. This was in the year 2000.

Within the next 5 years, Hersha Group established itself extremely well in the East Coast. There were numerous articles published about our Group and our family in leading newspapers, magazines, and business journals. Hersha Group had also won several awards.

By 2005, it was a completely different scenario for us at the AAHOA convention. Earlier, we had to literally kill time, whereas now, we had a killing schedule with not a moment to spare.

The AAHOA used to schedule seminars, speeches, press conferences for us. In addition to these, we had a number of invitations for lunch, dinner, and cocktails from the hotel owners present at the convention. And then there were also some hotel owners who dropped into our room for informal chats.

Where we once used to spend hours waiting to talk to people, now people approach us, they wanted to talk to us, the reporters wanted sound bytes. I will not deny that it feels great to get all that attention but at the same time we realized that this was only the beginning. We still had a long way to go.

We are often asked the question, 'What exactly happened between 2000 and 2005 which led to the spectacular growth of the company in this period?'

The answer to that is simple. The rapid development seen during that time cannot be attributed to these five years alone. The key also lies in the firm foundation that my parents had built over 20 years. They received invaluable support from their partners. Frankly speaking, a part of the credit goes to us and a big part is also due to the changed circumstances. In 1999 when America was hit by recession, it was the hospitality industry and real estate which were the most affected. But the IT industry flourished during exactly the same time. If one invested $10,000 in the IT industry, it could increase to $30,000 or $40,000 within a period of 3 months. Naturally everyone wanted to be a part of this boom. In contrast, the real estate and hotel industry suffered on two counts; on the one hand, the number of customers decreased considerably and on the other hand, nobody wanted to invest money in these businesses because of the minimal returns.

The IT bubble grew bigger and bigger until 2001 when it burst with a huge bang. Thousands of investors were ruined because of it. The small-time investor learned that slow and steady does win the race in the end and hence people started investing once again in real estate and hotels. The same stock market which had witnessed our debacle now saw the miraculous rise in hotel share prices. In 1999 we failed to raise capital from our public issue. But I was not disheartened. I continued with my efforts. We put together the money that we had got from underwriting the issue, sold our 8 hotels and bought 18 new properties. Some of these were existing hotels while others were lands at prime locations. The most important thing was that all these properties were in big cities like New York, Boston, and Philadelphia. We renovated the existing hotels and built new ones on the empty plots. All these hotels were of the limited service type.

What exactly is a limited service hotel? Let us take the example of Hampton Inn, our hotel which was started in Chelsea, New York in 2003. This was a 144 room hotel. All the rooms were well furnished with facilities including television etc. What we cut down on was the unnecessary space wasted in a hotel and items of luxury. Every room was one third size smaller. There were no Conference rooms, no bars, restaurants or swimming pools.

In a limited service hotel, customers are served only breakfast and that too is limited to cereals, coffee, milk etc... As the area is smaller, catering is cut down and service is limited, the overheads are reduced, and it is the customer who gets a better deal. He pays much less than at the other hotels in a big city. And as these rates are still higher compared to those in small towns, the owner also makes a good profit.

Another plus point is that thanks to the prime location of the hotel in the city, there is never a dearth of customers. These hotels run at full capacity throughout the year.

From 2000 to 2005, these limited service hotels did so well that gradually the number of hotels we owned went up to 20. And then the graph climbed from 20 to 50 and then to 70. We did not even realize when the number crossed 100. At the moment, we have several ambitious plans for an even brighter future.

Epilogue

The success story of Hersha and Hasu Shah and their sons, Jay and Neil, is worthy of the highest praise.

However, I personally feel that a good human being is someone who thinks beyond himself and helps out others. So let me tell you about the humane side of the Shahs.

Hasu and Hersha Shah were always firm believers in God. Their faith was strengthened by the wise counsel of their Guru Krishna Shankar Shastri who guided them in the right direction. It was Krishna Shankar Shastri's annual visit to America on the invitation of the Indians settled in the US. Hasu and Hersha attended a sermon by Shastri Maharaj who said, 'We can never repay God's debt for having given us this life but even if we cannot repay the capital, we can certainly try and pay the interest, isn't it?'

When everyone nodded their heads, he continued, 'So let us see how we can pay the interest. Some say that they give donations to holy places. But I feel why does God need our money? It would be better if you could give something even more precious, your time.' The audience was puzzled. How exactly does one give time to God? How can we make time from our impossibly hectic schedule?

Shastri Maharaj gave a small smile and said, 'I will tell you how you can make time. God has made the same amount of time available to everybody. There are 24 hours in a day. Even if you spend 10 hours sleeping, you are still left with 14 hours. Give only one hour of these 14 to God. When I say God, I do mean the idol that you find in temples. I mean give time for a good cause, for people who are needy. You will find God in every place and you will be able to repay his interest.'

Hasu and Hersha were completely convinced by his ideas. While returning, Hersha said, 'Hasu, until now, we have only thought about ourselves, our life, our family, our business. Our idea of happiness is to see a good film, wear good clothes, eat good food. But after listening to Shastriji's thoughts, I have learnt that there is greater joy in spreading joy and happiness amongst others.'

Hasu too was of the same opinion. 'Yes, today, my perspective of life and happiness has changed. Everything is clear now. I understand how we should live our life and what we should do to make it better.'

From that moment onwards, Hasu and Hersha made a conscious effort to dedicate a part of their money and more importantly their time for good causes. Their actions benefitted a lot of people and gave them immense satisfaction.

In 1974, there were approximately a 100 Indian families in Harrisburg. They used to rent a hall or the church on religious festivals and other occasions. Some used to say, 'We should have a temple in our town.' Hasu and Hersha understood the sentiments of the people and decided to do something about it. To begin with, they established a small temple in their home itself and then eventually after a lot of effort, succeeded in collecting enough money to build a temple in the town.

The Indian community in Harrisburg now had their own place where they could meet anytime they wished. Apart from being used for religious and social functions, it also became the venue for classes on Indian culture and Indian languages.

Hasu and Hersha also became members of the Rotary Club and participated actively in the various programmes; arranging to have the 'Jaipur foot' or the prosthetic leg fitted on handicapped people living in poor countries in Africa, arranging free camps on eye care for the tribal Adivasis of Champa forest, and helping those affected by natural calamities like earthquakes and the tsunami. Hasu and Hersha played an important role in all these activities.

They do not limit their participation to donating money or arranging funds for good causes. They liked to play a hands-on role and actually work in the affected areas themselves.

In spite of their enormous responsibility towards the Hersha Group, Hasu and Hersha still make sure that they find time to participate in these activities. If Hasu is unable to go, Hersha Ben does not mind going alone and lending a helping hand in any project undertaken by the Rotary anywhere in the world. She feels, 'There are doctors and nurses in most places but there is almost always a shortage of volunteers. This is where I step in to help. I am ready to help in any way I can. Once during the eye camp in the Champa forest, there was an electricity failure. The operations were conducted in the light of Petromax lamps and it was my job to hold the lamps. During a campaign against polio in Ethiopia, we went to remote villages by bus and gave the polio drops to children. We arranged to have the Jaipur Foot fitted for the handicapped in Kenya and Ethiopia. We had a team of doctors and nurses and we assisted them in every way possible.'

'Once, while walking through rough terrain, I fell down and hurt my knee. It was not possible to have any tests done in that remote region so I came back on a wheelchair. I had hurt my knee so severely that I had to undergo a major operation after returning to the US. My friend came to visit me and said jokingly "Why do you want to do these things and put yourself at risk unnecessarily?" I did not feel the need to explain myself to her as I knew exactly the amount of satisfaction it gave me. It may be to assuage a sense of guilt that we feel for having come here to the US and left our parents behind in India. Even though we wished to, we could not physically be there every time to help them. Now when we go to different parts of the world and offer our assistance to those who need it, we see our parents' image in them.'

When I spoke to Mr Hasu Shah about this, he agreed totally with his wife's thoughts. He added, 'I also have another thought in mind. I studied and worked in the US. I settled down here with my family and have been living here since so many years. I have a debt to repay. I must give back something to this land that has given me so much. With Hersha's permission, we set up an old age home here. We bought land for it, built the building, had all the necessary facilities installed, and employed responsible people to manage it. There is a manager who is in charge of the home.

Both Hersha and I spend a lot of time here. We celebrate Christmas, New Year, and other festivals with the residents. We take everyone shopping before Christmas. Once in a while we arrange a music concert or a dance party. Most of these ideas are Hersha's and it is her initiative completely. She takes care to ensure that the elderly people here do not feel neglected or lonely.'

I have to give 100 percent credit to Hersha Ben and Hasu Bhai in this respect. They have found the perfect balance between family, business, and social work.

Today they live a content and happy life and bring joy in the lives of so many others.

The chapter is entitled 'Not only Potels' because of a special reason.

In the 1970s the Gujarati community established its importance in the motel industry and the majority of them were Patels. In fact very soon, the number of Patels in this business increased to such an extent that motels began to be known as Potels. But it was basically a pejorative term and was used to poke fun at the Gujarati community.

Today, however, the ridicule has replaced by respect and the condescending tone by one of awe.

This is because according to the latest statistics, 50 percent of the Hospitality industry, including motels, 3 star and 4 star hotels, restaurants, 5 star hotels, is owned by Indians of which the majority are members of the Gujarati community and more specifically the Patels.

Today the Patels own not just motels but also reputed hotels like Marriot, Hilton, Holiday Inn etc.

Thus the fitting title 'Not only Potels' since this story illustrates the determination, perseverance, hard work, courage, and excellent business sense of the Shahs.

ACKNOWLEDGEMENTS

Thank you Mohanbhai Patel, Jaydev Patel and family, Dalpatbhai Patel and family, Maganbhai Patel and family, Hersha and Hasubhai Shah, Jay and Neil Shah and family, Bhimjibhai Patel, Gauri Dange, and Sanyukta Diwan. Without your support, help, and cooperation, this book would not have been possible.

A NOTE ON THE AUTHOR

Shobha Bondre is a celebrated and much-published Marathi writer. She has been writing for the last 25 years and has published 13 books, many of them bestsellers that have gone into over 25 editions.

The non-Marathi reading world is now keen to read her works and her books are being translated into English, Hindi, and Gujarati. She has written articles, short stories, and columns for prestigious publications like the *Maharashtra Times, Loksatta, Lokprabha, Maher, Kirloskar,* etc. She has also written dialogues for many popular Marathi TV serials like *Abhalmaya, Manasi, Oon Paaus,* and *Ardhangini.*

In the last few years, personality profiles of people from various walks of life has become Shobha's forte. For this, she interacts closely with her subjects, understanding them in their social, familial, emotional, and economic settings. She has won many literary awards for her work, including the Maharashtra State Award for Best Novel in 1997, for *Saata Samudrapar.*

Bhimjibhai Patel

Bhimjibhai's three brothers

Shivbhai   Kurjibhai   Dhirajlal

Bhimjibhai's son—Lalji Patel

Krishi Mandir, Mohanbhai Patel's residence at Supa Farm

Mohanbhai at work at Supa Farm

Mohanbhai getting his fourth generation, great granddaughter
Aanya interested in horses

Mohanbhai with his girlfriend—great granddaughter Aanya

Two lovers—great nanaji Mohanbhai and great granddaughter Aanya—looking into each other's eyes

Mohanbhai speaking at a seminar

Birds of paradise—peacocks—at Mohanbhai's Mumbai residence

Patel Family Portrait: Front Row (sitting): Samir, Neetaben, Kunal, Priti, Chetan, Karina

Standing: Maya, Champak, Dalpatbhai, Maganbhai, Manjuben, Rakesh, Neil, Anjana

State of New Jersey

THE SENATE AND GENERAL ASSEMBLY
STATE HOUSE, TRENTON, N.J.

JOINT LEGISLATIVE RESOLUTION
By Senator SINGER and Assemblymen COTTRELL and MALONE

WHEREAS, The Senate and General Assembly of the State of New Jersey are pleased to commend and salute the Honorable Dalpat C. Patel, an esteemed resident of the Garden State, who has been selected by the Township Committee of Mansfield Township as Mayor for the year 2001; and,

WHEREAS, Dalpat C. Patel's record of inspired and effective civic leadership throughout many years has earned for him the respect and admiration of the citizens of his community; and,

WHEREAS, Dalpat C. Patel has especially distinguished himself through his tireless efforts as a member of the Mansfield Township Board of Education, and the depth of his knowledge and the breadth of his experience have contributed immeasurably to the quality of education within the Township; and,

WHEREAS, Dalpat C. Patel brings a deep and diverse cultural background to the administration and citizenry of Mansfield Township; and,

WHEREAS, The people of Mansfield Township and of the State of New Jersey are genuinely indebted to hard-working and inspiring individuals, personified by Dalpat C. Patel, whose time and energies are devoted to improving the effectiveness of their communities and the quality of life for their neighbors; and,

WHEREAS, It is altogether proper and fitting for this Legislature to recognize Dalpat C. Patel, and to salute him as an individual of outstanding character and exceptional determination; now, therefore,

Be It Resolved by the Senate and General Assembly of the State of New Jersey:

That this Legislature hereby honors and salutes Dalpat C. Patel, pays tribute to his meritorious record of service, leadership, and commitment within his community, and extends to him sincere best wishes for his continued happiness and success during his term as Mayor of Mansfield Township; and,

Be It Further Resolved, That a duly authenticated copy of this resolution, signed by the Senate President and the Assembly Speaker and attested by the Senate Secretary and the Assembly Clerk, be transmitted to the Honorable Dalpat C. Patel.

Attest:

Dolores A. Kirk
Secretary of the Senate

Linda Metzger
Clerk of the General Assembly

President of the Senate

Speaker of the General Assembly

Certificate proclaiming Dalpatbhai Patel as Mayor of
Mansfield Township, Columbus, New Jersey

Dalpatbhai being sworn in as Mayor at the Mansfield Township Hall in Columbus, New Jersey

Maganbhai and Dalpatbhai in the lobby of the Imperial Inn. Photo in the background is of the article published in the July 4th edition of the *New York Times* Magazine

From left: Maganbhai, Manjuben, Neetaben, and Dalpatbhai in the lobby of the Imperial Inn

Dalpatbhai outside Imperial Inn

Jaydev Patel

Sharan, Seema, Jaydev, and Sachin Patel

Receiving 30 years of service award from Seymour 'Sy' Sternberg,
Chairman and CEO of New York Life in 2003

Seema, Sharan, and Sachin Patel

Jaydev and Purnima at the 1983 Council meeting in Toronto

'As a new agent he worked harder than he ever did as a chemist
and he almost never had any time to spend with
Sachin and me'—Purnima Patel

Before and After: M.M. High School in Sojitra, India

Purnima, Seema, and Jaydev Patel

The Hersha Group's Hyatt 48 LEX New York

On a family vacation to Cape May, New Jersey
From Left to Right: Neil, Simrin, Juhi, Arhan, Hasu P. Shah, Hersha, Aryana, Susie, Avikar, and Jay

At the Michigan State Endowment and Award, November 2012 when Jay & Neil Shah were unanimously selected as the 2012 Industry Leaders of the Year by The School of Hospitality Business Alumni Association at Michigan State University (MSU)

At a black tie gala dinner at Pierre Vimont's home, the Ambassador of France honouring Mr and Mrs Shah's bestowment of the 2009 National United Way Tocqueville Society Award
From Left to Right: (Back row) Juhi, Neil, Hasu, Jay (Front row) Hersha, Susie

Entrance to the library bar at the Shah's Rittenhouse Hotel